D1083293

SABBATH LIGHT

*BY THE SAME AUTHOR*

The Social Life of the Jews in Northern France in the XII-XIV Centuries. 1938

Soldiers from Judea. 1942

The Herem Hayyishub: a Contribution to the Medieval Economic History of the Jews. 1945

Jewish Merchant Adventurers: a Study of the Radanites. 1948

Out of the Depths: Sermons for Sabbaths and Festivals. 1951

Far East Mission. 1952

Sparks from the Anvil: Sermons for Sabbaths and Festivals. 1955

# SABBATH LIGHT

## SERMONS ON THE SABBATH EVENING SERVICE

RABBI LOUIS I. RABINOWITZ

M.A., Ph.D.,

**Chief Rabbi,** Federation of Synagogues of the Transvaal **and** United Hebrew Congregation of Johannesburg. **Professor** of Hebrew, University of the Witwatersrand.

FIELDHILL PUBLISHING CO. - *Johannesburg*

5719 - 1958

EXCLUSIVE SELLING AGENTS

FOR THE UNITED STATES OF AMERICA

BLOCH PUBLISHING COMPANY

31 West 31st Street, New York 1

Printed by Eagle Press Limited,
19, Rockey Street, Doornfontein,
Johannesburg, South Africa.

# *CONTENTS*

## *CONTENTS*

# PREFACE

## AN APOLOGIA FOR THE TITLE

THE choice of the title for this volume, my third published volume of sermons, deserves an explanation, and an apology for what can only be considered a feeble pun!

In their desire to ascribe as hoary an antiquity as possible to the institution of the statutory three daily prayers, Shacharit, Mincha and Ma'ariv, our Rabbis ascribe the institution of those three daily prayers to the three patriarchs, Abraham, Isaac and Jacob. Abraham is regarded as the originator of Shacharit, the Morning Prayer, Isaac of Mincha, the Afternoon Prayer, and Jacob of Ma'ariv, the Evening Prayer. Each of these ascriptions is justified by a Scriptural proof-verse, and the proof that Jacob instituted the evening prayer is found in the verse of Genesis xxviii: 11, the translation of which in the Authorised Version is, "And he *lighted* upon a certain place, and tarried there all night for the sun had set." The word translated "And he lighted," can, according to the Rabbis, also be translated "And he prayed," and they therefore derive from it the origin of the Evening Prayer.

And since these sermons, as explained in the Preface, are all based upon the Sabbath Evening Service, with apologies to the reader, I have called it SABBATH LIGHT!

I have decided to include in this volume the complete text of the Friday night service in Hebrew and English in order that the reader may not only have the complete text available for reference, but that this volume may be used for Friday evening devotions.

# INTRODUCTION

I THINK that it can fairly be claimed that the present volume of sermons, my third, is unique. It is a well-established tradition of Jewish preaching that the preacher selects his text from the current Sidra of the week, and the two previous volumes, "Out of the Depths" and "Sparks from the Anvil," have followed this tradition.

At the Great Synagogue of Johannesburg in particular, however, and in South Africa as a whole, the Friday evening services attract much larger congregations than do those of Sabbath morning. The reason is a simple one. If on the one hand the widespread non-observance of the Sabbath—which is by no means entirely due to economic reasons—is the most unpleasing feature of the religious life of the Community, the tradition of regular attendance at Synagogue on Friday evenings is one of the most encouraging. There is hardly a Community which contains ten males which does not muster a "Minyan" regularly on Friday night, while in the more popular Synagogues in the towns the regular attendances number hundreds. Whatever one's views may be of an attitude to Sabbath which expresses itself in attendance at Synagogue on Friday night, at business on Sabbath morning and at the Sports Club in the afternoon, the fact remains that this tradition of Synagogue attendance is one of the most powerful of contributory factors towards the maintenance of religious cohesiveness and loyalty.

It has been my invariable custom to preach both at the Friday evening and at the Sabbath morning services, but whereas at the latter I have continued the practice of taking my text from the Sidra, it was borne in on me that such a practice on Friday night suffered from a disadvantage which did not apply to Sabbath morning, namely, that the Congregants do not have their Bibles in front of them.

The late Dr. J. H. Hertz, Chief Rabbi of the United Hebrew Congregations of the British Commonwealth, was unwearying in his insistence on the vast untapped wealth of homiletical and ethical treasures to be found in our prayer book and used to urge preachers to avail themselves of that material. (For some reason or other he always used to accompany this wise counsel with the statement that on three occasions he had preached on the simple text "Our Father, our King, we have sinned before Thee," and the opportunity it gave on dwelling on the concept of God as Father, God as King, Sin and awareness of the Presence of God.) I finally decided to take this sound counsel to heart and apply it, and conceived the ambitious scheme of taking my text for the Friday Night sermons during the course of a whole year from the Friday Night Service.

In point of fact the series took slightly more than a year, and from the outset it met with a most gratifying and unexpected success. Attendances at Synagogue increased, and the increase was sustained right through the year. What was especially pleasing to the preacher, who is rarely able to gauge the extent to which the Congregation is associating with the sermon, was, as I have mentioned in the last sermon, the rustling of the pages of the Prayer Book by the hundreds of worshippers as they turned to the page which I indicated for the text.

These sermons are published as they were delivered, and I make no apology for the plain and perhaps even homely language in which they are couched. In my desire to awaken a deeper interest in that imperishable treasure of the Jewish soul, I deliberately and studiously avoided any straining after effect or such "purple passages" as adorn or mar my previous publications in the genre of sermonic literature. If some of them will be found to be pedestrian it was because of set purpose I avoided flights—of imagination or of oratory.

Three of the sermons, as indicated, were delivered by three of the Ministers serving the United Hebrew Congregation of which I am Chief Rabbi and of which the Great Synagogue is the main Synagogue. They are Rabbi A. H. Lapin of the Yeoville Synagogue, Rev. Dr. H. Abt of the Oxford Synagogue, and the Rev. D. Isaacs, B.A., now of the Cyrildene Congregation, but at that time Assistant Minister to the Great Synagogue.

It is my earnest prayer that the publication of these sermons may effect for a wider public what I feel they effected for those who heard them delivered, a deepening of understanding of our sublime prayers and a strengthening of the never completely absent bond which joins Israel to their Father in Heaven.

# INTRODUCTORY

## אדני שפתי תפתח ופי יגיד תהלתך

## O LORD, OPEN THOU MY LIPS, THAT MY MOUTH SHALL DECLARE THY PRAISE

WHEN I was a child I received my introduction to Hebrew through the medium of a Prayer Book called Vallentine's Prayer Book. The only indication that it had been specially printed for Jews in English-speaking countries was that at the beginning it had a number of laws concerning prayer and mourning printed in English, and a number of brief rubrics, instructions as to when specific prayers were to be recited, also in English. That Prayer Book represented the height of anglicisation and modernisation in the Beth Hamidrash of which my father was Rabbi and in which I was brought up. Apart from that, the Siddurim used were what are called "Heimische Siddurim," printed on cheap paper, devoid of any embellishments or aesthetic content, and produced solely for the utilitarian purpose of enabling the pious worshipper to recite the statutory prayers. The measure of the attachment to, and knowledge of, the prayers by those simple, pious and learned Jews—learned at least in the Siddur—can perhaps be seen mirrored in a favourite quip which was current there; "Since *every Jew* knows Ashrei by heart, why is it necessary to print it in the Siddur?" To which the answer was that if it was not in the Siddur every Jew would *not* know it by heart!

It was only when I entered the service of the United Synagogue in London that I became acquainted with what is now to a large extent the standard Prayer Book of all English-speaking Congregations, the Authorised Daily Prayer Book of the United Hebrew Congregations of the British Empire, commonly known as "Singer's". Apart from its fine format, its main distinction was its elegant and meticulous English translation. First published in 1890, it has since gone through twenty-two editions and the twenty-second edition in 1956 brought the total number printed to over 400,000. It has therefore obviously filled a need, and that need in itself is obvious—the Jew not only felt the need for prayer, he wanted to know *what* he was praying.

Fifteen years ago the next stage towards the greater understanding of the Prayer Book by English-speaking Jews saw the light, with the publication of the first part of the Annotated Prayer Book by that great leader and educator of Anglo-Jewry, the late Chief Rabbi, Dr. J. H. Hertz. It has not "caught on"—to use a colloquialism—to the same extent as Singer's, but I hope that with the passage of time it will. One may assume, I think, that the purpose behind its distinguished editor was that the worshipper should know not only *what* he was praying more thoroughly but also *why* he was praying.

These four stages, from the "plain" Siddur to the fully annotated one, can superficially be regarded as a sign of the decline of Jewish knowledge, but such a diagnosis is not, to my mind, necessarily correct. I am not sure that these simple Jews who said their prayers with such fervour were Hebrew scholars who knew the meaning of what they were saying any more than I, who find pleasure and delight in the Annotated Prayer Book, fail to understand the Hebrew text. I believe that the truth lies much deeper than this simple diagnosis. I believe that it is a question of faith more than of knowledge.

I am indebted to Chief Cantor Alter for a brilliant and simple interpretation in the name of a Chassidic Rabbi of what is otherwise one of the most difficult verses in the liturgy of the High Festivals. It is as simple as it is brilliant, as brilliant as it is simple. He explained the phrase הודאי שמו כן תהלתו as "to the extent that one is certain of His Name, to that extent is he prayed to." When the knowledge of God is a certainty then man prays unquestionably, and when the certainty of God is lacking, prayers come stammeringly, if at all. The faith of these simple and pious Jews was complete and their acceptance of the statutory prayers unquestioned. "This is what one has to say" they were taught, and so they said it.

That simple unquestioning faith, that delight in treading the old paths is now largely a thing of the past. We are no longer prepared to sign on the dotted line without first perusing the document. The answer "this prayer was instituted by the Anshei K'neset Ha-Gedolah" is no longer regarded as a suitable answer. The modern worshipper is more critical and less unquestioning. He wants to know what it is he is saying and once he knows that, he wants to know why he should say it, and what exactly it intends to convey. And the text of the prayers in English is the first concession to that enquiring mind and the annotations are the second, and the decision which I have come to, and which I have already announced, of devoting my sermons every Friday night this year to the Friday evening service is the third.

I heartily concur with the sentiments expressed in the opening paragraph of Dr. Hertz's Annotated Prayer Book: "The Jewish Prayer Book, or the Siddur, is of paramount importance in the life of the Jewish people. To Israel's faithful hosts in the past as to its loyal sons and daughters of the present, the Siddur has been the Gate to communion with their Father in Heaven; and at the same time it has been a mighty spiritual bond that united them to their scattered brethren the world over. No other book in the whole range of Jewish literature that stretches over three millennia and more, comes so close to the life of the Jewish masses as does the Prayer Book. The Siddur is a daily companion, and the whole drama of earthly existence—its joys and sorrows, workdays, sabbaths, historic and Solemn Festivals; birth, marriage and death—is sanctified by the formulae of devotion in that holy book. To millions of Jews, every word of it is familiar and loved; and its phrases and Responses, especially in the sacred melodies associated with them, can stir them to the depths of their being. No other volume has penetrated the Jewish home as has the Siddur; or has exercised, and continues to exercise, so profound an influence on the life, character and outlook of the Jewish people, as well in the sphere of personal religion as of moral conduct.

"Surely the story and nature of such a book should be known not only to Jews, but to all who are interested in the classics of Religion. Yet the Jewish liturgy is the one branch of religious literature that is generally neglected by Christian scholars; and as to the Jews of Western lands, a well-known theologian not so long ago wrote, it would be well for the Jewish religion if the beauty and emotional power so largely manifested in its prayers were more intelligently appreciated by its adherents to-day."

To that task I wish to devote myself, at least with regard to the Friday night service.

But it is not the only reason for my decision. There are at least two more. The whole purpose of a sermon is to develop a text and apply it to the problems which face us. It is, or should be, but an extension of the text, deepening its message, revealing unsuspected depths, showing its eternal validity and application to conditions of life. It is for that reason that it has become the tradition to select one's text from the Sidra of the week. The fact however that the Torah is not read on Friday night, and that you have not your Chumashim in front of you, renders the sermon unrelated to the whole service. Whereas, therefore, I shall continue to preach on Sabbath morning on the Sidra or Haftarah, I shall take my text from the prayers which are read, with exactly the same intention in mind.

Thirdly, the Friday evening service includes two fundamental portions of Scripture, a selection of Psalms and three paragraphs of the Shema. If you will look at the last page of Singer's Prayer Book you will find that no less than 74 of the 150 Psalms which make up the Book of Psalms are to be found in the Prayer Book, but the fact remains that they come at such a time in the service that they are hardly known. And although the eight Psalms which are included in the ordinary Friday night service are by no means the most soulful of the Psalms, they will afford an opportunity of pointing out the depth of spirituality in that book. Similarly, I hope that by the time the service is ended you will begin to appreciate the central role which these three paragraphs from the Pentateuch occupy in our Prayer Book.

Lastly may I say that I shall welcome any suggestions which may be put to me to deal with any aspect of the sermon which may interest you.

It is my earnest prayer and hope that the result of this series will be to deepen our appreciation of that classic expression of the Jewish soul, our Siddur, the product of two and a half thousand years of the outpourings of a God-intoxicated people, that it will strengthen the bonds between Israel and their Father in Heaven, that as a result "our lips will be opened, that our mouths shall declare God's praise."

## GOING OUT TO MEET GOD

לכו נרננה לה׳ נריעה לצור ישענו
נקדמה פניו בתודה בזמירות נריעה לו.

*O Come. Let us exult before the Lord; let us shout for joy to the Rock of our Salvation. Let us come before His presence with thanksgiving.*

(Psalm 95, vv. 1 and 2.)

A Chief Rabbi is not without honour in his own country—at least when he goes out of the confines of Johannesburg and pays a visit—all too infrequently—to one of the country Communities. I say without conceit that such a visit is often regarded as a red-letter day in the life of some Communities and they signalise it by sending out a convoy of cars to meet me on the road some miles out of the town to escort me into that Community. If those who have paid me this honour were to express their intention in Hebrew, they would say נקדמה פניו which means simply that one does not sit in one's place and wait for a visitor to come to him, but one goes out to meet and to greet the person and thus show him honour.

You will therefore realise that, as I have had occasion so often to point out, the English translation fails to convey the true inwardness of the Hebrew. The phrase does not mean "Let us come before his presence" but it means "Let us go out of our way to greet him and usher him in ceremoniously and with joy."

It is this sentence and this correct translation which gives us the clue to the reason for the selection of these six Psalms, Psalms 95-99 and Psalm 29, and their addition to the ordinary weekday evening service, and it will not be without interest to explain how it was that they came to be added.

Following upon the Expulsion of the Jews from Spain in 1492, many of the exiles made their way to the Holy Land, and repopulated the ancient historic centres of Israel, Jerusalem, Hebron and Tiberias. But in addition to those centres, a new centre was established, Safed, and there developed a Community the like of which has never been seen in the world, a community of which it has been said that "it had the atmosphere of a permanent revivalist camp." It is the subject of a brilliant essay by Solomon Schechter in the second series of his Studies in Judaism, but for the moment it is sufficient to point out that it was in Safed in the 16th century that there was written the Shulchan Aruch, the authoritative code of Traditional Judaism, that the Practical Cabbala of the Ari was founded and developed, that the first attempt was made to reintroduce Semicha upon which the much debated question of the re-establishment of the Sanhedrin to-day depends, and lastly it was in Safed that the two additions to the Friday Evening Service, the Introductory six Psalms and the beautiful poem L'cha Dodi were introduced and composed respectively. To those mystics and saints in Safed the Sabbath was a day of joy and spiritual recreation, and as Schechter says "Indeed, the Sabbath should give man a foretaste of the blissful Messianic times when sin and sorrow shall have disappeared from the world. Reluctant to part with these hours of peace and unalloyed joy, and anxious to prolong them as much as possible, the Sabbath received an extension both at the beginning and the end. Thus they would, early Friday afternoon, dress in their best clothes and set out in groups to receive Queen Sabbath with song and praise, reciting certain Psalms and singing certain hymns composed for the occasion. In like manner, they would refrain from work for several hours after the Sabbath sun had set, and spend them in chanting hymns and in feasting. They had even a special society whose members would meet and spend the end of the Sabbath, reaching way into the night, with song and dance" (p.249). For exactly as one goes out of one's way to greet a welcome guest, so one tries to prolong the pleasure of his company even beyond the due time for his departure. And if there was a welcome guest whose departure was regretted as much as its arrival was welcomed, it was the beloved Sabbath Queen and Bride. The reluctance to let it go which is referred to in the concluding paragraph of that quotation gave rise to the beautiful and neglected Melave Malkah, the chanting of the hymns and feasting which was interpreted as accompanying Queen Sabbath on her way out, while the welcoming was expressed in the beautiful language of what has been rightly called "perhaps one of the finest pieces of religious poetry in existence", the "Lecha Dodi, Likrat Kalah" "Come my beloved to meet and intercept the Bride Sabbath". In a very real sense therefore the words נקדמה פניו "Come, let us go out and meet it" expressed in even a physical sense the Inauguration of the Sabbath. The "certain Psalms" were those six Psalms with which we open the service, and the "hymn composed for the occasion" was the L'cha Dodi.

But if the Psalm uses the phrase נקדמה פניו with regard to God, and the Lecha Dodi with regard to the Sabbath, Rabbinic Judaism has extended the conception to the performance of every single Mitzvah, and makes the question whether one sits at home with folded hands and waits for a Mitzvah to come to one, or whether one goes out to meet that Mitzvah half way, so to speak, the acid test not of observance, but of the *fervour* of observance, and expressed the idea succinctly in three Hebrew words זריזין מקדימין למצות. The eager man does not wait for the Mitzvah to come to him, he goes out to meet the Mitzvah.

The proof verse which is adduced for this doctrine is well known. It harks back to the father of the Jewish people Abraham, of whom it is recorded וישכם אברהם בבקר "And Abraham rose up early in the morning." It is in connection with the immortal story of the Akedah* when Abraham is

* But see Tos. Hullin 81 b.

put to the supreme test of faith by being commanded to sacrifice his only beloved son Isaac for whose birth he had prayed, and in whom he saw the fulfilment of his life. Would his faith have been questioned had he, while still fulfilling the dread commandment, put off the evil to the last possible moment? But Scripture records "and Abraham *got up early* in the morning." No more cogent proof could be adduced that זריזין מקדימין למצות, that one shows one's zeal for God by going out to meet the Mitzvah rather than wait for the Mitzvah to come to him.

None of us is called upon to be put to the test to which Abraham was put, but each of us fulfils Mitzvoth in one way or another, the Mitzvah of Sabbath, the Mitzvah of charity, the Mitzvah of succouring the poor and of helping the unfortunate, the Mitzvah of keeping the communal machinery going or of assuring the survival of the State of Israel. And the test of loyalty is not *whether* one fulfils the Mitzvah but *how* one fulfils it. For in every aspect of life there are two approaches, the static and the dynamic, or what is called in Rabbinic literature שב ואל תעשה the sitting with folded hands and doing nothing, or the קום עשה the get up and doing. To which of these categories do we belong when the question of fulfilling a Mitzvah arises? Do we content ourselves with being of the שב ואל תעשה of the static and the passive, and when a Mitzvah comes our way we fulfil the commandment מצוה הבאה לידך אל תחמיצנה "when a Mitzvah happens to come your way, we do not let it get sour?" Do we wait for it to come to us, and when it comes fulfil it grumblingly, grousingly and reluctantly? The Mitzvah has been fulfilled; it has not been allowed to go sour and rancid, but how much greater is the test of religious loyalty when we fulfil נקדמה פניו that we go out to meet the Mitzvah half-way! In the one case we show ourselves the servant of God, but a reluctant servant, while on the other we can lay claim to the title of Zerizim, of fervent, loyal and eager servants, delighting in fulfilling God's law, of those who can say נקדמה פניו בתודה Let us go out to meet him in thanksgiving.

## WHY WE DO NOT INDULGE IN MISSIONARY ACTIVITY

ספרו בגוים כבודו בכל העמים נפלאותיו

*Declare His glory among the nations,*
*His marvellous works among all the peoples.*
*For great is the Lord, and highly to be praised.*
*He is to be feared above all gods.*

(Psalm xcvi, 3-4.)

Even to the superficial reader it is obvious that the first five Psalms of the Friday evening service form a close unity with one single theme, and that theme is the ultimate ideal for which we strive and pray, the final establishment of the Kingdom of God upon earth, when his sovereignty will be complete when, in the immortal words of the beautiful Alenu prayer "All the inhabitants of the world shall perceive and know that unto thee every knee must bow, every tongue swear. . . . Let them all accept the yoke of thy kingdom and do thou reign over them for ever and ever. For the kingdom is thine, and to all eternity thou wilt reign in glory." If, however, you will read these first two Psalms in conjunction, you will see clearly indicated the successive stages whereby this ideal may become a reality until the third of the Psalms opens up with the positive triumphant, exultant declaration ה׳ מלך תגל הארץ ישמחו איים רבים "The Lord is enthroned, let the earth rejoice, let the multitude of isles be glad."

The first stage is indicated in the first Psalm. It is the struggle between God and the children of Israel to bring them to acknowledge his sovereignty. "For forty years was

I wearied with that generation and said 'It is a people that do err in their heart, and they have not known my ways.'" God almost abandons them in despair, and "swore that they would not enter the Holy Land." And then (although this verse precedes it) suddenly the barriers are withdrawn "For he is our God, and we are the flock of his pasture." How has this surrender taken place? היום אם בקולו תשמעו "To-day! If you will hearken to his voice." Israel at last submits and accepts the sovereignty of God.

That is the first stage. The second is the extension of that conquest with which the second Psalm opens. The glory of God has to be proclaimed to the nations. Israel has the duty of spreading the knowledge of God and his glory in the world. And as a result of that activity, הבו לה׳ משפחות עמים, הבו לה׳ כבוד ועוז the families of the nations will ascribe unto the Lord glory and strength, and not only the Jewish people, but they also will bring an offering and come unto his courtyard. Then and only then can one proclaim the sovereignty of God in the world.

That is the ideal picture which emerges from this exultant Psalm of the ultimate enthronement of God and the establishment of his sovereignty in the world. It is obviously a picture which represents the ultimate Messianic age, but it raises the acute question which the Rabbi is often seriously asked. If the purpose of the Jew is to bring the world, in the beautiful phrase of the Rabbis, "under the wings of the Shechinah," why do we, alone of all religions in the world, refrain from missionary activity? Why do we not go out into the world and try and make converts? Why, on the contrary, do we place every obstacle in the way of conversion?

This question becomes peculiarly apt this week when we read of the Call of God to Abraham and of the fact that he and Sarah arrived in the Promised Land with הנפש אשר עשו בחרן which our Rabbis beautifully translate "the souls which they made by converting them to a knowledge of the true God." It is as a result of this that Abraham is regarded not only as the racial father of all Jews, but as the spiritual father of all converts; it is for that reason that every convert to Judaism is given the patronymic of בן אברהם אבינו . Why then do we not go and declare the glory of God among the nations in order to bring nearer the day when the Lord will reign?

The question is much too comprehensive to be encompassed in the course of one sermon, but there is one fundamental fact which is not sufficiently appreciated. The Jewish religion is the only one of the major religions of the world which does not make salvation depend upon the acceptance of a specific creed. Where Christianity, for instance, proclaims "He that believeth in me shall be saved," with the natural corollary that "he who does not believe in me shall not be saved," and no matter how upright or God-fearing an individual may be in his life and actions, as long as he does not accept that specific belief salvation is denied him, it naturally follows that in their desire to bring about the salvation of the world they have to undertake that missionary activity which is so characteristic a feature of their faith. Judaism alone maintains that salvation does not depend upon the acceptance of a specific creed, but upon the uprightness of one's life, and maintains as a principle of faith that חסידי אומות העולם יש להם חלק לעולם הבא that "the pious of all nations have a portion in the world to come." Nor does Judaism content itself with enunciating a vague principle, but enunciates a programme of righteousness for the world as a whole which are called the שבע מצות בני נח the seven Commandments which were given to the sons of Noah. It will surely be of interest to hear what these Commandments are:—

They are:—

1. The prohibition of idolatry.
2. The prohibition against blaspheming God.
3. The prohibition of adultery.
4. Not to kill.

5. Not to steal.
6. Humane killing of animals for food.
7. The establishment of Courts of Justice.

According to our belief the non-Jew who adheres to these seven basic principles of humanity and faith, of what might be termed natural religion, is regarded as equal to the Jew who fulfils the traditional 613 Commandments, and who shall deny, with all the vaunted progress of Western civilisation, that it has still a far way to go before it can be said that these principles form the fundamental bases of that civilisation, the "eternal verities."

Once that conception is accepted, that it is not necessary to become a Jew in order to achieve salvation, the very need to convert mankind to Judaism as a spiritual boon falls away. And it is at least noteworthy in this connection that of all the "souls which Abraham and Sarah made in Haran," of all the allies who are mentioned, Aner, Eshcol and Mamre, of the 318 followers חניכיו ילידי ביתו not one became a follower of Abraham in the specifically Jewish doctrine. His task was complete when he brought to them an awareness of God and of the above-mentioned principles which stem from that awareness. We acknowledge that there are many paths which lead up the mountain of the Lord, and each one can choose his own.

That remarkable and unique doctrine in which is enshrined the ideal of religious toleration, does not, however, answer the question as to how the Jew is to fulfil that mission of bringing mankind to an awareness of God, of fulfilling the verse of my text ספרו בגוים כבודו בכל העמים נפלאותיו "Declare his glory to the nations to all people his wonders." How then is the Jew to fulfil this, and how does he fulfil it? To that question Judaism gives a clear and unequivocal reply. The Jew teaches the existence of God by the example of his own life. It is in the manner that the Jew shows himself to be imbued with the spirit of God, to that extent he influences mankind. The Jew lives up to the precepts of

Judaism and, since he is the standard-bearer of the word of God, he either glorifies God or desecrates his Name. It is this idea which has given rise to the glorious conception of קדוש השם and חלול השם. Where the Jew does an honourable act he brings glory not only to himself but to God, where he is guilty of a dishonourable act he brings the name not only of the Jew, but of God himself into disrepute.

Our Rabbis always prefer homely practical examples rather than theoretic speculations to drive home the truth of a message. And this point which I am trying to make is beautifully illustrated by a simple story of one of the fathers of Rabbinical Judaism, Simeon b. Shetach. Once his disciples presented him with an ass which they had purchased from an Arab. Round its neck was tied a pebble which on examination proved to be a precious stone. Joyfully his disciples congratulated him on his windfall and told him that now he could be independent. Simeon replied that the Arab had sold him a donkey, and not a jewel, and promptly returned it to its owner, who exclaimed, "Praised be the God of Simeon b. Shetach" (Deut. R. III, 5). Had he not thereby declared the glory of God to the nations? Had he not performed an act of Kiddush Hashem?

And I would invite all you business men—nay, and professional men also—who are here, to think whether in the course of your business activities you have at any time perpetrated such an act, where, despite the fact that legally you could uphold a certain claim, you nevertheless decided to act in a spirit of equity and justice, with the result that the recipient of the boon has cause to praise not only you, or the people to whom you belong, but the God of Israel also. For if you have, you have helped to declare God's glory in the world, and brought nearer his ultimate sovereignty.

# THE HATRED OF EVIL

## אוהבי ה׳ שנאו רע

## YE THAT LOVE THE LORD HATE EVIL

(Psalm XCVII, 10)

A few days ago I received the current number of the Anglo-Jewish Association Quarterly, published in London. It contains an article by Rev. Alan Miller entitled "On Love, Hatred and Jealousy" and it opens with an account of what must have been a most moving incident. It was during the war, when the full truth of the gruesome details of the Nazi Concentration Camps had at last been revealed. The writer was present at an Oneg Shabbat which was held on a Friday night at the Bachad Kibbutz in Bromsgrove in England. Various people had been asked to read extracts from Jewish and general literature which appealed to them. And one of the girls, actually a German refugee, read the following passage from Dostoyevsky's "The Brothers Karamazov."

"Brothers have no fear of men's sins. Love a man even in his sin, for that is the highest semblance of divine love, and is the highest love on earth. Love all God's creation, the whole and every grain of sand in it. Love every leaf, every ray of God's light. Love the animals, love the plants, love everything. If you love everything, you will perceive the divine mystery in things . . . and you will come at last to love the whole world with an all-embracing love!"

As he was musing on the incongruity of a plea for love under these circumstances, his thoughts were rudely disturbed by the stern voice of Rabbi Unterman, at that time

Rabbi of Liverpool, and now Chief Rabbi of Tel Aviv, who was the guest Rabbi for that Sabbath. "Enough of this talk of love," said he slowly and deliberately, "God is a God of Love, but he is also a God of Vengeance!" And pounding on the table at each phrase, he enunciated

אל נקמות ה׳ אל נקמות הופיע הנשא שפט הארץ השב גמול על גאים

"O God of Vengeance, Lord, O God of Vengeance, shine forth, lift up thyself, thou judge of the earth, render to the arrogant their desert." (Psalm XCIV 1/2). Which of them was right, and which, under the circumstances which prevailed at that awful time, expressed Jewish ethics? Should we have loved the Nazis "even in their sin" with an all-embracing love, or should we have hated them with a deep hatred, and called on God to avenge the blood of his servants?

Let me give you another quotation dealing with the same contemporary events. "Who will condemn the hatred of evil which springs from the love of what is good or just?" asks Menachem Begin in the Introduction to "The Revolt." "Such hatred has been the stimulus behind progress in the world's history . . . And in our case, such hate had been nothing more or less than that of a manifestation of that highest human feeling, love. For if you love freedom you hate slavery, if you love your people you cannot but hate the enemies that compass their destruction. If you love your country you cannot but hate those who seek to annex it. Simply put, if you love your mother would you not hate the man that sought to kill her? Would you not fight him at the cost, if need be, of your life?" And again I ask, is this active, positive hatred in accordance with the principles of Jewish ethics?

To that question surely the four simple Hebrew words of my text give the final answer. "Ye that love the Lord, hate evil." Hatred can be the most ignoble and destructive of vices, and there is no vice which looms larger in Jewish ethical thought, and one from which the Jew in the course of history has suffered more than שנאת חנם, baseless hatred, irrational hatred, hatred without cause or rhyme or reason. To it for instance is ascribed the Destruction of the Second Temple. But the very use of the phrase שנאת חנם "baseless hatred," surely presupposes that there is a hatred which is not baseless but which has a sure foundation in Jewish ethics, a hatred which, as Begin rightly says, is "a manifestation of that highest human feeling love." One cannot love God without hating evil, and the hatred of evil stems from that love of God.

But if ואהבת את ה׳ אלהיך "Thou shalt love the Lord thy God" expresses the highest ideal of man in relationship to the divine, surely ואהבת לרעך כמוך "Thou shalt love thy neighbour as thyself" expresses the highest ideal of the relationship of man to man. How then can we combine it with that feeling of noble hatred?

To that question Judaism gives a complete and wholly satisfactory answer, and again it illustrates it not by a bald statement of ethics or theology, but by a vivid incident. R. Meir had some neighbours who were persecuting and distressing him, and in a burst of anger he prayed for their death. Whereupon his brilliant and learned wife Beruria said to him, "The verse יתמו חטאים מן הארץ ורשעים עוד אינם (Psalm CIV., 35) need not be translated "Let *sinners* perish from the earth, and the wicked will be no more," but "Let *sins* perish from the earth, with the result that the wicked will be no more. Hate sin, but not the sinners, pray for the destruction of their evil, not for their destruction." R. Meir heeded the noble interpretation of his wife, prayed for their betterment and they repented of their evil ways. And it is noteworthy that the verse of my text emphasises "Ye that love the Lord, hate *evil*" not "*evildoers*." Once that essential qualification is made, the way is surely clear for an examination of the justification of a feeling of noble hatred. I make bold to say that the greatest ethical drawback from which the modern world suffers is its inability to hate evil. Instead of hating it with an utter hatred, in the blessed name of tolerance and of "live and let live" we dismiss it with a shrug of the shoulders. It has become positively bad form to say that one hates anything or anyone and as a result our professed love of God is either diminished or becomes hypocritical. For, as the verse of my text clearly implies, hatred of evil is the corollary to love of God.

With what a wholesome and full-blooded hatred of evil do the Scriptural authors express themselves! "Do I not hate them that hate thee?" asks the Psalmist, "And am I not grieved with them that rise up against thee? I hate them with an utter hatred, I count them mine enemies (Psalm CXXXIX., 22) and the author of Proverbs states a simple syllogism "The fear of the Lord is to hate evil. (Therefore) Pride and arrogance and the evil way and the froward mouth do I hate" (Prov. VIII., 13).

How many of us ever experience that noble frenzy of hatred of evil and intolerance of wrong doing or injustice which acts as the spearhead of the attack upon its bastions? The noble frenzy of a Moses who, at the sight of the orgiastic worship of the Golden Calf, in a fit of anger smashes the Tablets of Stone written with the Finger of God? The sublime anger of a Mattathias who at the sight of the act of apostasy rushes forward in uncontrolled passion and, slaying the apostate Jew and his Syrian taskmaster, raises the standard of revolt and thereby saves the world for God? Their love of the Lord made them inevitably into haters of evil and from that hatred there was generated a spiritual force whose currents still flow to this day. Alas, we fail to be roused to hatred at the sight of evil, we fail to raise a finger to remove it. Can it be said that such an attitude reveals love of God? Can it be equalled with the ethical doctrines of Judaism?

We do not hate evil enough! I tell you that I do hate! I hate the doers of evil. I hate those who grind the faces of the poor. I hate the wealthy man who has amassed his fortune out of the tears and blood of others. I hate the upholders of unfair privileges and the protagonists of discrimination. I hate the retailer of malicious gossip and tittle-tattle. I hate those who hate the Lord and rise up against Him. But because I do not hate them with an "utter hatred" my love of God is thereby diminished. For the yardstick of the measure of our professed love of God is the extent to which we hate evil.

## THE PROHIBITION OF INSTRUMENTAL MUSIC.

SING PRAISES UNTO THE LORD WITH HARP, WITH THE HARP AND THE VOICE OF MELODY, WITH TRUMPETS AND THE SOUND OF THE SHOFAR SHOUT FOR JOY BEFORE THE KING, THE LORD.

(Psalm XCVIII., 5/6)

The kingdom of God has been established; God is King. He has made known his salvation and revealed his righteousness in the eyes of the nations. Sing therefore unto him a "new song." And in that new song everyone and everything participates. "Shout for joy unto the Lord all the earth, break forth into exultation and sing praises." It is not only man who will sing unto God. Everything in nature will join in that harmony of song "Let the sea roar and the fullness thereof, the earth and all that dwell therein. Let the floods clap their hands, let the mountains exult together." Nor is it with human voice only that man will break forth into praise of the Lord, but with every kind of musical instrument, the string instrument of the harp, the brass of the trumpet, the natural sound of the Shofar. In other words, whatever can possibly add to the swelling and triumphant melody of thanksgiving, animate and inanimate, is pressed into service.

It is by no means the only Psalm in which the praise of God with musical instruments is enjoined. The Book of Psalms as a whole reaches its culminating crescendo with the last Psalm, the 150th, which forms part of our daily service, and it enumerates a much fuller and exhaustive list of musical instruments for Halleluhu, Praise him! It adds to the forms of instruments in my text the percussion instruments. "Praise him with the sound of the Shofar, praise him with the harp and the lyre. Praise him with the stringed instruments and the pipe. Praise him with the clear-toned cymbals, praise him with the loud-sounding cymbals." And since all these instruments mentioned were used in the Temple, the question naturally arises, why is there such a complete prohibition of the use of instrumental music in the Orthodox Synagogue Service? And when I say complete prohibition I am choosing my words carefully. For in this prohibition there is more than the prohibition of playing instruments on the Sabbath, and there is more than the legal grounds for this prohibition. When, at the beginning of the 19th century the first organ was introduced into a Reform Temple in Berlin, albeit, let it be noted, a non-Jewish organist was employed to play it, the great Rabbis of the time issued a ban against it, which they based on three grounds:—

(1) That the playing of musical instruments is prohibited on Sabbaths and Holy days,

(2) That music in general is prohibited on religious occasions in mourning for the destruction of the Temple, and

(3) That the introduction of the organ is merely an aping of Christian worship.

It will be seen, therefore, that the custom which we have, and which is generally followed in Western countries, of permitting the use of the organ on weekdays does not remove the second and third objections, and I am prepared to admit that it is not strictly in accordance with Jewish law.

But it is not with the legal side that I am so much interested at the present moment, but rather with the psychological aspect; with the spirit of Jewish worship rather than with its regulations. And the more I consider this matter from that angle, the more I feel the aptness of the excellent word used by Rabbi Dr. M. Gudeman who, although himself a Moderate Reformer, objected to the introduction of the organ on the ground that it was a "Mésalliance." In other words, Jewish worship and musical instruments form an unsatisfactory union, it is a "Shlechter Shidduch."

When I was in Stockholm last year, I was informed by a member of the Congregation that when, about the middle of the 19th century, the Stockholm Jewish Congregation wished to introduce an organ — which incidentally they subsequently did — there was considerable opposition. In order to overcome it the advocates of the proposal wrote to two outstanding figures in the secular world to ask their views. They were the famous German poet of Jewish birth, Heinrich Heine (1797-1856) and the most famous Jewish composer of the time, Jacob Meyerbeer (1791-1864). They were confident that the reply would be in the affirmative, and to their astonishment both answered with a decided negative. Heine gave an answer typical of him "The God of Israel does not wish to be worshipped with brass, but with the human voice," while Meyerbeer, who remained a loyal Jew all his life, said that it is not in accordance with the spirit of Jewish worship, that whereas the organ fits in with church music, it is unsuitable for Jewish melodies.

Those striking replies have a peculiar support in Jewish tradition. According to the Bible, Jubal, the son of Lemech, was "the father of all that handle the harp and pipe" (Gen. IV., 21) and, therefore, as Dr. Hertz points out, "Music, according to Hebrew tradition is thus the most ancient art, dating from the beginnings of the human race." But on that verse Rashi comments, that the purpose of that invention was לזמר לעבודת אלילים, to sing to idols! There is surely an instinctive feeling in that comment that the use of musical instruments in the worship of the true God is excluded.

How can one explain or rationalise this attitude? I cannot lay claim to being a passionate lover of music, but ever since I first heard Beethoven's Ninth Symphony, the famous Choral Symphony, played by the then Palestine Philharmonic Orchestra in Jerusalem during the war, I have never failed to take every opportunity of hearing it again, and thus it was that I heard it a fortnight ago conducted by Sir Malcolm Sargent in connection with the Johannesburg Festival. As some of you may know that Symphony is unique. After the first three movements, rendered in the "Orthodox" manner by the Symphony Orchestra, in the fourth movement the orchestra is superseded by human voices, the choir singing Schiller's Ode to Joy. The transition from instrument to voice is provided by the introduction of the bass singing:—

"O Freund, nicht diese Tone! Sondern lasst uns angenehmere anstimmen, und freudvolle."

"O Friends, no longer let those sounds continue! Let us sing something more pleasant, more full of gladness and joy, let us praise thee."

As one of the musical commentators says, it is "the one and only solution of the emotional and symphonic issues raised by the first three movements." I am prepared to be told by the true cognoscenti of music, of whom I unfortunately cannot claim to be one, that my interpretation is wrong but each one is entitled to interpret music as he feels it, and the more I hear that symphony, the more I feel convinced that the inward meaning of that introduction is that no instrumental music, however melodious and moving and stirring it is, can serve as a suitable instrument for that exultant expression of thanksgiving and joy. It can only lead to a certain point, but when that point is reached the spontaneous outburst of joy which is engendered can be expressed only by the human voice, coming from the soul and raising itself in praise and thanksgiving.

And that, I am convinced, is the reason for the rejection of musical instruments in the Synagogue. And that, I am convinced, is the reason why, though it was permitted in the Temple, it is forbidden in the Synagogue. For in the Temple the worshipper was a *passive* participant. The priest performed the sacrifice, the Levites sang with voice and accompanied the voice with instrument. But the ordinary Israelite took no part and associated with worship merely with his presence. But the Synagogue knows no distinction between Cohen, Levite and Israelite in the approach to God through prayer. It demands the active, vocal participation of each worshipper, and in that participation the instrument acts as a bar instead of a channel to the establishment of communion with God.

For after the enumeration of the various instruments with which Halleluhu "Praise him" is to be performed, the Psalm ends, and with it the Book of Psalms כל הנשמה תהלל יה, הללויה Let the whole soul and every soul, praise God, Halleluyah! And when one praises God from the soul, there is no need for the adventitious aids of string or brass or drum. The words which emerge from the heart, says the Hebrew proverb, go direct to the heart of the hearer, and when we praise God from the heart, we do it with דברי שירות ותשבחות with *words* of song and praise.

# PEACE THROUGH STRENGTH

ה׳ עז לעמו יתן
ה׳ יברך את עמו בשלום

*The Lord shall give strength to his people;*
*The Lord shall bless his people with peace.*

(Psalm xxix: 11).

If there is one book to which the word timelessness can be applied, it is the Bible. It speaks to us for all times and for all circumstances. It never fails to give an answer to the problems and perplexities of the times. It acts as a light in our darkness, as a guide and a beacon to tell us "the way that we should go and the actions which we shall do." But how is it that a book which is essentially a collection of the history, poetry and literature of a people, a collection which ends nearly 2,500 years ago, can have its permanent and timeless message? I cannot do better in reply than to quote from a recently published work:—

"The quality of ever-renewed meaning renders the Bible a book of everlasting value. It is the work of religious genius."

"It is one of the characteristics of any genius that his words convey much more than he originally intended them to mean. Though apparently limited by the circumstances of their time, they are never ageing, inexhaustible in depth and meaning. Each new generation discovers more of their truth and message. This applies to any work of genius: to Beethoven's music, Wordsworth's poetry, Rembrandt's painting and Shakespeare's dramas. Time-bound, they are eternal; dealing with subject matters of definite dates and specific places, they are ageless. But no work possesses this quality of perpetual renewal and everlasting meaning more than the Bible.

The loyalty of Ruth, who was prepared to go anywhere just to keep faith; the faith in God of David, who feared no evil in the valley of the shadow of death; the endurance of Job, who in spite of all suffering, knew that his Redeemer lived; they all were time-conditioned, the outcome of definite historical circumstances and yet, immortal in their value, they will speak to us with undiminished dynamic force. God's call to guilt-stricken Adam and Eve — "Where art thou?" — as well as Cain's brazen refusal to recognise his social responsibility — "Am I my brother's keeper?" — these are not merely echoes from the dream-distant past, but possess shattering present-day reality."

And that is why, when my purpose this evening is to deal with the present emergency which has arisen in Israel, to discuss its implications and its background, I find the text which conveys our feelings. It is immaterial whether the author of the verse had that interpretation in mind; I do not believe he did, and I intend to devote another sermon to what I consider to be its true inward meaning.* The fact is that the verse speaks to us in the context of our thoughts and emotions, and directs them in the right channel.

"The Lord will give strength to his people, the Lord will bless his people with peace." It is with that verse that the six Psalms selected for the Inauguration of the Sabbath end, and the meaning appears to be clear. Only when Israel possesses sufficient strength to deter those aggressors who are bent upon its utter destruction; only when they will come to realise that such an attack would constitute a hazardous venture whose outcome is in doubt, only then can Israel be assured that the one boon which it desires

---

*See Sermon 8, p. 33: "Spiritual Strength."

above all others, the boon of peace for constructive development will be assured.

It is a sad commentary on the present state of civilisation that such a theory has to be adumbrated, it is one which to my mind runs counter to the whole spirit of Jewish ethics and to the Divine plan of God. I believe that in essence the increase of military power constitutes an almost irresistible temptation to resort to the grim arbitrament of war, that ultimately and in the last resort peace will be secured only when the ideal of Micah and Isaiah is realised "They shall beat their swords into ploughshares and their spears into pruning hooks. Nation shall not lift up sword against nation, neither shall they learn war any more."

And the irony and the tragedy of the present position lies in the fact that it was partly in order to be the instrument of the fulfilment of that ideal that the State of Israel was born and came into being those $8\frac{1}{2}$ years ago. Israel was to become the state which was to be the exemplar of the ethical ideals of the prophets, the principles of justice and right and democracy and peace. We wanted peace as an ideal, and we wanted peace as an urgent practical expedient and necessity. Rarely have ideals and expediency met in such harmony as in Israel's passionate desire for peace. For peace was necessary to bring in the hosts of Israel's exiled sons who wished or who were obliged to return to the bosom of Mother Zion, peace for the purpose of developing the country, of turning the desert into a garden and the Negev into a place of habitation, peace that Israel's sons might grow up free from the shadow of fear and insecurity which has haunted them during the long and bitter centuries of their exile. And to establish that peace we made our sacrifices. We agreed to an armistice at the time when our enemies were on the point of collapse and we could have occupied the whole country. We renounced — despite my conviction that a renunciation of divinely promised land was not within our power — our claims upon enemy-held territory, we agreed to impossible boundaries, we turned our backs wistfully upon the Old City of Jerusalem and the site of the Temple, we pleaded with the world and with the Arab nations to turn the armistice into a permanent peace, but all to no avail. The outstretched hand of friendship was rudely spurned and dashed away, the overtures of peace were met with a snarl of rejection, and with threats of a second round which would reverse the fortunes of the first round. Ceaselessly and continuously guerilla warfare has been waged against us on our abnormally extended frontiers, a warfare which has cost over 1,000 casualties, of soldiers as of civilians, of women and children as well as men.

In their determination to turn this guerilla warfare into an eventual overall assault the Arab States began to build up their armaments to a fantastic extent, and with a cynical and indecent importunity the Western Powers vied with the Eastern bloc in pouring in a wealth of arms of all kinds to the Arab States while resolutely refusing to furnish Israel with comparable quantities. Day by day the disparity between the arms so lavishly poured out to the Arab States and the arms so painfully acquired in the face of every opposition by Israel grew, and the bland assurance by England that the recipients had undertaken to limit them for defensive purposes received a strange and distorted echo when the recipients announced that now that they had received these arms they could proceed to liquidate Israel! And before the bar of history we arraign those nations who, in their cynical pursuit of international power politics, have made it necessary for Israel, reluctantly and agonisingly, to change the ploughshare for the sword and the pruning hook for the spear, and undertake the punitive action in which she is now engaged.

And with clear consciences, though with sorrow in our hearts we turn to God in prayer. O God, give strength to thy people, Israel, for thus alone, under present circumstances, will she be vouchsafed the one blessing she yearns for above all, the blessing of peace!

## THEY WHO CALL UPON THE NAME OF THE LORD

משה ואהרן בכהניו ושמואל בקוראי שמו
קוראים אל ה׳ והוא יענם

*Moses and Aaron among his priests, and Samuel among them that call his name, called upon the Lord and he answered them.*

(Psalm XCIX., 6).

In the first year of my ministry in Johannesburg, I was invited by the then New Zionist Organisation to deliver the Memorial Address at the Annual Commemoration to Herzl, Bialik, Jabotinsky and to Shlomo ben Joseph, the first of the rank and file martyrs of the New Yishuv. The leaders of the Community had not yet discovered that it was not their function to dictate to me where and when I should speak, and thought that it was within their right and their privilege to do so. One of them wrote me a letter in which he enclosed the newspaper advertisement of the proposed meeting, and, suggesting that I cancel my acceptance of that invitation, he wrote "I am sure that you will agree that it is a reflection on the great names of Herzl, Bialik and Jabotinsky to couple their names with that of Shlomo ben Joseph."

I answered him that I fully agreed that Shlomo ben Joseph could not very well be put in the same class as the other three, but knowing him to be an avowed opponent of Jabotinsky I was delighted to note that he agreed that

Jabotinsky's name could be coupled with that of Herzl and Bialik!

That incident of eleven years ago came back to my mind when I was pondering upon the Rabbinic comment upon this verse. I shall try to make the somewhat complicated reasoning of the Talmud, which is based upon the theory that things which are equal to the same thing are equal to one another, as simple as possible. One verse of the Bible couples the name of Samuel with three of the most disreputable Judges who judged Israel during the period of the Judges, Samson, Jephthah and Gideon. Our verse, on the other hand, couples Samuel with Moses and Aaron. Ergo, says the Talmud, the three most important of the leaders in Jewish history are equated with the three least important, in order to teach the important and far reaching lesson that there is no point in hankering after the"good old days." "Say not what was; that the former days were better than the present, for thou hast not enquired from wisdom concerning this" (Eccles. VII., 10). Gideon in his generation is equal to Moses in his; Samson in his generation is as Aaron in his; and Jephthah in his generation is as Samuel in his" (T.B. Rosh Hashanah 25 a and b).

My purpose however this evening — and it was this which reminded me of the incident to which I have referred — is not to pursue this subject, fascinating though it is. The Talmud limits itself to the fact that the three least important leaders are equated with the three most important. I want on the other hand to deal with the fact that Samuel is regarded in every way as being on a par with Moses and Aaron. In every way. The verses that follow emphasise the complete equality of the three. "They called upon the Lord and he answered them. He spake unto them from the pillar of cloud: they kept his testimonies and the ordinances he gave them. Thou answerest them, O Lord our God." For Moses, Aaron and Samuel represent not only three great leaders, but three almost entirely different types of leadership. To the veriest tyro there is an instant association of ideas with these three names, Moses—Prophet; Aaron—Priest; Samuel—Judge. Each of them is regarded as the outstanding example of the qualities represented by that type of leadership. It is true that Moses is coupled with Aaron as a "priest" but there is no need to emphasise that it is as prophet and not as priest that his importance is to be sought. The father of the Prophets, the divinely appointed leader, the Saviour and Deliverer of his people from bondage; the only prophet who, in the words of the Bible spake with God "Mouth to mouth, clearly and not in riddles, and he shall see the similitude of God" (Numbers XII., 8). The Faithful Shepherd, the Giver of the Torah, Moshe Rabbenu, Moses our Master.

His brother Aaron is equally predominant in his sphere. Chosen as the High Priest who alone could officiate before God in the Sanctuary, the priesthood is made hereditary in his descendants. They have the privilege of birth which is denied to every other Jew no matter what his talents or abilities, his piety or morality may be. And so Moses represents the gift of divine inspiration, while Aaron represents the aristocracy of birth. And Samuel? True that he is regarded as a prophet, but it is not as a prophet that he is distinguished, nor as a prophet that he is referred to in this verse. Samuel represents the dedicated life, the life of the person that even before his birth is dedicated to the service of God. והנער שמואל משרת את ה׳ "And the child Samuel acted as servant to the Lord" (1 Sam. III., 1) is the first notice we are given of him, and to that ideal of *Sherut*, service, he remains faithful from that day to his last. Because of his loyalty to that service he vigorously opposes the appointment of a king, because of that ideal of service he undertakes his periodical circuits of the country in order to dispense justice in the spirit of the Torah. And the importance of Samuel lies in the fact that whereas the Lord calls to Moses and Aaron, in his case Samuel calls unto the Lord, and the highest title which the Psalmist can give him is קורא שמו he who calls upon the name of the Lord. And all three of them, Moses who received a greater abundance of the spirit of God than any person who lived, Aaron chosen to minister before the Lord and Samuel who calls upon him — all three are placed on a plane of equality and of all three it is stated without distinction "God answered them. He spake unto them in the pillar of cloud, they kept his testimonies and the statutes that he gave them. Thou didst answer them, O Lord."

What lesson is there in this interpretation for us to-day? Surely it is written so large that he who runs may read. Prophecy is no more, and none of us can be endowed with its divine spirit. Priesthood depends upon birth and none who is not born a Cohen can claim its responsibilities or its privileges. And therefore to be a Moses or an Aaron is beyond the capacity of the ordinary Jew.

But it is not only to the Moses' and the Aarons that God speaks. God speaks to the Samuels as well, and the Samuels are the קוראי שמו, "Those who call upon the name of the Lord." There is no Jew who cannot rise to the level of a קורא שמו of one who calls upon His name, and of them it is said קרוב ה׳ לכל קוראיו לכל אשר יקראוהו באמת "The Lord is near to all that call upon him, to all that call upon him in truth." (Psalm CXLV., 18.)

There is no man, however humble of birth, however devoid of the higher spiritual capacities, who is thereby precluded from the loyal and dedicated service of God. Butcher and baker, and candlestick-maker, tinker, tailor, he can by his dedication to God's service deserve to rank with a Moses and with an Aaron אחד המרבה ואחד הממעיט ובלבד שיכון את לבו לאביו שבשמים.

"It matters not whether one gives much or little, as long as one directs his heart to his Father in Heaven," is the great message of Judaism, the great lesson of this verse. And God answers him as he answers Moses and as he answers an Aaron.

## SPIRITUAL STRENGTH

ה׳ עז לעמו יתן ה׳ יברך את עמו בשלום

*The Lord will give strength to his people;*
*The Lord will bless his people with peace.*

(Psalm XXIX., 11).*

Over the portals of the building of the Ministry of War in the mighty Austro-Hungarian Empire of the Hapsburgs, that empire which was broken up into fragments after the First World War, there is, or was, engraved the Latin proverb "Si vis pacem, para bellum," "if you desire peace, prepare for war." That slogan was regarded as the justification for the existence of a War Ministry, for the piling up of arms and the development of a mighty military force. Whether they said it with their tongue in their cheek or not, they maintained that the purpose of these massive preparations was not to wage war but to prevent war, that this was the best way of ensuring the blessing of peace.

And despite the fact that two devastating World Wars have proved the falsity and the illusion of this attitude of mind, it is still put forward as the justification of the mad race in armaments which is the most disturbing feature of our modern civilisation. The atomic bomb which devastated Hiroshima and Nagasaki, with its explosive power of 10,000 tons of T.N.T., is now obsolete and outmoded. The hydrogen bomb with its immeasurably greater capacity for destruction has taken its place and eager itching fingers of military scientists are burning to experiment with the cobalt bomb compared with which even the hydrogen bomb is a puny weapon. Guided missiles and rockets, supersonic

* See Sermon 6.

bombers and fighters, all are being developed with frantic energy by the great powers of the world, by America in the West and Russia in the East, and the statesmen and politicians of the world who are responsible for these developments reiterate with a bland and nauseating monotony that they are being pursued, not, God forbid, for the purpose of waging a devastating annihilatory war — perish the thought — but in order to ensure peace. Bigger and better bombs for a bigger and better peace, that is the alluring prospect which is set before us, and to which so many give their uncritical acquiescence.

In 1933, as a Territorial Army Chaplain, I was present at an Army Chaplains' Conference in England. The Chaplain General to the Royal Air Force gave a most moving address on the task of Chaplains during peace, and in the course of which he made a striking point. "Do you realise," he said, "the almost irresistible temptations which face young men in the Air Force in times of peace?" There they are, ardent, youthful, full of vitality and spirits, spending the best years of their lives training and perfecting themselves in the art of war, and year follows year and they have to content themselves with exercises and dummy bombing instead of the "real thing," and a feeling of frustration and exasperation gains increasing hold over them at the waste of their lives, and increasingly one hears from them the wistful thought expressed "When shall we have a chance at the real thing?" And he concluded by pointing out that the damping of that enthusiasm constitutes one of the most valuable of activities of a Chaplain in time of peace. The truth in that analysis applies not only to the airmen and to trigger-happy soldiers. It applies to all those who see themselves possessed of the power of imposing their will by might. The temptation to resort to the fearful arbitrament of war becomes irresistible. "Let us finish with them or with this — once and for all now that we have the power" becomes the approach. In short there is no greater lie, whether it be a lie on the lips or a lie in the heart than the slogan that "if you wish peace prepare for war." The truth is that if you prepare for war you will have war. It is only when swords shall be beaten into ploughshares and spears into pruning hooks that nation shall not lift up sword against nation neither shall they learn war anymore. That is the lesson of history and that is the teaching of Judaism.

If that is so, what is the meaning of the verse "The Lord shall give strength to his people, the Lord shall bless his people with peace"? You will no doubt remember that I preached on this self-same text a fortnight ago, on the occasion of Israel's attack upon the Sinai peninsula and, although, for the purpose of giving expression to our thoughts and emotions at the moment, I interpreted it to mean that only when the Arab nations, bent and resolved upon the utter destruction of Israel, would be deterred by the might of Israel from making it an unprofitable adventure, only then could Israel be assured of peace, I emphasised that this is not the eternal or abiding message of this verse. What then does it mean?

In his commentary on the Prayer Book Dr. Hertz gives the answer by the addition of one word "God . . . blesses his people with *moral* strength and lasting peace." And that interpretation of עז not as physical or military strength but as moral strength, is decisively supported by a verse in the Psalm read before this one, ועז מלך משפט אהב אתה כוננת מישרים משפט וצדקה ביעקב אתה עשית "The strength of the king lies in his love of justice. Thou didst establish equity, thou has wrought justice and righteousness in Jacob." (Psalm XCIX., 4). The strength of a king lies not in the size of his battalions but in his love of justice, and that strength is shown in the extent of his equity, his justice, his righteousness. That is the doctrine of Judaism, and that is the ideal which, despite its unpopularity and despite the tragic and grim necessities of the moment, we are bound to uphold and proclaim to ourselves and to the world. "Not by might nor by power, but by my spirit, saith the Lord."

There is a real fear that these grim necessities of the moment may cause a distortion of Jewish values, of these doctrines which Judaism has given to the world, and of which the Jewish people have been a living exemplar by the very miracle of their survival. Our pride in the massive and brilliant achievements of the Defence Army of Israel, the desperate need to remain on guard until the threat to our existence passes, must not at any price bring in its train a distortion of the ethical truths of Judaism. The hands are the hands of Esau and the voice is the voice of Jacob. True strength is moral strength, and peace will come through justice and righteousness. With all its brilliant successes Israel will remain as one of the smallest nations, inset in an unbroken stretch of territory with a population of, if I mistake not, 400,000,000 Moslems. It is neither our aim nor our future to become a mighty military power prevailing by its ability to hold the surrounding nations at bay by a show of force. The ideal of Judaism to which the State of Israel must and will corporately apply itself, as the Jewish people in the Diaspora must individually, is to bring about the supremacy of those divine ideals upon which alone the security and future of the world depends.

That is the inner meaning behind the otherwise peculiar juxtaposition of the verses. "The Lord sat enthroned at the Flood, yea the Lord sitteth as King for ever. The Lord will give strength to his people, the Lord will bless his people with peace." For the Lord who sat enthroned at the Flood was the Lord who with sorrow in his heart decreed the destruction of mankind "because the earth was filled with violence," because "All flesh had corrupted its way." When these ideas prevail destruction comes, for "upon three things the world depends for its continued existence, upon truth, upon justice and upon peace." (Ethics of the Fathers I: 18.) It is they which give moral strength to a people, and by their enthronement alone will the world be saved.

## ON LECHA DODI

I AM going to give you a lecture to-night, a lecture on the not very thrilling subject of Neo-Hebrew poetry. If I shall succeed in keeping you from yawning I shall be satisfied; if I can maintain your interest I shall be happy; if as a result of this lecture there will be aroused in you a desire to acquaint yourselves further with one of the most luscious of the fruits of the Jewish spirit, I shall be overjoyed. It is the first of three sermons—if indeed this can be called a sermon—which will be based upon the beautiful hymn Lecha Dodi, and in order to understand the structure of the poem, it is necessary to give that lecture.

Where Western poetry is characterised by the external features of rhyme and metre—I ignore for this purpose what is called blank verse—Biblical poetry relies for its external effect upon two other artificial expedients, the use of the successive letters of the alphabet in successive verses, and what is known as parallelism, the repetition of the same thought, but in different words, in the second half of the verse as is expressed in the first. I have taken the trouble of having a sheet roneoed which I hope you will study at your leisure, but the most common example of both the alphabetical and of parallelism is to be found in the 145th Psalm, commonly called, after the first word of the introductory verse, which is an addition to the Psalm proper, "Ashrei."

In the ninth or tenth century, under the influence of Arabic poetry, there took place a revival of the art of Hebrew poetry, which is called Neo-Hebrew poetry. Neo-Hebrew poetry entirely discarded the parallelism which characterised Biblical poetry, but it not only retained the alphabetical acrostic, but it developed it to an extraordinary degree. Not content with having a "straight" alphabet, the poets showed their ingenuity by writing poems in every conceivable permutation and combination of the alphabet. They would write poems with the alphabet backwards, with the first letter of the alphabet followed by the last, the second by the second last, and so on. But for one of these developments of the alphabetical acrostic the historian of Hebrew poetry has reason to be profoundly grateful, and that was the so-called "signing" of their poems by incorporating their names into the initial letters of the verses. We thus have an infallible proof of the names of the authors of countless poems which would otherwise remain anonymous or be the source of faulty speculation. In addition, Neo-Hebrew poetry introduced from their Arabic models the use of rhyme and metre. Thus to sum up this brief and perhaps boring lecture, Biblical poetry is characterised by the straight alphabet and/or parallelism, without rhyme or metre, while neo-Hebrew poetry employs one or more of the developed alphabetical acrostic, rhyme and metre.

Now neither parallelism nor acrostic, rhyme nor metre in themselves constitute poetry. "The big fat cat, stretched on the mat" happened to have both rhyme and metre, and in the sentence "a big cat dreamed easily for good hours," each word begins with a successive letter of the alphabet, but that does not make poetry out of them! In true poetry the elevated thought and the elevated language are such that these external aids come with such an effortless ease that they are scarcely noticed. There is no strain or forcing of expression, so that the external aspect is submerged in the sublimity of the thought.

Only after that introduction can we begin to appreciate the beauty and mastery of that wondrous hymn "Lecha Dodi" which Schechter rightly calls "Perhaps one of the finest pieces of religious poetry in existence."

In the Talmud (T.B. Shabbat 119a) we are told that as the evening shadows lengthened on Friday afternoons, Rabbi Chanina used to wrap himself in his Tallit and say בואי ונצא לקראת שבת מלכתא "Come, let us go out to greet Queen Sabbath," while R. Yannai similarly used to robe himself and say בואי כלה בואי כלה "Come, O bride, Come, O bride." They thus used to welcome the Sabbath under the name of both bride and queen, and the Sephardi formula of Lecha Dodi adds, after the words, בואי כלה בואי כלה "Come, O bride, come, O bride," the words: בואי כלה שבת מלכתא "Come, O bride, Queen Sabbath" to include both passages. Round about the year 1540 a Rabbi and mystic, Rabbi Solomon Halevi Alkabetz of Safed, a member of the school of mystics established there, of which I spoke in an earlier sermon, brother-in-law and teacher of the famous R. Moses Cordovero, took these words and made them the basis of this immortal hymn which was instantly accepted and introduced into all rites, Ashkenazi as well as Sephardi.

If you will refer to this hymn you will see that it contains two of the three characteristics of neo-Hebrew poetry to which I have referred. The first letters of the eight verses, excluding the refrain and the last verses are ש'ל'מ'ה' ה'ל'ו'י' which made שלמה הלוי "Solomon Ha-Levi" the author of the poem. Thus it has the characteristic of the alphabetical name acrostic.

In addition it follows a definite rhyme. Every verse consists of four phrases, of which the first three rhyme with one another, while the fourth, ending in ה, rhymes with the last word of each stanza.

When, in addition to that, almost every phrase in that beautiful poem is not the invention of the inspired author, but is merely a quotation from the Bible, making it a mere mosaic of Biblical phrases, the author could well have been excused if the result had been a certain artificiality and forcing of expression. Just consider the severe limitations which he had to place upon himself. He had to begin the first verse with the letter Shin and the second with

Lamed and the third with Mem; he had to find three successive phrases which rhymed with one another, and a fourth which ended in ה. He had to cull his phrases from the Bible, and yet is there anyone who will deny the opinion of Dr. Hertz that "the resulting whole is wonderfully fresh, fragrant and full of new charm." It fulfils the most exacting standard of the highest form of poetry and is an immortal and classical addition to Jewish liturgical poetry in particular and religious poetry in general.

Lecha Dodi inspired Heine, the famous German poet of Jewish origin, to write his famous poem "Princess Sabbath" and it will not be out of place if, with apologies to our Chief Cantor, I read to you a portion of that poem as translated by Aaron Kramer.

There, beside his praying table,
Stands the Congregation's singer;
Tidy man, who shrugs the shoulders
Of his cloak coquettishly.

While he fumbles at his neck,
Just to show how white his hand is,
Pressing thumb against the throat,
Index-finger on the temple.

Hums quite softly to himself,
Till, at last, exulting loudly,
He lifts up his voice, intoning:
*Lecho Daudi likras kallah!*

*Lecho daudi likras kallah*—
Lover, come, the bride awaits you,
She who soon shall lift the cover
From her bashful countenance!

This inspired song of marriage
Was created by the noble,
Greatly-honoured minnesinger,
Don Jehuda ben Halevy.

In this song he celebrated
The event of Israel's wedding
To the lady Princess Sabbath
Who is called "The Silent Princess."

Pearl and flower of all beauty
Is the Princess. Not more lovely
Was the fabled Queen of Sheba,
Bosom friend of Solomon.

I have read this extract for two reasons. First of all as an example of the manner in which inspired poetry breaks the bounds of the language in which it was written and invades, so to speak, foreign territory. And secondly because I wanted to put you to a test. For if you have followed me carefully you will be able proudly to say that you now know more about Lecha Dodi than Heinrich Heine! For that poet, so long estranged from his people, made the mistake of ascribing it to the infinitely greater poet Judah Halevi,* whom he calls Judah ben Halevi, and you are now able to demonstrate his error and say "It is not by *Judah* Halevi, but by *Solomon* Halevi, and the proof positive of it is that he "signs" his name in the initial letters of the verses. And it is to Solomon Halevi that we owe a debt of eternal gratitude for this immortal hymn to Sabbath the Bride and Sabbath the Queen.

---

* Leon Feuchtwanger makes the same mistake in his novel "Raquel, the Jewess of Toledo."

## ALPHABETICAL POEMS AND PASSAGES in SINGER'S PRAYER BOOK

1. In Psalm 145 "Ashrei" every verse begins with a successive letter of the Aleph-Beth, except that "Nun" is missing.
2. The famous passage from Prov. 31 "A virtuous woman who can find" (page 123) gives the complete alphabet in successive verses.
3. The hymn El Adon (p. 129) gives the consecutive alphabet in the first letter of every *phrase*.
4. In the first paragraph of p. 38 the complete alphabet is to be found in every successive *word*.
5. The 119th Psalm has an eight-fold repeated alphabet of which four verses are given on pages 301 and 302.
6. The Musaph prayer on p. 161 is an excellent example of the alphabet *backwards* from Tav to Aleph.

## "SIGNATURE HYMNS"

1. The initial letters of Lecha Dodi on p. 111 give us the name of the author שלמה הלוי (Solomon Ha-Levi Alkabetz).
2. Those of Ya Ribbon (p. 124a) give us ישראל Israel (Najara).
3. Those of Yom Zeh on p. 124c give us יצחק ל״ח It is an abbreviated version of a longer hymn the initial letters of which were יצחק ל(וריא) ח(זק) Isaac Luria, May he be strong.
4. The famous Maoz Tsur (p. 275) is similarly signed מרדכי Mordecai.

Adon Olam, page 3, follows a strict metre — — — ◡

## ON CHANUKAH. DAILY MIRACLES

*We thank thee also for the miracles, for the redemption, for the mighty deeds, and saving acts wrought by thee, as well as for the wars which thou didst wage for our fathers in days of old at this season.*

(Special Chanukah Prayer.)

THERE are two essential components of our daily prayer, supplication and thanksgiving, supplication for God's grace to be extended to us, and thanksgiving for grace and favour already received. That thanksgiving finds its beautiful expression in that prayer which forms an integral part of every single service thrice daily, "We give thanks unto thee, for thou art the Lord our God and the God of our fathers for ever and ever; thou art the Rock of our lives, the Shield of our salvation through every generation. We will give thanks unto thee and declare thy praise for our lives which are committed unto thy hand, and for our souls which are in thy charge, and for thy miracles, which are daily with us, and for thy wonders and thy benefits, which are wrought at all times, evening, morn and noon." On this Festival of Chanukah, however, we add to this daily prayer a special prayer of thanksgiving for the glorious victory and mighty deliverance achieved by the Hasmoneans after three years of guerilla warfare in 165 B.C.E. It was a victory in a war fought for the first time in human history for the sacred principle of freedom of worship and by that victory that right was established for all time. And we introduce that special prayer with the formula which I have selected as my text to-day.

If ever there was an apt description of a struggle, it is to be found in the words which follow: "Thou didst deliver the strong into the hands of the weak, the many into the hands of the few, the impure into the hands of the pure, the wicked into the hands of the righteous and the arrogant into the hands of those who occupied themselves with thy Torah." If on the one hand it contrasts the hopeless inequality of the struggle from the physical point of view between the two opponents, on the other hand it explains how it came about that despite that hopeless inequality, victory went to the heavily outnumbered Maccabees. For if it is true that they were the weak against the strong and the few against the many, it is equally true they were the pure against the impure, the righteous against the wicked and those who occupied themselves with the word of God against the arrogant. And as history has shown throughout the ages, where there is the conviction of right and justice, of purity of motive and passion for God, these moral and spiritual virtues, imponderable though they be, outweigh weight of metal and preponderance of man-power.

That, in the words of my text, that victory brought about a redemption, that it constitutes a "mighty deed," and was in the highest sense of the word a "saving act" is beyond doubt or cavil, but what is significant is that it is regarded by the composer of that prayer of thanksgiving as appertaining to the category of Miracles. Nor, as you will see from the rubric which precedes this prayer, is this introductory passage limited to the Festival of Chanukah alone. It is said both on Chanukah, the Festival of Light, and also on Purim, the Festival which celebrates the deliverance of the Jews of Persia from the evil machinations of Haman, through the courage and self-sacrifice of Mordecai and Esther. The events of both these festivals are thus specifically and explicitly referred to as "miracles," "Nissim."

When we think of the word miracle, or its Hebrew equivalent, "Ness," we unconsciously but inevitably associate the word in our minds with some supermundane happening when God, so to speak, intervenes on the side of man by an act which reverses the course of nature, or by some other abnormal occurrence. The parting of the Red Sea, when of fluid water it is recorded "The water became like a wall for them," the flowing backwards of the waters of the Jordan for Joshua, the sun standing still in Gibeon; it is happenings like these to which we usually refer as miracles, and in that context, however rational we may be in our attempt to explain them away, or however solid the faith that impels us to accept them literally, we say regretfully that "the age of miracles is past." Wistfully but in vain we prayed, for instance, for some *deus ex machina* to come and strike down Hitler, but the "miracle" did not happen. God appears to stand on the sidelines and merely look with compassion upon the unequal struggle between good and evil, between the weak and the strong.

And yet neither of the Crossing of the Red Sea nor the fact of man hearing the voice of God on Mt. Sinai do we say " We thank thee, O Lord, for the miracles," but we confine that word to Chanukah and Purim. And strangely enough it is just on these two Festivals that the divine intervention of God on the side of right is apparently conspicuous by its complete absence. The Book or Esther was even in danger of exclusion from the Canon on the very solid grounds that the name of God does not appear once in the whole book, and to the secular, rational reader the deliverance of the Jews which is celebrated on that day came about as a result of a number of strokes of luck, flukes, coincidences and accidental happenings. As someone once said, "If Esther had been born with a wart on her nose, the deliverance would not have come about!" Similarly with regard to Chanukah. No thunderbolt from heaven came down and discomfited the armies of the Syrians. No Red Sea was parted; no sun stood still. It was a ding-dong military struggle with swaying fortunes in which superior strategy and morale combined with military genius finally obtained the victory of the few over the many. There were defeats as well as successes and reverses as well as battles won. It is the military analyst and not the man of faith who studies profitably the campaigns of Judas Maccabeus! And yet it is these two events which are designated by the term Nissim, "Miracles." And above all on Chanukah the word is repeated with almost monotonous regularity in the prayer before the kindling of the lights and the prayer which follows it.

Is it not obvious that one has to reconsider one's view as to what constitutes miracles? And in fact, in the daily prayer of thanksgiving to which I have referred and to which the Chanukah and Purim passages are but additions, do we not thank God, "For thy miracles which are daily with us?" What then is meant by "Ness," the "Ness" of daily occurrence, the "Ness" of Chanukah, the "Ness" of Purim?

And as obvious is the need for reassessment, so obvious is the direction which that reassessment has to take. There is a greater miracle than the supermundane intervention of God on the side of man, a more constant miracle than the occasional violent upheaval of Nature which brings about a certain result. And that is the miracle of the spirit of man which impels him to sacrifice on account of an ideal, the miracle of faith which makes him reckless of every odds, and determined to fight to achieve the impossible. And because of that faith the impossible becomes possible and the miracle is achieved. It is the miracle which makes man rise above the consideration of his own selfish interests and put the interest of others, the interest of God, in the forefront of his mind. It is the miracle which produces saints and martyrs, men who devote their lives to the pursuit of an ideal without thought of self.

A Moses, by a strange quirk of fortune, out of the very persecution and genocide of his people, becomes an Egyptian prince. Every consideration of self-interest speaks to him and tells him to dissociate himself from his people, and find safety and comfort in his adopted home, and yet, "When Moses grew up he went out to his brethren" and, returning to his lowly and oppressed people, becomes their saviour. An Esther, similarly buttressed against the effects of the persecution which is imminent for her people, to whom similarly every consideration of selfish self-interest cries out to dissociate herself from them, comes to the fateful decision "And if I perish, I perish" and risks her life in the successful attempt to save her people. A Mattathias, living out his well-earned retirement in the village of Modi'in, engulfed by a passion of righteousness, rushes forward and strikes a blow for freedom, his son Judas Maccabeus with superb courage fighting the War of the Lord against impossible odds, or to turn from these ancient events to a modern one, an Albert Schweitzer, philosopher and musician, acknowledged world expert on Bach and on organs, devotes his life to operating a hospital for Natives at Lambarene, in the heart of equatorial Africa; these and countless other examples can be cited as "God's miracles which are daily with us."

And what applies to individuals applies to peoples as a whole. Whether it be the gallant band of Maccabean warriors so imbued with divine ideals that they cheerfully throw down the gauntlet to the immensely superior forces of the Syrians, whether it be the people of England after Dunkirk when inspired by the glow of a great ideal they wrested triumphant victory out of certain defeat, whether it be the hastily organised army of Israel warding off the attacks of the armies of five Arab States and forging the State of Israel, all these phenomena represent the miracle of the human spirit.

After the Israeli War of Liberation there was an animated discussion between the secularists and the men of faith in Israel. The secularists maintained that the glorious victory of the Defence Army of Israel had been achieved by secular means alone, by the human virtues of courage, gallantry and resolute determination, while the men of faith seeing in it the finger of God pointing the way to the ultimate redemption of which this was the beginning, regarded it as a miracle. One of the advocates of the former view was the Prime Minister of Israel, Mr. David Ben Gurion, while the Chief Rabbi, Dr. Herzog, naturally took up the other view. Mr. Ben Gurion, somewhat irritated at this view, which to him seemed to derogate from the glory of the achievements of Israel's army, said to the Chief Rabbi "Where was the miracle? It was a victory won by human agency alone," to which Rabbi Herzog solemnly and wittily replied "Mr. Ben Gurion, I regard you as one of God's miracles."

For in the phenomenon of man rising above circumstances and achieving the impossible lies the greatest of the miracles of God. It is on that phenomenon that depends the slow but sure and ever-increasing unfolding of the spirit of God in the world, until his sovereignty will be acknowledged by man, and for that continuing miracle we humbly render thanks to God to-day.

# THE ESSENCE OF JUDAISM

## שמור וזכור בדבור אחד השמיענו אל המיוחד

*"Observe" and "Remember the Sabbath Day" the only God caused us to hear in a single utterance.*

(From Lecha Dodi.)

WHEN, a fortnight ago, I spoke of Lecha Dodi, I referred to the effortless flow of the words, despite the severe limitations which the self-imposed demands of Hebrew poetry placed upon the author of this beautiful hymn.

The words which I have chosen for my text to-day represent what is, I think it will be agreed, the only exception to this appraisal. They are a cryptic allusion to a passage of the Talmud, and in order to make it comprehensible, Singer, as you can see, has had to have recourse to the rare expediency of a footnote. The Ten Commandments are found twice in the Bible, once in the twentieth chapter of Exodus, and once in the fifth chapter of Deuteronomy. The fact that the opening word of the Fourth Commandment, the Commandment of the Sabbath, differs in both versions, represents a difficulty to the Rabbis of the Talmud, to whom the literal inspiration of the words of the Bible was a fundamental assumption. The Fourth Commandment in Exodus begins זכור את יום השבת לקדשו "Remember the Sabbath Day to keep it holy," while the version of Deuteronomy reads שמור את יום השבת לקדשו "Observe the Sabbath Day to keep it holy." Which of these two words, then, issued from the mouth of the Almighty? Did he say שמור or did he say זכור? And the Rabbis ingeniously answer

שמור וזכור בדבור אחד נאמרו מה שאין הפה יכול לדבר ואין האוזן יכולה לשמוע Both שמור and זכור issued simultaneously from the mouth of God, which no human mouth can do, nor human ear hear.

Were that difference to be the only variation between the version of the Ten Commandments as found in Exodus and the version of Deuteronomy, the explanation, unsatisfactory though it may be, might be acceptable, but the fact is that there are other, and even more serious, discrepancies between the two versions. A reference to the two versions shows that the differences between them consist, not only in single words, but in one case of a whole verse, and it is more than passing strange that nowhere in the whole of Rabbinic literature does one find the same explanation of the other discrepancies.

It is that fact which lay behind a brilliant interpretation of that phrase by my late father-in-law, an interpretation which throws a flood of new light upon this comment, and which emphasises one of the most far-reaching and profound conceptions of the nature of Judaism. For the most serious discrepancy between the two versions of the Ten Commandments is actually found in the fourth Commandment, and it is much more significant than the change in wording between שמור and זכור. Of all the Ten Commandments the Fourth, the Commandment of the Sabbath, is the only one which gives the *reason* for the observance of the Commandment, and an entirely different reason is given in both versions. The version in Exodus says "For in six days the Lord made heaven and earth and rested on the seventh day, wherefore the Lord blessed the Sabbath and hallowed it." In this version, therefore, the reason for the injunction to keep the Sabbath is a *religious* reason. It depends upon the belief in God who created the world, it depends upon the acceptance of the story of creation as given in the first chapter of Genesis. When we turn to Deuteronomy, we find an entirely different reason given. "And thou shalt remember that thou wast a slave in the land of Egypt, and the Lord thy God brought thee out thence by a mighty hand and by an outstretched arm; *therefore* the Lord thy God commanded thee to keep the Sabbath Day" (Deut. v: 15). In this case the reason given is a *national* one, that the Sabbath signifies the emergence of the Jewish people from bondage to freedom, and the beginning of their independent national existence.

What is Judaism? Among the bewildering variety of definitions that abound there are two which represent apparently clear-cut and sharply demarcated distinctions. There is the definition of Judaism as a faith and a creed of life, that Judaism expresses itself in a belief in the One God who revealed himself to his people on Mt. Sinai and gave them the Torah with its 613 traditional commandments, its positive enactments and its negative, its regulation of the duty of the Jew to God and his duty to his fellowmen. The loyalty and adherence of the Jew to his faith is measured by the extent to which he adheres in thought and word, in practice and observance, to these precepts, in prayer and in action, in Torah, Avodah and Gemiluth Chassadim. A Jew who is an atheist is a contradiction in terms, and a Jew who fails to observe the dictates of Judaism is a renegade Jew, or at best a nominal Jew. It is the Judaism of Mitzvoth, the Judaism which regulates the life of the Jew according to the expressed will of God and which reaches its highest point in communion with God. Such a Judaism is independent of country or of territorial considerations; of that Judaism it has been finely said that "Judaism is greater than Judea."

The other definition of Judaism is strikingly divergent, and with the development of secular Zionism and the establishment of the State of Israel has received a tremendous fillip in modern times. It is the conception of Judaism not as a religious faith but as a national idea. It is Judaism as an ethnic concept. The Jew is the person who is a member of the Jewish Nation. Where the highest ideal of Judaism as a religion is found in the verse "And thou shalt love the Lord thy God with all thy heart, with all thy soul, with all thy might," the Judaism of nationality invents a new version, "And thou shalt love the land of Israel with all thy heart, with all thy soul and with all thy might." From the point of view of this concept, Mr. Ben Gurion is strictly logical in his contention that a Zionist who remains outside Israel is no Zionist, and to it one must add the corollary that a Jew who feels no bond with Israel is no Jew. From this point of view also, there is nothing absurd or paradoxical in the idea of a Jew being an atheist, any more than there is in the fact that an Englishman, a Frenchman or an American can be an atheist.

An excellent illustration of the divergence between these two points of view is provided by the delightful story I once heard told in Israel. The Orthodox section of the Community decided to undertake a propaganda drive for the better observance of the Sabbath, and in pursuit of that aim to undertake these demonstrations which are so common in Israel and which, when carried to excess, bring about these painful incidents which marred the peace of Jerusalem a few weeks ago and caused the death of one of the Neturei Karta. Among the zealous upholders of the sanctity of the Sabbath was a recently-arrived Yiddish-speaking Yeshivah student. Seeing a Chalutz walking along with a cigarette in his mouth, he approached him and irefully exclaimed in Yiddish, "Sheigetz! Shabbes reichert men?" (You good-for-nothing! Smoking on the Sabbath). But the Chalutz, nothing dismayed, and without even removing the cigarette from his mouth, retorted disdainfully in Hebrew, "Goy! Dabber Ivrit" (Gentile! Speak Hebrew!). To the one the essence of Judaism was observance, and the Jew who smoked on the Sabbath was thereby a "goy," while to the other the essence of Judaism was its national content and a Jew who did not speak the national language was a "goy."

And each point of view finds its passionate and strident advocates, and each one maintains with equal conviction that his interpretation of Judaism is the correct one, and each can bring chapter and verse to prove his case. Which of them is right, and in what does Judaism consist? Is it a religion or is it a nationality? Is the concept of "Zachor" which gives a religious reason for the keeping of the Sabbath the correct one, or is the "Shamor" which gives a national reason? It is to that question that the answer is given, "Zachor and Shamor were both uttered in one breath." Judaism is unique among all the religions in the world; Judaism is unique among religion and nationality; Judaism is a national religion and the Jews are a religious nation. Those who maintain that it is only a religion, a way of approach to God, are as guilty of a distortion of the essence of Judaism as are those who maintain that it is only a national concept. One cannot separate these two elements of Judaism into watertight compartments since it is an indivisible amalgam of both. And to those who wish to deprive Judaism of one of its essential components the words of Ecclesiastes can be applied: טוב אשר תאחוז בזה וגם מזה אל תנח ידך כי ירא אלהים יצא את כלם "It is good that thou seizest hold of this, but neither relax thy hand from that, for he who feareth God shall fulfil both of them" (Eccles. vii: 18), for שמור וזכור בדבור אחד נאמרו "Remember" and "Observe the Sabbath Day" were both uttered in one breath."

## THE RESIDUAL LEGACY OF JEWISH RIGHTLESSNESS

*For he is the Lord our God . . . who redeemed us from the hand of kings. Our King who delivered us from the grasp of men of terror . . . who wrought for us miracles and vengeance upon Pharaoh, signs and wonders in the land of the children of Ham.*

(Evening Service.)

THE text which I take to-day, on this special occasion when our thoughts are directed towards the unhappy position of our brethren in Egypt, and our prayers go up to God for their speedy deliverance, is the first in this series which is taken from that part of the evening service which is common to both Sabbath and weekday. That means, of course, that it is read on every single day of the year.

It speaks of God's faithfulness to Israel, a faithfulness which reveals itself by the very fact that the Jew is still alive to utter it, by the very fact of the survival of the Jewish people. Harried and persecuted, decimated and discriminated against, the Jew has nevertheless been granted, as no other people has been granted, the boon of collective immortality. Kings and men of terror, tyrants and dictators, barbarians and the so-called cultured and civilised nations, all have tried to destroy the children of Israel. "Grievously have they afflicted me from my youth up, yet they have not prevailed against me. The plowers plowed upon my back, they made long their furrows." (Psalm cxxix: 1-3.) Hardly a nation which has not at one time or another during the long course of Israel's tragic history, attempted to destroy the Jewish people, Pharaoh and Nebuchadnezzar, Haman and Antiochus Epiphanes, the Romans and the Holy Roman Church as exemplified by Torquemada, Chmielnicki and Hitler. As we say in the Haggada of Passover, "For not one alone rose up against us to destroy us, but in every generation they rise up against us to destroy us, but the Holy One, blessed be He, hath delivered us from their hand."

That passage which forms my text is the subject of a comment by me in my book "Far East Mission." Prior to my journey to India I spent a few days in Israel in order to be briefed for my difficult mission, and in the chapter entitled "Glimpses of Israel" I made the following comment:—

> "I turn on the wireless after Sabbath. 'Melave Malka,' the extension of the spirit of Sabbath after its conclusion, was on the air. The familiar words repeated daily in the evening serivce, 'Thank God, who holdeth our soul in life and hath not suffered our feet to be moved; who made us tread upon the high places of our enemies and exalted our horn over all them that hated us! who wrought for us miracles' are sung by a Cantor. But with what passionate pride are they charged, giving them added force and significance! They are the outpourings of a soul bursting with thankfulness that, Phoenix-like, Israel has emerged to triumphant independence out of the ashes of the greatest holocaust in world history."

These words surely expressed the hope and the confidence which filled the heart of every Jew after the State of Israel was established. We felt that with the attainment of our independence, the tragic odyssey of Israel's persecution throughout the ages was now a thing of the past. No more, we proclaimed, would the Jewish people be led like lambs to the slaughter; no more would we be the helpless victims of circumstances beyond our control. The State of

Israel would champion the cause of its people should they be faced with discrimination or persecution, and in the last resort it would serve as a haven of refuge for communities which found conditions of existence intolerable in the lands of its dispersion. The second hope has been, and continues to be fulfilled, but alas, recent events have shown that the era of persecution and discrimination is not yet over, and our daily prayers of thanksgiving for deliverance from Egypt at the dawn of our history is to-day combined with supplication and prayer to God that the Jewish Community which is in Egypt to-day shall be delivered from the persecution to which it is daily being subjected.

The events of the past weeks have revealed one fact to which I have given expression in the speeches which I have given on behalf of the I.U.A. Campaign which has recently been launched. Simultaneously with the abortive attack by Britain and France upon the Suez Canal, of which that persecution is the direct outcome, there took place the savage and brutal assault of Russia upon the Hungarians who made a desperate attempt to free their country from the yoke of Soviet domination. That assault has also brought in its train a refugee problem. Some 80,000 Hungarians have fled the country and taken refuge in Austria. Others have been deported to concentration and slave camps in Siberia. No one with a spark of human feeling, no one whose heart responds to the gallantry displayed in an unequal and desperate struggle can fail to be moved by this expression of the innate desire for freedom which burns in the heart of every people, and I have no doubt but that the Jewish Community in this country will do its duty equally with members of other communities. But at the same time, are we not permitted to express our distress and resentment at the inequality of the reaction to the plight of these Hungarian refugees and to those who are equally the objects of persecution in Egypt? Every country in the free world has geared itself to extend the maximum possible support, both moral and material, to the victims of Russian brutality. England has taken more than the rest of the world together, America has suspended the operation of the McCurran immigration laws to step up the numbers from the 6,000 permitted to 21,000, Canada has opened its doors wide; our own country, so cautious and even niggardly in its immigration, is to bring in at least 1,000 refugees. Their plight has become the subject of major discussions at the United Nations. And at the same time the similar plight of Egyptian Jews is almost completely ignored. The impassioned plea of Israel's Foreign Minister at U.N.O. is met with complete silence. A delegation of British Jews which came to the British Home Minister with a modest request to allow 500 Egyptian Jewish refugees to enter the country was met with a polite but cold assurance that consideration would be given to the request, though they are the direct victims of the British action in Egypt. They are abandoned, neglected and ignored.

And from these facts two considerations emerge, the implications of which we do well to take to heart. The first is that the State of Israel alone remains the one sure hope for the Jewish people, the one haven of refuge for its persecuted brethren. And the other is that despite the emergence of the State and the newborn dignity of the Jewish people, there still lingers in the background of the mind of the nations of the world the unexpressed but still present thought that the sufferings of Jews are not as the sufferings of other people, that Jewish lives are just a little bit more "Hefker" than non-Jewish lives. The murderous attacks of Fedayeen on Israelis is not expected to produce the same reaction as guerilla attacks on other peoples, the plight of Jewish refugees is not put in the same class as that of Hungarian. It is the sad residual legacy of 2,000 years of persecution and until it is eradicated the Jew cannot be regarded as having come entirely into his own.

## IF I FORGET THEE, O JERUSALEM!

On the occasion of the First Anniversary of the establishment of the reborn State of Israel, a banquet was held in Johannesburg. The function was graced by the presence of a large number of distinguished non-Jews, among them a member of the Cabinet. I was not one of the speakers on that occasion, but I was asked to recite Grace After Meals. I did so in an unusual manner. I prefaced the recital of the statutory Grace with the following comment: "I am about to recite the traditional Grace After Meals. It is the benediction which is recited by every observant Jew after every meal. In view, however, of the occasion, and of the non-Jews who are present, I intend making but a slight departure from the normal usage. Instead of reciting the whole Grace in Hebrew, I shall render in English those passages which give expression to the undying hope that God would one day in his mercy restore the Jewish people to their land, and which vividly kept that hope alive. You will then, perhaps, begin to understand the phenomenon of a people divorced from its homeland for nigh on two millennia, still maintaining the sublime faith in its ultimate return, and how the re-emergence of that State after that long period became a reality."

It being a festive occasion, I began by reading the 126th Psalm, the reading of which is prescribed as an introduction to Grace on all such occasions:—

> "When the Lord turned again the captivity of Israel, we were like unto them that dream. . . . Bring back our captivity, O Lord, as the streams in the south. They that sow in tears shall reap in joy."

I then proceeded to recite the statutory Grace After Meals, rendering the following passages in English:—

"We thank thee O Lord, our God, because thou didst give as an heritage unto our fathers a desirable, good and pleasant land."

"Have mercy, O Lord our God, upon Israel thy people, upon Jerusalem thy city, upon Zion the abiding place of thy glory, upon the kingdom of the house of David thine anointed, and upon the great and holy house that was called by thy Name."

"And rebuild Jerusalem the holy city speedily in our days. Blessed art thou O Lord, who in thy compassion rebuildest Jerusalem, Amen."

"May the all-Merciful break the yoke from off our neck and lead us upright to our land."

It read almost as a Zionist Manifesto, and the Cabinet Minister who was present, was sufficiently impressed—or sufficiently incredulous—to ask the Minister for Israel the next day to let him have a Jewish Prayer Book so that he could see it for himself! The fact is striking by its very incongruity. That in giving thanks to God for food we should pour out our hearts to God in thanksgiving for the Land of Israel once granted to us and in tearful supplication for a restoration of our independence must be startling to anyone but a Jew. To the Jew it was but a fulfilment of the vow in the 137th Psalm, the Psalm which is also read before Grace on non-festive occasions: "If I forget thee, O Jerusalem, let my right hand forget its cunning. If I do not remember thee, let my tongue cleave to the roof of my mouth, if I prefer not Jerusalem above my chief joy." In sadness and gladness, on weekday and Festival, after meals and in the Amidah, the Jew placed the thought of the restoration in the forefront of his mind and in his prayers.

It is that thought that I want you to have in mind when I ask you to turn again to consider the contents of Lecha Dodi. Here is a hymn composed in praise of the Sabbath Day, and in his passionate love for the Sabbath he personifies it as a bride whom he wishes to clasp in a loving embrace and lose himself in her love. And in the Sephardi version based upon the original statement of the Talmud, she is both Bride and Queen and therefore he is only the Prince Consort. And as bride he pours out his love, and as Queen he pledges his undying loyalty and allegiance. And so he pours out his heart to her. But for how long does he maintain this outpouring of love and allegiance? It possesses him for the first verse, "Come let us go greet the Sabbath, for it is a source of blessing." It is the theme of the second verse of which I have already spoken, but after that he seems to forget the object of his love and allegiance until almost forcibly he is dragged back to it in the last verse. He sings the message of hope and comfort to Jerusalem destroyed; and gives expression to his perfervid faith in its ultimate restoration to glory. And after devoting three verses to that, he prophesies the ultimate victory of the Jewish people, their increase and the restoration of the sovereignty of the House of David. Has not the beloved bride a right to complain? Would there not be justification in her allegation, "Is this your love for me? You hold me in your arms and profess to love me, but you have become tired of me already. You are not thinking of me any more. You love someone else. You are holding the Sabbath in your arms and singing a song to Jerusalem. You profess to love me, and your love song has turned from me to the Jewish people. Do you call that love?"

"A Queen am I to whom you swear allegiance? Traitor! You are guilty of dual loyalties! It is not to me that you are swearing allegiance any more, but Jerusalem and the Jewish people!" How can one call this a Sabbath hymn?

But surely from what I have said the answer is clear. There is no aspect of Jewish life or thought which is not shot through and permeated with the love of Zion. Just as in giving thanks for the satisfaction of one's hunger, one fulfils the injunction, "If I forget thee O Jerusalem, let my right hand forget its cunning," just as on Rosh Hashanah, which is the day of Judgment, we include the Haftarah of Jeremiah which deals with the return, just as we conclude the Service on Yom Kippur with the declaration לשנה הבאה בירושלים just as on no single occasion of one's life does one omit to bring to one's mind the undying hope of Israel's subsequent restoration, so even in one's passionate outpouring of love and allegiance to the Sabbath one turned from that thought to the rebuilding of Israel and the rebuilding of the people of Israel.

The effect upon the Jewish people of that phenomenon was finely expressed by Benjamin Disraeli in a well-known passage, "The vineyards of Israel have ceased to exist, but the eternal Law enjoins the children of Israel still to celebrate their vintage. A race that persists in celebrating their vintage, although they have no fruits to gather, will regain their vineyards."

And it is from that point of view that the sin against the very spirit of Judaism which was committed by the Reform Movement in savagely excising from their Prayer Book every reference to Zion has to be viewed. For in all their tampering with the traditional prayers none so sinned against the essential spirit of Judaism, against that fundamental idea to which I devoted the last sermon on Lecha Dodi than this denying that the ultimate redemption of the Jewish people was to be envisaged in the return to their ancient homeland and the regaining of their independence. They saw in the boon of emancipation and the equality of all men before the law the Messianic age, they ripped from the fabric of Judaism that golden thread which represented the very warp and woof of that fabric and left it a miserable and tattered rag. The truncation of the prayers, the introduction of the vernacular, the abandonment of the references to the sacrificial system, as of the doctrine of the Chosen People, none of these eviscerations of the body of Jewish prayer can be regarded as so serious as this operation, for if the former affected the body, the latter destroyed the soul. For when the Jew abandons the hope in the return to Zion he abandons his hope in the future of the Jewish people and to the possibility of its giving a message of hope and comfort to the world. For only from Zion shall the Torah go forth, and only from Jerusalem the word of the Lord.

# THE GOD OF HISTORY*

ברוך אתה ה׳ אלהינו ואלהי אבותנו אלהי אברהם אלהי יצחק ואלהי יעקב

*"Blessed art thou, O Lord God and God of our fathers, God of Abraham, God of Isaac and God of Jacob."*

(Opening Words of the Amidah.)

THE most important part of a Jewish service is the Amidah or, as it is more popularly known from the original number of blessings contained in it, Shemoneh Esreh, the prayer of the Eighteen Benedictions. And the importance of this part of the service is emphasised by the fact that in the Talmudic literature it is called simply "Tefillah" prayer, *the* prayer.

Although the intermediate blessings of the Amidah vary according to the occasion, and are completely different from one another on weekdays, Sabbath and Festivals, there are certain statutory blessings which remain constant and do not change—these are the first three introductory paragraphs, the blessings of praise, and the concluding three, the blessings of thanksgiving.

It is of the first of these introductory blessings, that which in the Mishna is called "Aboth," the blessing of the patriarchs, that I wish to speak this evening. How does the Jew commence the most important prayer of his liturgy? By what appellation does the Jew address God? And to

---

* By the Rev. D. Isaacs, B.A.

anyone who reads this passage carefully and thoughtfully it must surely come as a surprise to find that *the* prayer of our liturgy speaks of God not as the creator of heaven and earth, not as the God who brought the world into existence, which is the primary and most essential concept of God as seen by the devout, but as the God who appeared to our fathers, the God of Abraham, Isaac and Jacob!

That question assumes an even greater importance when we realise that not only in the Amidah, where the question can be answered quite easily on the grounds that it has a specific *Jewish* significance and that is why it refers to God as the God of Jewish history, the God of *our* ancestors, but even in the Ten Commandments which are a "summary of human duties binding upon all mankind," and which have been accepted as the very basis of civilisation itself, and which are therefore not so limited in their application, even in these Ten Commandments God is described as the God of history, of Jewish history — "I am the Lord thy God who brought thee out of the land of Egypt, out of the house of bondage." Here the difficulty is even more pronounced — surely it would have been more in keeping with their universal message if God had been described as "Creator of heaven and earth"!

The answer to that question was given by the medieval philosopher-poet Yehudah Halevi in his immortal classic of Jewish religious philosophy—the Kuzari. This work is written in the form of a dialogue between the king of the Khazars, a pagan tribe living in the Crimean Peninsula, and a Jewish scholar. The Khazar king had decided to abandon pagan worship and become converted to one of the great religions. But neither the teachings of Christianity nor Islam were acceptable to him, and when the representatives of these two faiths each in turn agreed upon the superiority of Judaism over the faith of his rival, the king sent for a representative of Judaism, and in the discussion which takes place between the two of them Yehudah Halevi sets forth his presentation of the fundamental teachings of Judaism.

The Jewish scholar opens his discourse by saying that the Jews believe in the God of Abraham, Isaac and Jacob, the God who brought the children of Israel out of the land of Egypt and led them through the desert to the Promised Land. But on hearing this the king became angry. "I knew I shouldn't have asked a Jew," he exclaimed. "Surely you should have told me that you believe in the God who created heaven and earth, as any other religious person would have done! Why did you tell me that you believe in the God of your ancestors?" And Yehudah Halevi puts the answer to that question, to our question, into the mouth of the scholar. "No," he says, "I could not tell you that we believe in the God who created heaven and earth, because that is a point of bitter controversy among the philosophers and theologians; there are many people who deny categorically the truth of that statement, but historical fact no one can dispute, and none can deny the facts of Jewish history and Jewish history itself is the most conclusive proof of the workings of God in the affairs of mankind. For God had revealed Himself to His people in a great historic deed—the redemption from Egypt. It could never have come about were it not that God guides the process of history, for without the intervention of the Divine, as the Pesach Haggadah puts it, we would still be slaves in Egypt."

In this striking answer of Yehudah Halevi there is enshrined one of the most fundamental principles of Judaism, a principle which imparts a uniqueness to Judaism in that it bases its claims and demands not upon natural or supernatural phenomena, but upon the facts of history. It posits the fundamental concept of the appearance of God in the unfolding of history, it gives expression to the unquenchable optimism of Judaism that there is a pattern to and a meaning in history, and that the events which take place are not the haphazard products of chance, but are directed by God to a goal to be attained here on earth.

This important doctrine of Judaism was summed up

clearly by a distinguished contemporary Jewish scholar when he said:* "Considering the part played for good or for evil by the unforeseen and fortuitous in the development of human destinies, and man's inability to control the heightened potency of his destructive powers, there is surely little ground for the belief in the inevitability of progress. It is precisely here that Jewish teaching has most to say to us. In its conception of history are to be found principles of permanent validity determining the meaning of progress. History in the Jewish conception is not a chaos leading to nowhere, but an overall progression with a definite goal which it derives from God who is above history, and who rules and controls history. For God in Jewish history is not only the Lord of Nature, but also the Lord of History. History is the arena wherein God's activity on behalf of man is made manifest, and in which, and through which, His eternal purpose is being fulfilled. It is this which gives history its significance. All events in history are full of meaning, and it is in terms of that meaning that all historical happenings have to be interpreted."

The idea of the participation of God in the events of the day is the dominant note of Biblical history. No one reading the Bible can fail to be impressed with the plan and purpose its narratives unfold. The call to Abraham, the Egyptian bondage, the Exodus, the Revelation at Sinai, Israel's Election and entry into the Promised Land, are not isolated and unrelated episodes, but are all parts of a closely-knit drama, in which the end is already foreshadowed in the beginning; and it is this idea which is fundamental to prophetic teaching and the Jewish thought it inspires. The Exile, the Restoration, the subsequent destruction of the second Hebrew State and Temple, and the dispersion of the Jewish people among the nations, are not viewed as mere products of the contingent and unforeseen, but as parts of a divine plan, working towards the fulfilment of a

* Epstein—Faith of Judaism, p. 258.

purpose that was with Him from the beginning, for the individual, the nations and the human race. Empires may rise and fall, civilisations may flourish and decay, but everywhere there is the persistent activity of God, giving to all the movements of history, unity, direction and purpose."

And yet there are times when it is difficult, almost impossible, to see the hand of God in the events of history. When one recalls the ghastly tragedy of European Jewry, who in those dark days could see the finger of God in a holocaust which annihilated the great centres of Jewish life and learning, and brought about the hideous massacre of six million of our brethren? And today again in front of our very eyes the lights of freedom are being ruthlessly and brutally snuffed out in different parts of the world. Again right and justice are being mercilessly trampled underfoot, and the forces of iniquity gloat triumphantly. There are many who will ask: "Is this the work of God? Is this how God appears in history?" But there is one important consideration that we have to bear in mind—it is only when we are in a position to view such events from afar, when we are able to look back upon them and see them in their correct historical perspective, that we can see that God does guide the process of history, and we are able to say with the psalmist, בפרוח רשעים כמו עשב ויציצו כל פועלי עון להשמדם עדי עד "When the wicked spring forth as the grass and the workers of iniquity flourish—it is to destroy them forever." The forces of evil may triumph for the moment, yet their glory is but short-lived, and in the long run justice does prevail and right emerges triumphant.

These sentiments are not just the outpourings of the pious heart, they are substantiated and corroborated by a world-famous historian who, with his vast knowledge of the whole panorama of world history, felt impelled to say with absolute conviction: "One lesson, and only one, history may be said to repeat with distinctness, that the world is built somehow on moral foundations; that in the long run it is well with the good; in the long run it is ill with the wicked. But this is no science; it is no more than the old doctrine taught long ago by the Hebrew prophets" (Book of Jewish Thoughts, p. 151).

These then are the implications and the force of that age-old blessing which the devout Jew repeats three times a day, and the lesson they convey is of the deepest significance for us in these difficult times through which we are living. The world is in a turmoil, perched precariously on the brink of an abyss in danger of being thrust over the edge at any moment. And the Jew blesses the God of his fathers, Abraham, Isaac and Jacob, and calls to mind the miracles performed for him in the past, and he realises that it is this same God who guides history today, and he takes comfort in the thought that no matter how thick the darkness may be, the day is at hand when the sun will come streaming through to proclaim the dawn of that glorious era which will usher in the establishment of the Kingdom of God upon earth.

## GREETING THE MOURNER

## THE BROTHERHOOD OF ISRAEL

**המקום ינחם אתכם בתוך שאר אבלי ציון וירושלים**

*May the All-Present comfort you together with the other mourners of Zion and Jerusalem.*

I WANT to speak this evening about the beautiful custom of greeting mourners on behalf of the Congregation when they enter the Synagogue on the Sabbath of the week of their shiva. Before dealing with the main point which I wish to bring to your particular attention this evening, I feel it necessary, however, to say something about the Jewish laws of mourning as a whole which, I regret to say, are becoming increasingly honoured in the breach rather than in the observance.

Some years ago a book written by a Reform Rabbi of America, Joshua Liebman, entitled Peace of Mind, attained a fantastic success. It became a best seller overnight and its sales reached millions. The main distinction of this book, however, lies in the fact that the author, a profound and enthusiastic believer in the comparatively new science of psychiatry, applies its principles to Judaism as he sees it, and interprets it in the light of this new revelation.

As to how he succeeds in his main purpose is a question which has still to be answered, but he is most impressive in his assertion that the age-old traditional Jewish laws regulating mourning are strictly in accordance with the most advanced theories of modern psychiatry. He points out correctly that the laws regulating mourning represent a "gradual tapering of the intensity of grief." First there is the week following the funeral when the mourner, abandoning himself to the enormity of his grief, turns his back, so to speak, upon the world and its pleasures, upon his economic problems, and secludes himself in his house. During this time it is the duty of his friends to come and visit and comfort him, and give him an opportunity to release his pent-up sorrow by speaking of his loss. Then come the next 23 days which make up the "Sheloshim" during which, although he resumes his normal vocation, the burden of his sorrow is still heavy upon him. For the next eleven months, during ten of which he says Kaddish, he adheres to the ordinary laws of mourning which consist in abstention from gaiety and pleasure. When the year is ended the claims of life with their joys can be met.

Liebman proceeds to give the following interpretation of these laws, in accordance with the findings of psychiatry, in the following words:—

"The conclusion, then, of the newest psychological research is that when we face the loss of a dear one, we should allow our hearts full leeway in the expression of their pain. We should not pretend to grieve when we do not feel it, when, for example, an aged parent who has has been suffering from an incurable disease is given surcease by death. On the other hand, we must not be afraid to articulate the wildness of our sorrow if that is what we genuinely feel. We must never falsify our emotions in conformity with conventions. Nor should we prematurely seek for speedy comfort and consolation. Let us understand that the experience of pain somehow has a curative function and that any evasive detour around normal sorrow will bring us later to a tragic abyss. After all, we were given tear-ducts to use for such hours of darkness. Not only should we be unashamed of grief, confident that its expression will not permanently hurt us, but we should also possess the wisdom to talk about our loss and through that creative conversation with friends and companions begin to reconstruct the broken fragments of our lives.

"We should not resist the sympathy and the stimulation of social interaction. We should learn not to grow impatient with the slow healing process of time. We should discipline ourselves to recognise that there are many steps to be taken along the highway leading from sorrow to renewed serenity and that it is folly to attempt prematurely to telescope and compress these successive stages of recuperation into a miraculous cure. We should not demand of ourselves more than Nature herself will permit. We should anticipate these stages in our emotional convalescence: unbearable pain, poignant grief, empty days, resistance to consolation, disinterestedness in life, gradually giving way under the healing sunlight of love, friendship, social challenge, to the new weaving of a pattern of action and the acceptance of the irresistible challenge of life."

And yet, despite the prescribed intensity of mourning during the first week, as soon as the Sabbath comes that mourning is suspended—the joy and serenity of the Sabbath takes precedence over, and precludes, any outward expression of mourning—and since the reading of the Sabbath Psalm is regarded as the official commencement of the Sabbath, the mourner waits outside until the conclusion of Lecha Dodi and then he is ushered into the Synagogue.

That is why the mourner comes to Synagogue on the Friday evening of his Shiva, and that is why he remains outside until the Sabbath Psalm is due to be read. But it does not explain the announcement of the Cantor נחום אבלים "The comforting of mourners (will now take place)," nor the formula which is uttered by the Rabbi. And may I say at once that the confining of this formula to the Rabbi is but one instance of many, of which prostrating oneself on Yom Kippur is the most recent example which I have quoted, whereby an increasing formalism restricts a Mitzvah or a custom to the Rabbi, when in truth it belongs to every Jew. In my father's Beth Hamidrash the whole Congregation used to turn to the mourner and recite the formula, and the classical Ozar Ha-Tefillot prayer-book has the following rubric:—

> "In many congregations it is the custom that the beadle proclaims that the congregation shall greet the mourner. The Rabbi, followed by the elders of the city, proceeds to the entrance of the Synagogue and they stand within the Synagogue, forming two rows, and the mourner passes between them."

And this original custom helps us to understand its true import.

In order to understand that true import let me tell you of a little incident that happened this Tuesday during the morning service. I looked round the congregation and went up to the officiating Minister and told him not to recite Tahanun, the supplicatory prayers which are omitted on any occasion of communal joy. That instruction was not, as some may imagine, because it was New Year's Day, but because a young man the circumcision of whose son was to take place that morning had felt the impulse to come to Synagogue in a spirit of thanksgiving. He was probably unknown to the whole congregation apart from myself, yet the fact that he was in Synagogue was a reason for not saying prayers of sadness. And the same regulation applies even if the Mohel or the Sandek is in Synagogue.

When we consider the implications of both these beautiful customs together, the whole congregation joining in giving utterance to a formula of comfort to bereaved mourners, the whole congregation relieved from the obligation to say Tahanun because one of those present has an occasion of joy, do they not say more eloquently than words can do "The mourning of one Jew is an occasion for sorrow for the whole Jewish Community, a joyous event in the family circle of one individual Jew is an occasion for joy for the whole community. The Jew shares in the joys of his fellow-Jews and thereby adds to them, the Jew shares in the sorrow of his fellow-Jews and thereby tends to lessen it." For, if, as the proverb says, צרת רבים חצי נחמה the fact that a misfortune is shared by many constitutes a partial consolation, is it not equally, if not more true, to say that נחמת רבים חצי צרה the comforting by many makes the tragedy more bearable?

It was in this tangible way that expression was given to the concept of חברים כל ישראל of the brotherhood of Israel, and to the mourner we say "As far as possible we share your sorrow. May it be granted to you to have joys, that they also, in a spirit of fellowship and brotherhood, we may also share with you." For we believe and should act up to the belief of אחינו כל בית ישראל of the whole house of Israel forming one brotherly band, associating ourselves with their joys as with their sorrows.

# THE SABBATH PSALM

## מזמור שיר ליום השבת

*A psalm—a song for the Sabbath Day.*

(Psalm xcii: 1.)

As will, I hope, by now be clear to those regular worshippers on Friday evening who have been following this series of sermons, the six introductory Psalms and Lecha Dodi constitute an introduction to the Sabbath evening service, and were only introduced as late as the sixteenth century. The Friday evening service proper commences with the reading of the Sabbath Psalm, Psalm 92, to which Psalm 93 is added. According to the Din, it is with the reading of this Psalm in Synagogue that the incidence of the Sabbath takes place, even though the sun may not have set, in accordance with the principle that מוסיפין מחול על הקודש that one may extend the length of the Sabbath day by adding to it a portion of the weekday, and once the congregation has recited it, the Sabbath is deemed to have begun. It is for that reason, as I pointed out last week, that the suspension of mourning on the part of the mourner begins with its reading and that he enters the Synagogue at this point of the service.

That is as far as the regulation of the Sabbath is concerned, but it is with another point that I wish to deal this evening.

Of the beauty and the elevated thought in this Psalm there can be no question, but the astonishing thing is that the contents of this beautiful Psalm appear to bear no relation whatsoever to its superscription. It purports to be "a Psalm, a Song for the Sabbath Day," and yet one searches in vain throughout the whole Psalm for a single reference to the Sabbath day, to the sanctity of the Sabbath, the spiritual and physical recreation of the Sabbath, the joy of the Sabbath. It almost reminds one of the sensational headlines of the yellow press, when one reads the paragraph underneath the headline and finds that it does not give the news which that headline purports to convey. Of what theme then does this Psalm deal? It is not only a praise of the greatness of the works of God and the deep wisdom of his plan in the world, but a defence of it against the age-old and ever recurring criticism that that justice and right which ought to prevail in the world if indeed it is ruled by an all-merciful and compassionate God, are not always evident to the eye. It is the ancient problem of the apparent prosperity of the wicked, the misfortune of the righteous. It is the problem of "When the wicked sprang up as the grass and all the workers of iniquity flourished." How can this be squared with God's justice? And almost contemptuously the author of the Psalm says that the person who poses that question belongs to the category of "the brutish man" who "knoweth it not" and the fool who cannot understand it. The answer to that problem according to the author of the Psalm is simple, and is expressd in three Hebrew words. The wicked are raised up on high in order that their ultimate downfall may be all the more catastrophic and complete. It is "that they may be destroyed for ever." For God is in his heavens and the enemy shall be destroyed, and the workers of iniquity shall be scattered. The righteous shall ultimately triumph, they shall spring up like the palm-tree and grow majestically like the cedars of Lebanon, and the Psalm ends with the triumphant assertion of faith "To declare that the Lord is upright: he is my Rock, and there is no unrighteousness in him."

The man who does not understand this is brutish and foolish, for the characteristic of the brute is that it sees only that which is in front of its nose; it possesses neither memory of the past nor prescience to look beyond the present to the future. And the characteristic of the fool is his inability to be a רואה את הנולד to see the development of events.

For the mills of God grind slow, but they grind exceeding fine. Injustice and wickedness may reign supreme for the time being, the wicked may spring up as the grass and the workers of iniquity flourish for the moment, but it is but a poor, vainglorious strutting upon the stage of history for a brief moment—the result inevitably is "that they are destroyed for ever." Have we not seen it in our own days and in our own time? When during 1939-1944 the most evil man ever to hold the destiny of a great nation and of the world in his hand seemed to flourish mightily, when the Nazi Colossus strode from the Arctic Circle in the North to the Southern shores of the Mediterranean in the South, from the Atlantic seaboard in the West to Stalingrad in the East, when England alone, defeated and disarmed, held out, how many of us were there who believed that there was no power on earth which could dislodge him? Yet how long did it take for him to be destroyed for ever? For a world lacking in faith to be convinced that "Thou O Lord art on high for evermore. For lo thine enemies O Lord, for lo thine enemies shall perish; all the workers of iniquity shall be scattered"?

It is easy to be wise after the event, but to maintain one's belief in the justice of God when every thing which one sees with the eyes of flesh belies and derides that justice, demands a sublime faith in the goodness of God which it is not always easy to call upon. But that faith is fortified by the undeniable facts of history which reveal the slow and unsteady yet sure development of divine civilisation.

All this may be true, but still it does not answer the question which I posed at the beginning of this sermon, what has this to do with the Sabbath, why is this theme made the subject of the Sabbath Psalm?

To that person who has penetrated into the inner, essential spirit of the Sabbath, to that person who observes the Sabbath not as a day upon which one goes to Synagogue, not merely as a day of negative cessation from work, but as a day, in the beautiful words of the Amidah of Sabbath afternoon, of "rest granted in generous love, a true and faithful rest, a rest in peace and tranquillity, in quietude and safety, a perfect rest wherein thou delightest," the answer to that question is beyond doubt. It is called a Sabbath Psalm not because it sings of the Sabbath and extols its virtues, but because it represents the kind of thoughts which are liable to enter and possess the thoughts of that person who observes the Sabbath in its true spirit.

It is in a very qualified sense that the adage "arbeit adelt," that "work ennobles a man," is true. It is true insofar as idleness has a demoralising and even corrupting effect upon a person, it is true insofar as the feeling that one is following a gainful occupation gives one a sense of self-respect and dignity. It is true in the case of the craftsman whose pride of achievement and the knowledge of creative effort give a similar feeling. But on the other hand, the preoccupation with the needs of gaining a livelihood, the hurly-burly, the hurry-scurry, the turmoil of the weekdays tend to have just the opposite effect. They brutalise instead of ennobling, they make a man sottish instead of wise. Just as of the enslaved children of Israel in Egypt, it is recorded that they rejected the vision of the redemption מקוצר רוח ומעבודה קשה "from the shortness of spirit which comes from hard labour," so to-day, even though it be not "hard labour," it takes man away from the contemplation of things of the spirit. He sees only that which is before his eyes. He has not the time, and if he has the time he has not the inclination, for contemplation of things *sub specie aeternitatis*, under the aspect of eternity.

It is only when the Sabbath comes, and he is relieved of material cares, when he makes of the day a day of recreation that in the serenity and tranquil peace of that blessed day he can give himself over to meditation and contemplation. It is then that he can sing of the greatness of God and of the ultimate triumph of right and justice. It is then that he can declare that the Lord is upright, that there is no iniquity in him. He can attune himself to the spirit of God and enter into communion with him, and spiritually refreshed and strengthened in his faith, face the future with confidence and trust.

Therein much more than in the enforced abstention from work lies the true value of the Sabbath of the Lord, and he who disregards it does it to the detriment of his immortal soul.

# MA'ARIV

If you will look at the top of the pages of the Friday evening service you will see that there are two different headings. Pages 108a to 113, that is, the six Introductory Psalms, Lecha Dodi and the Sabbath Psalm which we have been discussing during the last three months are headed קבלת שבת in Hebrew, and "Inauguration of the Sabbath" in English.

From page 114 onwards it is headed ערבית לשבת "The Evening Service for the Sabbath."

In other words, from the invocation to prayer ברכו את ה׳ המבורך "Blessed be the Lord who is to be blessed" we commence the evening service proper, and from this point until the end of the Hashkivenu prayer the wording of the evening service is identical on weekdays, Sabbaths and Festivals. Only in the Roman rite do the blessings which precede and follow the Shema contain additional and specific references to the Sabbath; in our rite as in others there is no distinction.*

It is therefore a convenient opportunity to discuss a question which ought to perhaps suggest itself more to a congregation of regular worshippers than it appears to do. What is the structure of our daily prayers? Why do we say this, and why that? Who is responsible for the order of prayers, and what authority attaches to them? Are they of Biblical origin or Rabbinical? Are they early or late? These, and a number of cognate questions, should from time to time suggest themselves. And when these questions

* I ignore the insertion of Piyutim on Festivals.

are answered it will be seen that far from our statutory prayers being a haphazard collection of liturgical passages, they follow a well-defined pattern, and their architectonic structure is one which compels our admiration.

The first paragraph of the Shema enjoins that it shall be read בשכבך ובקומך "When thou liest down and when thou risest up." In other words it has to be read both in the evening and in the morning, and the very first Mishnah of the first Tractate of the Talmud opens with a discussion as to what time of the evening that reading has to take place. To that discussion the Fourth Mishnah adds the regulation that "In the morning two Benedictions are said before the Shema and one after; whereas in the evening two Benedictions precede the Shema and two follow, the one long and the other short." The Mishnah was compiled at the end of the Second Century, but it includes material going back as much as seven centuries earlier. There is no doubt that this Mishnah represents one of the earliest portions of the Oral Law, going back to that period when the Synagogue first emerges on the scene of Jewish religious history, a period whose origin is lost in the mists of antiquity but which is almost universally regarded as being the Babylonian exile. From that pattern our evening prayer has not departed throughout the centuries. As the Shema with its accompanying Benedictions constitutes the earliest form of prayer, to which the Amidah was added a few centuries later, but also over 2,000 years ago, so it has remained to this day. It is to me, and I trust to you, a thrilling thought that as our ancestors have prayed to God during these millennia, so we continue to pray today, and our prayers therefore represent an element of continuity and stability in a world of whims and passing vagaries to which due tribute must be paid. But when we realise that in addition to this ancient and primal element of our prayers, the earlier part of our Friday evening service, the six introductory Psalms and Lecha Dodi are the latest substantial addition to our statutory prayers, dating as they do from the sixteenth century, one gets an insight into the vitality of our prayers. It surely dispels the oft-repeated allegation, based upon ignorance, malice or special pleading, that the orthodox Jewish liturgy is stereotyped and fossilised, that it is rigid and inflexible. As will, I hope, become apparent during the course of this series of sermons, every age and every epoch has added its contribution to our order of service. The Shema and its blessings, instituted over 2,000 years ago and the comparatively recent Lecha Dodi constitute two extremes between which there are intermediate stages of development. It is as though our ancestors, those great explorers in the realm of the spirit, with an intuitive genius of spiritual topography, hacked a path and blazed a trail between heaven and earth, from ground level to the peak of the mountain of the Lord where His Spirit dwells. That path having been made, subsequent generations trod it, and having trodden it they widened it, paved it, lighted it and signposted it, turning it into a broad highway. The ancient landmarks have not been removed; still we tread in the footsteps of these pioneers of the spirit, but we have added to their original trail-blazing. It is in that combination of the ancient and the modern, of the new growing out of the old, that the essential spirit of the combination of conservatism and progress which is characteristic of traditional Judaism is to be seen.

This, then, is the simple structure of the Evening Service, the three paragraphs of the Shema preceded and followed by two Benedictions, and the Amidah which, constituting as it does Prayer proper, prayer par excellence, is statutory to all services.

These four Benedictions will be dealt with in fuller detail during the course of this series, but in this review of the Evening Service as a whole, a few words about the themes of which they deal will not be out of place. The first deals with the daily recurring phenomenon of the setting of the sun, the coming of twilight, the light of day giving way to the darkness of night, and there is, of course, no need to dwell upon the appositeness of this introductory blessing. The second one deals with the love which God has shown to the children of Israel which expresses itself in the fact that he has given us the Torah. And if God has shown us His love for us in this precious and priceless boon, we on our hand return that love by making full use of that divine gift. If this Benediction has as its theme the love of God for His people in giving them the Torah, the next one, the first Benediction after the Shema, deals, as I have already mentioned, with God's faithfulness to Israel in redeeming them from those who would in every age destroy us, and we bless God for our redemption.

These three Benedictions, the two preceding the Shema and the first one following it, are closely paralleled by the three equivalent blessings in the morning service. Where in the evening we thank God for the change from day to night, naturally in the morning the thanksgiving is for the dawn and the daylight. As in the evening the second Benediction is God's love in giving us the Torah and our consequent duty to study it, and the first (which in the morning is the only) Benediction after the Shema, is similarly on the redemption of Israel. Surely that repetition speaks eloquently to us and gives utterance to one of the sublimest expressions of faith of the Jewish people, the acid test of submission to God's will. For it is a commonplace that the day and the sunshine symbolise well-being, prosperity, and joy, while the night and darkness symbolise sorrow and misfortune and tragedy. And however much the emotions may rebel against the impassable injunction, Judaism nevertheless enjoins כשם שמברך על הטובה כך מברך על הרעה

*In exactly the same way* as one blesses God for boons, so

one should bless him for misfortunes. We thank God and bless him for the night as for the day, for the removal of the sun from our lives as for its dawning; we rejoice in God's Commandments and the Torah when the sun rides high in the heavens, but בשכבנו ובקומנו נשיח בחוקיך ונשמח בדברי תורתך "Even at night as in the morning we will meditate in Thy commandments and *rejoice* in the words of Thy Torah." We thank God for the redemption of Israel when that redemption is as clear and as pellucid as the day, but we go further—we thank Him for our redemption even during the long night of the exile. In the words of the popular dance tune, we say to God "Night and Day You are the One."

The only additional theme in the evening, which obviously can have no counterpart in the morning, is the fourth Benediction, the beautiful Hashkivenu prayer wherein we pray to God for a peaceful and undisturbed night, that lying down in peace we may awake to life, and confident that though we may sleep, the Guardian of Israel neither slumbers nor sleeps. We commend our souls to Him in faithfulness and trustfulness.

That is the essence of the Evening Prayer, unvarying through the ages, since it gives expression to that which is constant in our lives. May the result of this exposition be a deeper sense of prayerfulness that the outpouring of our hearts may be acceptable before God. Amen.

## THE STUDY OF THE TORAH.

*"Therefore, O Lord our God, when we lie down and when we rise up we will meditate on thy statutes, yea, we will rejoice in the words of thy Torah, and in thy Commandments for ever. For they are our life and the length of our days, and we will meditate on them day and night."*

(From the Evening Service.)

Shortly after my arrival in this country I addressed a largely attended meeting of University students. In the course of my address I told them one of my late father's favourite stories. It is a story which belongs to those halcyon days of Jewish social and religious life when the Rabbi was regarded as standing on the top rung of the intellectual and social ladder of Judaism, while the "shuster," the humble cobbler, was regarded as being at the bottom. And the story was of a cobbler who came protestingly to the Rabbi, and said, "I do not understand why the fact that one is a Rabbi should be a cause for such pride and distinction. And if you answer me that it is because the study of the Torah is unending and fathomless, let me assure you that the art of cobbling is also unending and fathomless."

And I told these students that I had a great sympathy with the point of view expressed by that cobbler. As long as one regarded the purpose of study as vocational and not educational, I could see no difference in kind, but only in degree, between the person who studied law in order to qualify as a lawyer so that he could earn his living as a lawyer, the person who studied medicine so that he could be authorised to practise the art of healing to make a living as a doctor, the person who acquired a Rabbinical diploma in order to earn a competent salary as a Rabbi, and the person who studied cobbling in order to become an expert cobbler and make his living as a cobbler. On what, then, does the professional man, or the University graduate, base his claim to a superior status and prestige to that of an artisan or craftsman? It is surely upon the assumption that over and above the particular and specific knowledge which a student acquires in order to equip himself to earn a living in his profession, a University education, as indeed the word University implies, broadens his intellectual and spiritual horizon, opens his mind to the humanities, and gives him that refinement of character and breadth of outlook which education should bring in its train. For there are two kinds of learning for which our Rabbis have coined the expressive phrases לשמה and שלא לשמה, respectively, the acquisition of knowledge for its own sake, without any ulterior motive, but solely for the purpose of improving one's mind, and the acquisition of knowledge which shall act as קרדום לחפור בה "a spade with which to dig," as an instrument for personal advancement. The former alone constitutes true education; the latter is merely vocational training. And it is the former alone which knows no bounds or limitations, it continues as long as life continues, and its highest stage is reached when the searcher after it reaches the stage of יודע שאינו יודע of knowing how little he knows and how much he has still to learn.

No people in the world has raised this doctrine of לשמה of study for its own sake to a more exalted or sublime pinnacle than has the Jewish people in their conception of the place which the study of Torah should have in the mind and thought of the Jews. It is that conception which is so beautifully expressed in the words of the second Benediction which precedes the Shema, which emphasises that the Torah was given by God to the Jewish people as the expression of God's eternal and all-embracing love for his people. And with it is coupled the expressed resolve to meditate in it day and night as long as we live, for it is our life and the length of our days.

When we consider the woeful decline of Jewish loyalties which is characteristic of the present age, we are apt to point, with a certain justification, to the disregard of Jewish observances, the desecration of the Sabbath, the disregard of Kashrut, the lack of observance of the Festivals, the neglect of daily prayer. But these signs, ominous and distressing though they are, are but the outward symptoms of a deep-seated disease which do not take into account its root cause of which these are but the inevitable and ineluctable manifestations. Infinitely more serious than them, and representing the poisonous root from which these evils stem, is the taint of professionalism which has attached to the study of the Torah, which has transformed it from what it ought to be, and what throughout the ages until the present day it always was, "an inheritance of the congregation of Jacob," to the professional equipment of the Rabbi and of the teacher. It is because we have failed lamentably to "meditate in the word of Thy Torah when we lie down and when we rise up," it is because we fail to live up to the implications that it is "our life and the length of our days," that all these evils have befallen us, and a vast and limitless ignorance has overtaken the people who were once proud to call themselves "the people of the Book." Many of you were present at a function which was held some years ago at the Sive Hall. Almost without exception each speaker who preceded me quoted in his speech from the Bible, the Talmud or the Midrash, but any delight which I might have felt in this gratifying display of Jewish knowledge on the part of laymen was marred by the senseless formula of apology with which each speaker, with unvarying monotony, preceded his quotation, "With the permission of the

Chief Rabbi, I should like to quote," or "I hope the Chief Rabbi will excuse me if I quote," etc. When I got up to speak, I was stung to comment with an acid humour that I relinquish and renounce any copyright to the words of the Torah, and I hereby give full and unqualified permission to any and every Jew to regard himself as having the same right to it as I have! And however small the progress which has been made in rolling away the reproach of ignorance of Jewish knowledge which attaches to our Community it is gratifying to note that some progress has been made, and that probably the number of laymen who in our Community are taking advantage of the ever increasing facilities for acquiring Jewish knowledge is steadily on the increase.

Rarely have I felt such a glow of spiritual satisfaction as I did on receipt of a letter from one of my congregants. He is a regular worshipper in this Synagogue; he is the possessor of a higher degree from the University of the Witwatersrand, but in the Faculty of Science, and in a subject which is as far removed from theology or religion as one could possibly imagine. The letter was written almost exactly a year ago, on January 24th, 1956, and I was so impressed by it that I asked, and was granted, his permission to quote it in a sermon. He probably thought that I had been guilty of a gushing compliment, and I am glad that he will now realise that I have treasured this letter for this whole year, waiting for this opportunity to read it. In the course of that letter he wrote:—

> "I derived the greatest benefit and pleasure by reading your sermon on the relevant Sedrah each Friday evening after supper. At that time I made a point of glancing at Dr. Hertz's commentary and notes, so that during the course of a year I in fact 'completed' a highly superficial reading of the whole Chumash without delving too deeply into the multiplicity of arguments which require a life-time of intensive study. The odd hour spent privately in meditation

each week in this way I found so beneficial and instructive that I unhesitatingly recommend the same procedure to the average Jewish layman who is devoted to our culture but unfortunately cannot spare too much time in its study."

In that moving letter one sees mirrored the old spirit of Jewish learning for its own sake, the spirit of this beautiful prayer which is the subject of my sermon this evening. I have read it not only for this reason, but to bring to your notice the accessibility of text-books to the layman desirous of acquainting himself with the inexhaustible treasure house of the Jewish spirit. May I echo the hope expressed by him, that this prayer may become a reality, that through a knowledge of the word of God our loyalties and our observance of his statutes and judgments may be strengthened and reinforced?

## A TIME FOR EVERYTHING*

### לכל זמן ועת לכל־חפץ תחת השמים

*To everything there is a season, and a time to every purpose under the heaven.*

(Ecclesiastes iii: 1.)

It is a platitude to say that one requires time for everything that is to be done; but there is meaning and urgency in the second part of this verse which states that if any purpose is to be achieved then there must be appointed the hour in which it must be done. זמן is time in its broad and abstract sense, whereas עת denotes the divisions of time—hours, minutes and seconds—time in its specific sense. Although the statement remains a simple one, nevertheless its truth is never realised fully by the individual, and the years pass by and lives lack fulfilment because the hours and minutes (עתים) are wasted.

For this reason, among others, the Jew has been given set times for prayer, morning, afternoon and evening. It is not left for each person to pray as and when he is moved, but rather, it is prayer which becomes the means and instrument for the achievement of a regular and frequent daily religious experience. Let me say at this stage that in the whole of the Prayer Book there are very few prayers of supplication. The Jew hesitates to ask God for that which he considers he needs. Does not God know all our needs? Might we not ask God in our ignorance for some bounty

* By Rabbi A. H. Lapin.

which may be our undoing? Those few pages, which form a negligible proportion of the whole Prayer Book, in which we do make requests for our needs are devoted to petitions for health and that the earth should give forth its produce, for knowledge and repentance. The Prayer Book consists of praises and blessings and these bring to us a realisation of God's greatness, love and kindness. In other words, the purpose of our prayers is not to receive, but to become better human beings. By praying thrice daily we are forced for short periods to divorce ourselves from the humdrum existence we lead and from the materialism of everyday life, and we become elevated from the commonplace to the spiritual. Even if we do not remain on this plane for long it must, however, have a salutary effect on ourselves and on our business, professional, social and family relationships for all the intervening hours of the day.

With typical insight the authors of our prayers perceived the difficulty of coming straight from our earthly occupations to the sublimity of prayer, and the approach, therefore, is that the opening blessing of the morning and evening service should be on the theme of that which we are immediately experiencing. In the case of the former we bless God who "gives light to the earth and to them that dwell thereon," and in the latter "who bringest on the evening twilight." And it is from the concrete that we move to the more abstract ideas contained in the subsequent passages of the service and culminating in Kaddish and Kedusha.

Let us turn to the first blessing of the evening service on page 113a with which the Ma'ariv proper commences. Here we bless God "who brings on the evening twilight. . . . And with understanding changes times and varies seasons and arranges the stars in their watches in the sky." If by seasons is meant spring, summer, autumn and winter then there are two questions which I find myself asking. The subject of this blessing is twilight and night, and although we might permit ourselves in this context to speak of day, surely the seasons of the year are quite irrelevant to the whole theme.

Furthermore, the logical sequence is incorrect as we commence with day and night, then speak of the seasons, and immediately revert back to the stars and the subject of day and night. The words משנה עתים refer to the finer divisions of time, the minutes and the seconds, and the interpretation is that the change from day to night is wrought by a gradual process. We are not plunged into sudden darkness but God brings on the night slowly and gradually and by the time it overtakes us we have become accustomed and attuned to it. Psychologically the effect of being overwhelmed by darkness without any warning would be harmful. Thus ומחליף את הזמנים He changes day into night. Even now he does not leave us in complete and utter darkness, but "arranges the stars in their watches in the sky," giving light and symbolising God's watchfulness and guardianship over his children in times of darkness. As we recite these words with a full knowledge of their meaning we become aware of how God continually manifests himself in Nature, and we are led to an appreciation of his merciful goodness, and this and other daily natural phenomena assume a significance and importance to what would otherwise have been cloyed minds.

God created not only the day but also the night בורא יום ולילה. We do not consider darkness to be merely the absence of light, and night the negation of day, but darkness and night are positive concepts, creations in their own right having intrinsic values of their own. The peacefulness and tranquillity that come with the evening twilight are like balm to tired and frayed nerves. Years ago I took a short holiday in Finland. It was midsummer and my first evening was spent with friends in Helsingfors. They would not allow me to leave and it was shortly after midnight that I rose to go. My host said that he had purposely kept me so long as he wished to show me Helsingfors, and the best time to see its beauty was at the dead of night. As he opened the front door there was a burst of daylight. I was in the land of the midnight sun, and it was then that I realised that the windows were heavily shuttered and I asked him why did we have to sit indoors with artificial lighting when it was so unnecessary. He replied that to me it was a novelty, but unless they who lived there the summer months had a few hours of darkness daily their nerves would be shattered and they themselves would become nervous wrecks.

The Vilna Gaon is reputed to have said that God gave us the night for study of the Torah. The measure of concentration needed to understand its deeper meaning could only be attained in the still of the night when man was more or less free from his worldly cares. How strongly does this attitude contrast with that of those who "tarry late into the night till wine inflame them"?

To us all the hours of evening and night could be a time of religious and spiritual resuscitation. Our whole day is devoted to our business and professions and if the evenings are to be spent entirely in social gatherings, in amusement and pleasure or even in meetings, then there is time for everything excepting for those things which instil in us an appreciation and understanding for the eternal values. Each Jew must be a קובע עתים לתורה, set aside an appointed time, be it an hour or two or even a few minutes daily every evening for prayer, for the study of the Torah and for the building up of a family relationship between husband and wife and parents and children. It is in this spirit that, after a tiring day, we recite each evening ברוך אתה ה׳ המעריב ערבים Blessed art Thou, O Lord, who bringest on the evening twilight.

---

For the main theme in this sermon I am indebted to S. R. Hirsch.

# THE SH'MA

אשרינו שאנחנו משכימים ומעריבים... ואומרים פעמים בכל יום
שמע ישראל ה׳ אלהינו ה׳ אחד

WE Jews have always glorified in the fact that we are a people who every morning and every evening, twice every day, proclaim the unity and oneness of God . . . שמע ישראל

It is my privilege tonight to make my modest contribution to a venture initiated by the Chief Rabbi some time ago: to explain our prayers and to make them intelligible to every worshipper, so that the final result will be a greater understanding and a deeper devotion, when we offer our prayers to God.

In accordance with an old Jewish principle, all prayers should begin with a praise of God. It is for this reason that the first blessing of the evening service is devoted to singing the praise of God, the Creator. The second blessing is called Ahavah, love. In this prayer we rejoice in the love of God, who has given us the Torah, the words of which are "Our life and the length of our days." These two blessings which introduce the Shema were explained to you last week. It is my task tonight to speak about the Shema prayer itself. Its source is the Torah, and thus it is amongst the oldest prayers in our Siddur. It was recited in the Temple of old, every morning and every evening.

To-day, it is the first prayer we teach our children, and it is our last confession before we die. And yet, it is not a prayer in the proper sense of the word. It is not expressed

* By Rev. Dr. H. Abt.

in a form which we think is typical of prayers. In the Shema we do not address God. We address Israel, our people. But it is nevertheless a prayer in which our communion with God is this: To think of God and to think of His will. Instead of speaking to God in prayer, we think of the relation between Man and God. To us serious, honest meditation has always been a legitimate form of prayer.

But the Shema has become more to us than a prayer and a confession. All our hopes and all our agonies have been expressed in the few words: שמע ישראל ה׳ אלהינו ה׳ אחד

שמע Hear: we hear the voices of all generations before us. We hear the voices of our Jewish brethren from a thousand lands. We hear the voices of innocent children, of scholars, of saints. We hear the last cry of our martyrs who died על קדוש השם, for the sanctification of the name of God.

ישראל: we, who hear, we are Israel, an ancient people, a people very old, but also very young, like the Land of Israel, an ancient land, but a young new land in our own days.

ה׳: There is a God in this world, a God who is eternal and everywhere. We know of His presence in the lonely longing of our heart no less than in the happy experience of a Kehilla, whose Congregation, united in prayer, an experience which gives us the right to say: אלהינו: He is our God.

ה׳ אחד: And this Our God is one. He alone is God. We Jews do not believe in polytheism, in the worship of many gods. Nor can we Jews accept the doctrine of Trinity, of a God divided into three spheres, a doctrine which Christianity, the daughter religion of Judaism, regards as fundamental dogma. And likewise, we Jews reject the dualism of other religious systems in some Eastern countries, as if there were two divine powers in the world, the power of good and the power of evil, of light and darkness.

We Jews believe in one God only, a God of whom Isaiah says: יוצר אור ובורא חושך עושה שלום ובורא רע "who createth light and darkness, who maketh peace and createth evil in the form of human suffering" (xlv 7). He has the power to unite the most contradictory and hostile elements. He combines as our mystics say, אש and מים, fire and water, into שמים the heavens. There he makes peace in nature, and a spark of this, His sublime, divine gift, Shalom, enters the heart of man and of all our people Israel. This is the deeper meaning of the well-known sentence with which we conclude every Amidah and every Kaddish: "He who maketh peace in heaven, may he also make peace for us and for the whole of Israel."[1]

---

It was no digression from my theme when, in an attempt to explain the Shema prayer, I quoted עושה שלום with the conception of כל ישראל. The Jewish concept of the oneness of God leads naturally to the concept of the oneness of Israel, the Jewish people. שמע ישראל has been the spiritual heritage of all Jews, the passionate confession of one nation proclaiming their belief in the unity of one God. You cannot divorce the Jewish people from God, nor can you divorce God from the Jewish people. It is nothing but a shocking blasphemy when, at an international sporting event held in Israel not so long ago, a banner was displayed with an inscription showing a garbled and mutilated paraphrase of שמע ישראל. It read שמע ישראל עם ישראל עמנו עם אחד "Hear, Israel, the people of Israel, our people, are one people."

You cannot eliminate God. The oneness of our people cannot be separated from the oneness of God. In this our age, in which so often a narrow and stupid nationalism raises its ugly head, let us not forget that the oneness of God is a greater and wider denominator than the oneness of a nation. No sovereignty can be recognised by the Jew, neither that of a human being nor that of a nation or a state, claiming

1. Targum and Rashi to Job xxv: 2.
See also Num. Rab. xii: 8.

totalitarian powers. There is only one sovereignty, that is the sovereignty of God.

We well understand why the sentence ברוך שם כבוד מלכותו לעולם ועד "Blessed be His name, whose glorious kingdom is for ever and ever" should accompany the opening verse of the Shema prayer. Incidentally, it is not a Biblical verse. We recollect from our Yom Kippur Machzor that it was used in the Temple, when in the solemn atmosphere of Yom Kippur the High Priest pronounced the Ineffable Name and the people responded with this sentence. We Jews, and mankind as a whole, have still a long way to go before God's kingdom will be established on earth. The kingdom of God remains our hope. It is a belief embedded deep down in our heart, and our rabbis say that this hope for the future as expressed in this verse should not be profaned and, so to speak, made "wochedik" by uttering it every day in a loud voice. We say this line softly. But once a year, on our holiest day, on Yom Kippur, when we purify our heart and are willing, in all sincerity and intellectual honesty, to take upon ourselves the yoke of the kingdom of heaven, then we say this line aloud like in the days of old. The universalistic character of Yom Kippur impresses upon us to anticipate the messianic time, when our God ה׳, who is at present only אלהינו our G-d, the G-d of Israel, will be ה׳ אחד, the one God, whose sovereignty is recognised by all. This is the messianic hope of Judaism, as expressed in the first two lines of the Shema prayer.[2]

One final remark: In the Sefer Torah the last letter of שמע the "Ayin," and the last letter of the word אחד, the "daleth" are written large. I always regret that the Singer Prayer Book, the standard Prayer Book which is in the hands of most of you, does not follow the example of other Siddurim in which these letters are printed in large letters.

---

2. Orach Chayim 61, 13 and 619, 2 (Ture Zahav). Pessachim 56a.

Many reasons have been offered, trying to explain the large Ayin and the large Daleth. The most convincing one is this: the two large letters form the word עד witness. Every Jew who says the Shema prayer is a witness testifying to the oneness of God. This has always been our noble calling, our specific task as Jews. As long as there are Jews in the world, they will glory in the fact אשרינו שאנחנו משכימים ומעריבים ערב ובוקר ואומרים פעמים בכל יום שמע ישראל ה׳ אלהינו ה׳ אחד. that we are a people who every morning and every evening, twice every day, proclaim Shema Yisrael.

## THE REWARD OF VIRTUE

*And it shall come to pass, if ye shall hearken diligently unto my commandments which I command you this day . . . that I will give the rain of your land in its season.*

(Deut. xi: 13-14.)

THE first half of the second paragraph of the Shema posits a comforting doctrine on the reward of virtue, or of obedience to God's commandments, which in Judaism is the same thing. It is a doctrine which belongs to the same ethical standard as the proverb "Honesty is the best policy," and the ethical standard of that doctrine can hardly be called an exalted one. It teaches that one should be honest not because of one's personal integrity, not because it is wrong and immoral to steal, but because it is expedient and in the best personal and material interests of man. In similar fashion does Moses apparently hold out to the Children of Israel the enticing prospects of the reward of virtue. If you will hearken to God's commandments, he says, the blessed rain upon which the material prosperity of an agricultural community depends will fall at the right time. The harvest of corn and wine and oil will be bountiful, the cattle will grow sleek and fat on the lush pastures, your belly will be filled. But if on the other hand you turn aside and serve false gods then a drought will ensue, the land will not yield its harvest and they will die of starvation. In other words, it is to man's selfish and material interests to obey the commandments of God.

When I prepared the first draft of this sermon, I made the comment that of such a doctrine one could only say tritely "It would be wonderful if it were true," but on further consideration I do not think it is so. Such a doctrine cuts the ground from under every moral foundation for right action; it makes it a matter of expediency instead of principle; it says to man "Do right not because it is right but because it pays material dividends." It presents the obnoxious doctrine that material prosperity is to be equated with virtue, and apparently poverty with vice!

The first attempt to refine the crudity of this conception appears to have been taken in the very earliest period of Rabbinic Judaism, and is seen in the noble and sublime statement of Antigonos of Socho, the first Rabbinical authority we know by name after the Anshei K'nesset Ha-Gedolah, the Men of the Great Synagogue, "Be not as servants who serve their master in the hope of receiving a reward, but be as servants who serve the master without thought of reward, and let the fear of Heaven be upon you" (Ethics 1: 3). Without denying that virtue brings its rewards, he pleaded and taught that the virtue should be dissociated from the thought of the award it brings. This ideal of service without thought of award was, according to the Aboth of Rabbi Nathan (v. 2) too exalted a conception for two of the disciples of its author, and brought about the first schism in Rabbinic Judaism. These two disciples, Zadok and Boethus by name, took the doctrine to mean that there was no reward, and arguing "How can one expect a labourer to toil all day and not receive his wages in the evening?" they broke away from the teachings of their master, and formed the two sects of the Zadokites (Sadducees) and Boethusians.

The next stage in the refinement of this doctrine of reward is given by the Rabbis in their comment on one of the most dramatic personal incidents in the life of the Tannaim, the apostasy of one of the greatest scholars of his time, Elisha ben Abuyah, the arch-apostate of Talmudic

Judaism, or, as he has been called, the Faust of the Talmud. Our Rabbis are at pains to find a reason for his betrayal of Judaism, and the most authoritative explanation is connected with this doctrine of material reward in this world for good. There are two commandments in the Bible of which Scripture says that he who fulfils them will live long upon the earth. One is the Fifth Commandment, "Honour thy father and thy mother that thy days may be long upon the land which the Lord thy God hath given thee." The other is the Commandment to drive away the mother bird from a nest before rifling it of its eggs. It happened, says the Talmud, that a man said to his son, "Climb up on the roof of the house and you will find there a bird's nest. Be careful to drive the mother away before taking the eggs." The son complied, and by complying fulfilled both Commandments which promise long life as a reward for their fulfilment. On the way down the ladder broke and the boy fell to his death. When Elisha ben Abuyah saw this incident he exclaimed, "Is this then the Torah and its promised reward?" and so utterly shaken was he by it that he rejected the whole of Judaism.

What then is the answer to this problem? asks the Talmud, and it is the grandson of Elisha, R. Jacob, who gives the answer. "The land which the Lord hath given thee" is not this world but the world to come, and lays it down as a principle for all time, שכר מצוה בהאי עלמא ליכא "There is no reward for virtue in this world."

This re-interpretation of the doctrine of reward for virtue, which removes it from the material plane to the spiritual, and from this world to the next, is summed up in the well-known statement of R. Tarfon, also to be found in the Ethics of the Fathers, "Faithful is thy employer to pay thee the reward of thy labour, [but] realise that the grant of reward unto the righteous is in the world to come." (Ethics iii: 21.)

But even that does not represent the last stage in the development of the Jewish doctrine of reward. It was left to ben Azzai, the outstanding example in Talmudic Judaism of "der ewiger student," the eternal student who renounced everything, position of authority and domestic happiness in his great love for study, to reach and to teach the final stage in this concept of reward for right doing. Is there שכר מצוה, the reward for good deeds? Of course there is! Is there punishment for transgressions? Of course there is! What then is this reward and the retribution שכר מצוה מצוה ושכר עבירה עבירה The reward of a good deed is the good deed itself and the punishment for a transgression is the transgression. (Ethics iv: 2.) Ultimately it is to no external reward, whether in this world or in the next, that one looks for the satisfaction of one's actions, but in the joy of performance itself, and for its own sake. It is in the knowledge of having done the right thing, in the fact that one has made the world a better place to live in, that one has brought a ray of sunshine into the otherwise overcast and gloomy lives of others, that one has caused in one's own being the spiritual to transcend the material that one has followed the path along which the finger of God beckons — it is these and cognate things and thoughts which provide the sole reward for good. And in the same way does evil bring its own nemesis.

The question, however, naturally arises, if there is no reward for virtue in this world, why does Moses explicitly state that there is? If virtue is in itself its own reward, why does R. Tarfon hold out an external reward, even if he projects it from this world to a hereafter?

To that question a brilliant comment of Maimonides in another connection provides a wholly satisfying answer. He takes the parallel of a child being introduced to the study of Hebrew. "If you will learn to read this properly," says his teacher to him, "I will give you a sweet." And in order to obtain the coveted sweet the child applies himself to his letters. And if he is asked why he is studying, he will promptly answer "Because I want a sweet!" When he grows older the enticement of a sweet no longer holds out the necessary attraction to him, and the teacher, still eager that he should acquire knowledge, says to him, "If you will study diligently you will be top of the class, and you will get a prize." And in order to be top of the class and get that prize the boy applies himself with due diligence to his studies. When he reaches adolescence that inducement palls and he is encouraged to continue his studies by having dangled before him the inviting prospect that he will become a Rabbi, that men will respect him and give him honour. And for that purpose he continues his studies. But, concludes Maimonides, it is only when he has reached this stage that the realisation dawns upon him that the real purpose for which one studies is not that one should get sweets, and not that one should be top of the class, and not that one should become a Rabbi and be the recipient of men's respect and honour, but the sole purpose of study is the acquisition of knowledge for its own sake. But one cannot tell that to a child or even to a boy or even an adolescent. For them one has to hold out more or less material inducements, until a certain stage of mental development is reached. The whole process represents a perfect example of the psychologically sound principle of which the Rabbis are so fond מתוך שלא לשמה בא לשמה a good deed done at first for an ulterior motive eventually comes to be performed for its own sake.

So in the early stages of Israel's history, as Maimonides points out also with regard to the sacrificial system, the stage of mental and moral development of the people, recently emancipated from a body-breaking and soul-destroying slavery, has to be taken into consideration. In a special sense דברה תורה בלשון בני אדם the Torah speaks in language which can be grasped by man. "You toiled in Egypt and received no material rewards, but if you toil for God you will receive rewards. Servants to Pharaoh see no blessing from their service, but servants to God will," Moses says to them, and it is a concept which is within their moral and mental grasp. It is only with the gradual development of that moral sense that a refinement of this crude doctrine can be enunciated. First comes the dissociation of the act from the thought of reward, and the rebellion of the two disciples of its author shows how advanced the doctrine was. Then comes the transfer of the thought of reward from the material to the spiritual sphere, until at last the noblest and finest conception of all can be propounded, the idea of virtue being its own reward, and the joy and satisfaction, the tranquillity and serenity which comes to that man whose soul is in communion with God gives the reward. For "Happy is the man that heareth the Lord, and findeth great delight in his Commandments" (Psalm cxii: 1).

## KINDNESS TO ANIMALS

ונתתי עשב בשדך לבהמתך ואכלת ושבעת

*And I will give grass in thy field to thy cattle, and thou shalt eat and be satisfied.*

(Deut. xi: 15)

THE value of the Scriptures to us Jews lies not only in the superficial and literal meaning and message of the Biblical narrative, however important and profound it may be, but in the beautiful moral lessons which our Rabbis derive from the text, which in their totality give us what is known as the Oral Law. It is this Oral Law, both Halachic and Aggadic, which represents the distinctive feature of Judaism. So important is this interpretative aspect of the Bible that there are times, as I have had so many occasions to point out, when the literal meaning of the Scripture may make no appeal to us, but its value remains, and is even enhanced, by virtue of that homiletical interpretation.

The verse which I have selected as my text affords an excellent example of that truth. It is part of that passage which formed the subject of my address last week which holds out the promise of material reward for the performance of God's will, and it is a doctrine, as I pointed out, which was virtually rejected by our Rabbis two thousand years ago. That being the case, one might well be tempted to regard this and similar passages as being devoid of any spiritual value, since it conveys a concept which is no longer acceptable. Yet no graver error could be committed, or one which would deprive us of some of the finest thoughts of our Rabbis. For, curious though it may sound to those uninitiated in the ways of the Rabbis, it is from this verse that they derive one of the details of one of the ethical teachings of Judaism, kindness to, or what I would prefer to call humanitarian consideration for, dumb animals. How so? You may ask. Perfectly simple! God says that he will give grass in the field to the cattle, and *then* "thou shalt eat and be satisfied." The giving of food to animals therefore precedes the satisfaction of man's desires. "Go and do thou likewise!" Before you sit down to a meal and "eat and be satisfied" see that you have first fed your animals!

This, as I say, is only one detail of the whole grand concept of the prohibition of צער בעלי חיים of inflicting any pain and suffering upon any living creature and I could, I am sure, give you a long and impressive account of the teachings of Judaism on this subject. I refrain from doing so for two reasons, firstly because I regard it as a self-evident statement, and secondly because kindness to animals is one of those ethical concepts which has become a common feature of civilisation, or at least of Western civilisation. There is probably no country in which legislation to enforce consideration for animals does not exist, which has not its Society for the Prevention of Cruelty to Animals. But at the same time let us remember that for centuries it was an ethical concept which Judaism alone maintained and raised to the level of a virtue. And those to whom these facts are unknown I would refer to the long note on the subject on page 854 of the one volume edition of Hertz's Pentateuch.

There is, however, in that note, one incident referred to which throws light upon the basis of this doctrine of consideration for animals which, as far as I am aware, has never been commented upon. The greatest and last of the Tannaim, Rabbi Judah the Prince, the compiler of the Mishnah, suffered intolerable agony for thirteen years. For seven years he suffered from stones in the bladder, or the kidneys, and for six years from another excruciatingly painful disease. After those thirteen years of suffering he was cured. And the Talmud makes both his suffering and his cure a direct result of his attitude towards animals. A calf was being led to the slaughter and with that instinct of imminent doom which is characteristic of animals, it managed to break away from its rope and, rushing over to Rabbi Judah, hid its face in his cloak and moaned pitiably. Rabbi Judah sternly repulsed it. "Go," he said, "since for this purpose wast thou created." And according to the Talmud the cry, so to speak, of that poor dumb animal reached the very throne of God's glory as an accusation against the Rabbi and there it was decreed, "Since he has no pity for the suffering of dumb brutes, let us bring suffering upon him." And to that thoughtless act of lack of consideration his thirteen years of agony was attributed.

But equally was his cure attributed to his attitude to animals. It was after these thirteen years of suffering, continues the Talmud, that his maid-servant was sweeping the house, and seeing a nest of rodents in a corner of the room, she was about to sweep them away and destroy them when her master said to her, "Leave them in peace! Is it not written ורחמיו על כל מעשיו "And God's tender mercies are over all his works" (Psalm cxlv: 9). And when this statement was heard in Heaven, they said, "Since he has shown compassion to animals, let us show compassion to him," and he was cured of his sufferings.

It is a beautiful and moving story in itself. The intervention of God in the affairs of man in the interests of dumb creation; the punishment brought upon the greatest figure of his age, and one of the greatest of all ages, for a mere lack of consideration for a calf—despite the fact that theoretically he was in the right; the intervention in the opposite direction in approbation of his consideration for a nest of rodents, is pure poetry and religion at its highest. But is there not a profounder thought enshrined in this incident? Does it not provide a perfect rationale for the concept of Kindness to Animals? Does it not say more eloquently than words, "As is the relationship of God to Man, so should be the relationship of Man to animals"?

What is that relationship of man to animals? Already in the first chapter of Genesis is that relationship expounded. "And God said, Let us make man in our image, after our likeness, and let them have dominion over the fish of the sea, and over the fowl of the air, and over the cattle and over all the earth and over every creeping thing that creepeth upon the earth" (Gen. i:26). It is this verse which gives man the title of Lord of Creation. He is master over the animals, the beasts, the birds and the fish. He can do with them as he wants and there is none to stop him. He can treat them with kindness and consideration, he can treat them with cruelty and heartlessness. He is their Lord and they are his creatures over whom he has full and unfettered dominion.

But if Man is Lord of Creation, God is Lord of Man. He is *their* Master and can do with them as he wants, and there is none to stop him. He can treat them with kindness and consideration, he can treat them harshly. He is our Lord and we are his creatures over whom he has full and unfettered dominion.

How shall God exercise his dominion over those who are subject to him? Surely those two beautiful incidents of Rabbi provide the answer. "Let us see how man exercises his dominion over those who are subject to him!" You have not considered the suffering of those committed to your care. See how you like it if I do not consider the suffering of those committed to my care. You have shown mercy to your creatures? Then I will show mercy to mine. And in a sense which is an inversion of the accepted meaning, man can plead for God's mercy only to the extent to which he can say מה אני רחום אף אתה רחום "Just as I am merciful, so be thou, O Lord, merciful." And kindness to helpless animals becomes the acid test of man's goodness of heart and his entitlement to God's mercy.

And now perhaps one can begin to understand the true inwardness of that beautiful and popular legend which is given in the Midrash as the reason for the choice of God of Moses as the "Faithful Shepherd" of his flock. According to this legend, while Moses was a shepherd of sheep and not of men, one of the lambs entrusted to his care ran away. Moses followed it beyond the desert and found it exhausted from want of water. "Poor lamb," said Moses, "I did not know that thou wast thirsty," and hoisting it on his shoulders he made his way back to the flock. And the Almighty, looking down from heaven, said, "Thou hast shown compassion to the flock given into thy charge. Thou art worthy to be the Shepherd of my people." "And God called unto him out of the bush and said Moses, Moses" (Exodus iii: 4).

And to the words of the Midrash, "As is the compassion of the Holy One, blessed be, over man, so is his compassion over animals," one can add "As is the compassion of man over animals so is the compassion of the Holy One, Blessed be He, over man."

I conclude with a comment which can be regarded in the nature of a postscript to the general theme. That the method of slaughter of animals for food enjoined upon Jews, the method of Shechitah, which, as has been amply proved, represents the most humane method of the dispatch of animals should be attacked on the grounds of cruelty, and the Jews impugned as a result, surely represents one of the grossest and most unfair of Community libels. For the record of Judaism in the matter of consideration for dumb animals is one for which we have no reason to be ashamed, and which will bear proud comparison with that of any other people.

## TEACHING BY EXAMPLE

**ולמדתם אותם את בניכם לדבר בם בשבתך בביתך ובלכתך בדרך ובשכבך ובקומך**

*And ye shall teach them your children to talk of them when thou sittest in thy house, and when thou walkest by the way and when thou liest down, and when thou risest up.*

(Deut. xi: 19.)

THERE is, in South African waters, a fish called Kingclip, and when I came to this country it was universally accepted by the Jewish Community that kingclip was not a kasher fish. Now, unlike in the case of poultry where one has to rely upon tradition, one can easily ascertain whether a fish is kasher or not. It may be a coelecanth, or it may be some other exotic fish which no human eye has ever beheld. If it has fins and scales it is kasher; if it has not it is treifa. When therefore we were informed by a large firm of fishmongers that kingclip had fins and scales, that humble denizen of the deep was afforded a signal honour. The Chief Rabbi accompanied by four learned Rabbis descended upon it and subjected it to an examination. That examination proved conclusively that the scales had been wrongly weighted against the innocent fish. It possessed scales and was kasher, and we duly made an announcemnt to that effect. The result was astonishing. It was met with reactions varying from total unbelief to vigorous protest. How can anyone dare to assert that kingclip is kasher? "Die mame hot gezogt" that it was Treifa, and against what "die mame hot gezogt," no decrees of Rabbis, however eminent or authoritative, were of any avail.

I have often thought of that experience as an excellent example of the two manners in which the doctrines of Judaism are inculcated in the heart of the Jew, and of the infinitely greater impact which the one makes on its subject as compared with the other. On the one hand there is the formal education which the teacher imparts to the pupil, the education of bench and desk, of blackboard and chalk, of exercise book and homework. It is the education of precept, and none will deny its vital importance or its effect. And on the other hand there is the education which comes in no formal way. There are no fixed lessons and no text books. It is the education of example which the child sees in the home. It is this education which is reflected in the verse which I have taken as my text, and which finds its close parallel in a similar verse in the first paragraph of the Shema. It is the teaching which is given not at formal sessions but "when thou sittest in thy house and when thou walkest by the way, when thou liest down and when thou risest up." It is in the manner in which the father conducts himself in casual sitting at home, in the manner in which he conducts himself outside the home when walking by the way. It is the education which is given, so to speak, even while apparently asleep, and it is as effective as that which is given when one rises up. And it is that education which makes an infinitely greater impression upon the plastic mind of the child than the formal conning by rote. Its effect is beautifully emphasised by the use of the unusual word ושננתם in the first verse. It is translated "And ye shall teach them diligently" but it means literally "you shall impress them sharply" or "you shall prick them in." It conveys the idea of something etched in in sharp, unmistakable outline, without blurring. If, as is rightly said in the Ethics of the Fathers, "He who learns as a child is like ink written on clear paper," he who absorbs the unconscious teaching of the home is like lines etched in on a clear surface. It retains the doctrine vividly, and with a great degree of permanence, and once it receives this sharp impression the second result naturally follows. From ושננתם לבניך ודברת בם teaching sharply to thy children and speaking to them, it follows that ולמדתם אותם את בניכם לדבר בם you teach your children that *they* shall speak of them. The doctrine and standard of the father becomes the doctrine and standard of the child and the continuity of Judaism is assured. That is why, incidentally, when mother said that kingclip is Treifa, the contrary ruling of the Rabbis was so coolly received.

That, of course, assumes that the doctrines and standard, the teaching and the example of the parents is in the right direction. But when, as so tragically often happens, the example of the home is in direct conflict with the precepts of the school, the teachers and Rabbis on the whole beat their wings ineffectually against an impenetrable wall. I once pointed out that I could quote you a hundred statements from the Talmud, beautifully enunciated, cogently argued and persuasively adumbrated, to the effect that when there is a conflict of loyalty between teacher and parent, priority must be given to the view of the teacher; that the honour, respect and obedience due to the teacher takes precedence over that due to the parent, but, as I wryly pointed out, all these statements suffer from one serious drawback, that they were enunciated by the teachers and not by the parents, and I went so far as to say that I would gladly relegate all those noble statements to the scrap heap for one simple statement from parents to that effect! But alas, that happens to be only a *bon mot*. For even a *statement* like that would be of no avail when set against the contrary *example* set by the parent. The plea by the parent, "Do not as I do, but do as the teacher tells you," runs contrary to every psychological instinct. The precept afforded by the parent when he sits in his home and when he walks by the way, when he lies down and when he riseth up is the most potent contributory factor in moulding the mind of the child. And the home and the street do more than the school in giving these sharp outlines, in transferring the "thou shalt speak of them" of the parents to the "they shall speak of them" of the children.

It is so much of a truth that it has become a truism; it is so obvious a statement of fact that it ranks as a hackneyed platitude, and I hope that my Congregation will be sufficiently impressed by the realisation that it constitutes by and large a confession of failure by the teacher and the Rabbi to overcome the obstacle of the silent but all-pervasive opposition of the parents to his efforts.

It was, however, with a definite degree of satisfaction that I came across a powerful support of this thesis from what was to me an unexpected source. In the current issue of Jewish Affairs there is a thought-provoking article by Mr. Edgar Bernstein, who if on the one hand is one of the thinking Jews of our Community, is so far removed from allegiance to traditional Judaism that he would, I am sure, not be offended at being called an opponent thereof. The article is entitled "Are We Rearing *Jews?*" and he concludes that article, which is the first of two, the second of which is still to appear, with the statement: "Unless the home can surround the child with the atmosphere of Jewishness, there is little hope of the Hebrew School filling the vacuum." When I expressed to him my appreciation of that article and told him that I was looking forward to the forthcoming concluding article, in which he undertakes to "offer a number of suggestions" as to "How to fill our homes with the atmosphere of Jewishness," he informed me that I would probably take serious objection to some of these suggestions. But even with that forewarning I welcome this positive support to the thesis which forms the subject of this sermon. I ask you parents whether the hours which will follow this service, the meal of which you will partake when you go home, will reinforce the message of Judaism which you hear here or be in flagrant contradiction to it; whether your child coming home from Hebrew School finds an atmosphere which is consistent with what he has been taught there or represents a denial of it. It is upon the answer which you and you alone can and will give to that question that the future of Judaism in the Community depends.

# ON PURIM: DIVINE AND HUMAN JUSTICE

ואתה ברחמיך הרבים הפרת את עצתו וקלקלת את מחשבתו
והשבות גמולו על ראשו ותלו אותו ואת בניו על העץ

*Then didst thou in thine abundant mercy bring his counsel to nought, didst frustrate his design, and return his recompense upon his own head, and they hanged him and his sons upon the gallows.*

(Special Prayer for Purim).

To-morrow night is Purim and we shall again read the Megillah and rejoice at the downfall of Haman, the archetype of the anti-Semite, and the deliverance of the Jewish people from imminent destruction. That Festival, like the Festival of Chanukah, is the occasion of the insertion of a special prayer in the Amidah—as in the Grace After Meals both of which are introduced by the same formula, rendering thanks to God for the miracles performed by him on those occasions, which formula is followed by a brief description of the events of the respective Festivals.

On Chanukah I dealt with this introductory formula and pointed out that the word "Nissim" ("Miracles") is employed just for these two events in which the supermundane intervention of God in the affairs of man by a reversal of the course of Nature, which is usually regarded as the sign of a "Miracle," is conspicuously absent. As I commented on that occasion, "The Book of Esther was even in danger of exclusion from the Canon on the very solid grounds that the name of God does not appear once in the whole book, and to the secular rational reader the deliverance of the Jews which is celebrated on that day came about as a result of a number of strokes of luck, flukes, coincidences and accidental happenings. As someone once said, if Esther had been born with a wart on her nose, the deliverance would not have come about." But despite that fact, as a glance at the two prayers will readily reveal, both the victory of Chanukah and the frustration of the "knavish tricks" of Haman are directly ascribed to God. "Thou delivered the strong into the hands of the weak," "Thou" and not Judas Maccabeus; "Thou didst bring his counsel to nought, and didst frustrate his design," "Thou" and not Mordecai and Esther.

This ascription of human activity to God is so commonplace that it hardly needs to be commented upon. Man is regarded as the instrument whereby God's purpose is fulfilled in the world, and so consistent is Judaism in this that it ascribes not only those incidents in which Israel is delivered, but also those in which it is defeated to this cause. When Assyria destroyed the Kingdom of Israel and put an end to the existence of the Ten Tribes, the prophet apostrophises him אוי אשור שבט אפי, Woe Assyria, the Rod of my Wrath. Assyria is but the stick which the Lord has chosen to beat the recalcitrant children of Israel.

What is remarkable, however, is that this ascription of the downfall of Haman to God is not consistently followed. Read this verse again and you will surely be struck by the sudden change of person from the second to the third. "Thou didst bring his counsel to nought; thou didst frustrate his design; thou didst return his recompense on his head," but "*they* hanged him and his sons upon the gallows." It is God to whom is ascribed the bringing of the counsel of Haman to nought, the frustration of his design, the return of his recompense to his head, but it is not to God that the dire and condign punishment which is meted out to him and to his sons is attributed, but to human agency.

To the student of Jewish history this significant change of person reminds one of one of the most tragic episodes in Jewish history, and one of the saddest in the history of Christianity. During the fifteenth century the Pope gave permission to Ferdinand and Isabella of Spain to establish the Inquisition in order to bring to book those Marranos who, unable to withstand the pressure of persecution and discrimination, had outwardly accepted Christianity but secretly adhered to Judaism.

In their ruthless determination to stamp out this growing heresy they condemned thousands upon thousands of these Crypto-Jews to the stake. For over three centuries the odour of burning human flesh went up from the stake as a "sweet savour" to the God of the Catholic Church, in Spain, Portugal, Sicily, America and India. An idea of the extent of this human sacrifice can be gauged from the fact that during the reign of Philip V (1700-1746) 1,564 persons were burned alive, 782 in effigy, apart from 11,730 who received other punishment. Of these 90% were Marranos.

And yet, incredible though it may sound, the Catholic Church claimed that it never put a person to death. In order to maintain an outward semblance of that pity and compassion and regard for human life which should be the characteristic of the religion of love, the Inquisition tried and sentenced the accused person, but for the act of execution they handed him over to the secular power, so that they could say "Our hands have not shed this blood."

In other words the Church could say "We have discovered his backsliding, we have arraigned him, we have tried him, we have found him guilty, but it is they who have burned him at the stake." And in this respect it represents a striking parallel to the formula of this prayer.

I should hate to think, however, that anything approaching this idea underlies this significant change of person. Judaism could never, under any circumstances, be guilty even in thought of, to use a colloquialism, "passing the buck" from God to Man in this way. When Man is guilty of the extreme penalty it is regarded as Divine Punishment, and in its execution, as in all other things, Man is regarded as the instrument of God's will. Why then does it say "*They* hanged him and his sons upon the gallows" and not "*Thou* didst hang him"?

I believe that in this change there is a profound and moral doctrine which goes far to answer the perplexing problem of evil in the world, and which places human justice and injustice in correct relationship with Divine Justice. The first atomic bomb is dropped on Hiroshima and over a hundred thousand persons, men, women and children are killed or horribly maimed. Hitler wreaks his evil will upon the innocent and helpless Jews of Europe and six million precious souls are destroyed. And we rail against God and question his justice. "Where is the God of Mercy?" we ask, "where the compassion of the Heavenly Father for his children?" And surely the answer is that it was not God who pulled the lever which released the bomb which created such havoc. It was General Doolittle of the American Air Force or one of his pilots, and the order to do so came from the Pentagon and not from Heaven. It was not God who led the Jews like lambs to the slaughter to the crematoria and the gas chambers. It was Hitler and his myrmidons, many of whom now hold high and honoured place in the counsels of Germany and the world. They were human acts of evil and not divine.

Where then does God come in in the mundane affairs of Man? Is there then "neither Judge nor Judgment?" And the answer is that of course there is. God has given unto Man the Freedom of Will to choose the way that he should go. He says unto Man "Behold, I have set before thee this day life and good and death and evil. . . . I call heaven and earth to witness against you this day, that I have set before thee life and death, the blessing and the curse: therefore choose life that thou mayest live, thou and thy seed" (Deut. xxx: 15 and 19). But Man, instead of choosing life chooses death, instead of good he selects evil, and for blessing a curse. And having thus chosen the results of his actions come down upon him through human agency. It is the failure of Man to live up to, and to act according to the Will of God which brings the ineluctable Nemesis upon him. When the time comes, as I am sure it will come, when the white population of South Africa will pay the penalty for its flouting of the law of God in its treatment of its Native population, when all the bitterness and frustration, the rankling injustice and discrimination which is at present being kept in bounds, breaks those bounds and releases a flood which will sweep us off our feet, shall we turn to God and say "Lord, what hast thou done unto us? My God, my God, why hast thou forsaken me?" Or shall we be fair and just and say "Thou hast given us thy commandments of justice and right, thou hast shown us the way that we should go. But we have not hearkened and we have followed in the way which has brought us to this pass, and *they* have done this thing unto us." "They" hanged Haman because he followed a path which flouted the will of God, for God in the end will be justified and Man becomes the instrument either of his own happiness and well-being, or the reverse.

## THE VALUE OF CEREMONIAL

**וראיתם אותו וזכרתם את כל מצות ה׳ ועשיתם אותם ולא תתורו אחרי לבבכם ואחרי עיניכם אשר אתם זונים אחריהם**

*And ye shall look upon it, and remember all the commandments of the Lord and do them, that ye go not about after your own heart and after your own eyes, after which ye use to go astray.*

(Num. xv: 39.)

The third and last paragraph of the Shema, apart from its last important verse, deals exclusively with the commandment to wear the Tzitzit, the four-fringed garment which, in the form of the Tallit, is the characteristic outward feature of a Jewish congregation, and is as honoured in the observance as its other form, the Arba Canfot which should be worn by every Jew, is honoured in the breach. But despite the fact that I have called it the characteristic outward feature of a Jewish congregation, to-night, as on all nights except Kol Nidrei, it is worn only by the Cantor and by the Rabbi when he is preaching. The reason is that by interpreting the words **וראיתם אותו** "Ye shall see it" as meaning that it shall be worn during the daylight hours, the Rabbis do not necessitate the wearing of the Tallit at night. This being so, there is no inherent reason for this paragraph to be included in the Evening Service, and in point of fact, its inclusion is due solely to that last verse. As you will remember from the well-known passage in the Haggada of Passover, the Mishnah decides that **מזכירין יציאת מצרים בלילות**, that the Exodus from Egypt must be mentioned in the evenings as well as in the mornings, and it is the reference to the Exodus in the last verse which justifies the inclusion of the whole paragraph in the evening Shema.

And so twice a day, morning and evening, we read the verse "And ye shall look upon it and remember the commandments of the Lord," but there is a difference between the two occasions. In the morning we fulfil it as we are reading it, while in the evening we read it without fulfilling it, and the difference affords us the opportunity of discussing the question of the value of outward ceremonial.

Man has five physical senses, those of sight, hearing and smell, taste and touch. But it is a well-known fact that the effect and potency of these senses differ in different persons. One man may have an acute sense of smell and an insensitive palate. One may have eagle eyes and impaired hearing, and it is a well-known fact that when a person is deprived of one sense, by a process of compensation or as a result of training the other senses are correspondingly developed. These are well-known facts which, as I say, differ with individuals and with circumstances, but, over and above those differences our Rabbis lay it down as a general rule that אינה דומה שמיעה לראיה that the effect of hearing something cannot be compared for intensity of effect with the effect of seeing. The sight of something is infinitely more impressive, in the literal sense of the word, than merely hearing about it. In other words, visual objects have a lasting effect that audial objects cannot hope to possess. It is surely in order to impress that lesson that the Midrash says that Moses found it difficult to comprehend four of the Commandments transmitted by God to him through his sense of hearing, until God brought in the aid of the sense of sight and *showed* them to him.

That truth has fully been realised by modern educators and from its realisation has grown that branch of education which is called visual education which is to-day a *sine qua non* of modern educational methods. Films, slides, pictures, models, all these are examples of the application of the truth that אינה דומה שמיעה לראיה. And that truth was realised by the Bible and by our Rabbis long before it was grasped by modern educators. The object seen by the eye conveys a thought, an idea, an emotion to the heart, reinforcing the message conveyed by other means. Therein lies the justification of that so much derided aspect of Orthodox Judaism, the outward ceremonial Tzitzit and Tephillin, Ethrog and Lulab, Succah and Hoshanah—with all of these the outward act of ceremonial makes use of the powerful sense of sight in order to awake a spiritual feeling in the heart of the person who fulfils the act, which persists long after the act is no more.

Whereas, however, with regard to all these other acts of ceremonial, they are enjoined without reason or explanation, in the case of Tzitzit a full and explicit explanation is given. The complete silence with regard to other ceremonial acts and the expansive explanation with regard to Tzitzit should occasion no surprise to the student of the Talmud. He instantly realises that this is a classic example of the hermeneutical rule of בנין אב., that it is necessary to state it only in one instance, which is called the "father," and it automatically applies to all other cases, in accordance with the well-known phrase זה בנין אב לכולם., this "father-example" applies to all. As Singer translates it, "A general law may be derived by induction from different cases which, occurring in the same or in different verses, have yet some feature in common." The common feature is the outward act, and we can now proceed to examine what our verse says about Tzitzit.

The potency of the eye applies both to good objects and to bad. The roving, questing eye of man can lead him astray as well as keep him on the right path. And the eye looks upon a world in which the spirit of God is not visible. It looks upon material things, it looks upon evil things, it looks upon unworthy things, and the sight of them makes its powerful impression and can decide that he will follow in the path indicated. And the warning goes forth, "Go not about after your own heart and after your own eyes, after which ye use to go astray." But as long as these are mere words, they suffer from the fact that they make use of the sense of hearing which is impotent against the vivid effect of the sense of sight. And so, to the audial commandment there comes the reinforcement of the visual ceremonial. Place upon your garments the fringes, and what is the result? The eyes, from looking upon that which tends to lead them astray, away from God, rest upon this other side. וראיתם אותו "And ye shall see it." A counterpoise is presented against the other things which he sees, and as he sees it וזכרתם את כל מצות ה׳ he remembers. He remembers all the commandments of the Lord.

And here one must pause for a moment, and give expression to another concept about which I have spoken on so many occasions and which is fundamental to Judaism. It is the wonderfully optimistic view which Judaism has of human nature. Judaism believes that man is not inherently wicked or vicious. Judaism believes that if man sins and goes astray it is not out of any perversity or evil in his nature, but because of apathy, sloth and negligence. If only man would consider, if only man would remember, he would not sin. "Reflect upon three things, and thou wilt not come within the power of sin" is an example of that conviction which occurs twice in the Ethics of the Fathers (ii: 1 and iii: 1) as is the famous explanation of Maimonides of the meaning and effect of the Shofar on Rosh Hashanah, "Awake ye sleepers from your sleep, and ye that are in a trance, rouse yourselves from that trance!"

And that being so, the consequence of seeing the Tzitzit, and by seeing them remembering, is a natural one וראיתם אותו וזכרתם את כל מצות ה׳ ועשיתם אותם ולא תתורו אחרי לבבכם ואחרי עיניכם אשר אתם זונים אחריהם "Ye will observe them and ye will not go about after your own heart and after your own eyes, which ye use to go astray after them." That is the effect and the justification of ceremonial which applies not only to the Tzitzit. The most frequent of all those acts of ceremonial is the laying of Tephillin, obligatory as it is on every common day. The Bible specifically states that "it shall be a sign," and a sign is important not in itself, but as an indication of something else. It is for that reason that with a clear psychological perception our Rabbis rendered the fulfilment of this duty unnecessary on Sabbath and Festivals since they themselves constitute the "sign" which shall bring man to a contemplation of the divine and of his religious duties. But on the ordinary day of the week, when all "signs" point in the direction away from God instead of towards him, we must set up this sign. Of what? The beautiful if mystical meditation before putting on the Tephillin which is found on page 15 of the Authorised Daily Prayer Book tells us: "He hath commanded us to lay Tephillin upon the hand as a memorial of his outstretched arm, opposite the heart to indicate the duty of subjecting the longings and designs of our heart to his service, blessed be he; and upon the head over against the brain, thereby teaching that the mind, whose seat is in the brain, together with all senses and faculties, is to be subjected to his service, blessed be he." With him who puts on his Tephillin these sublime thoughts remain throughout the long day. But he who fails to don them, and rejects them as mere ceremonial, whence shall these thoughts come into his mind? The signpost is lacking and he wanders away from the way of the Lord. For he who abandons ceremonial lets slip from his fingers the Ariadne thread which will lead him through the maze of the world to a contemplation of the way of God.

## EVERLASTING FREEDOM

המכה בעברתו כל בכורי מצרים ויוצא את עמו ישראל מתוכם
לחרות עולם..., ברוך אתה ה׳ גאל ישראל.

*Who in his wrath smote all the firstborn of Egypt, and brought forth his people Israel from among them to everlasting freedom. . . . Blessed art thou O Lord, who hast redeemed Israel.*

(Evening Service.)

No people in the world has suffered from bondage, and from the denial of national independence, as has the Jewish people. It is almost symbolic of the Jewish people that alone of all nations in the world it first became a nation, not in its own territory but as an enslaved people in Egypt. If, as is now almost universally accepted by Biblical scholars, the turn of the tide which changed the descendants of Jacob from a favoured group in the land of Goshen to the victims of the hostility and ill-will of the Pharaohs of the Oppression is to be attributed to the defeat and expulsion of the Semitic Hyksos Shepherd Kings in 1580 B.C., the Jewish people as a people has a continuous history of almost exactly 3,500 years. For how much of that long period has the Jewish people known the boon and blessing of freedom? The answer to that question is little short of startling. Again following the most recent accepted chronology we date the complete independence of Israel from the reign of David about 1000 B.C. This independence lasted until the destruction of the Temple by Nebuchadnezzar in 586 B.C., giving us a period of just over 400 years of independence. And that ignores the fact that the Northern Kingdom, consisting of Ten of the Twelve Tribes, ceased to exist nearly 150 years before that. The remnants of the Jewish people were permitted to return following the Declaration of Cyrus in 537 B.C., but the returned exiles did not achieve independence from foreign domination until the time of Simon the Hasmonean in 142 B.C. That independence was tragically short-lived. It came to an end in 60 B.C., when Pompey made Judea tributary to Rome. The second period of independence therefore lasted for a mere 82 years. In 1948 the third Commonwealth, the present State of Israel in a portion of its historic territory came into being and restored the long lost political independence of the Jewish people. And in two months' time, in an atmosphere of tension and crisis, we shall celebrate the ninth anniversary of the young State. When we therefore add together the 414 years of independence of the First Commonwealth, the 82 of the Second and the 9 of the Third, we arrive at a total of 506 years of independence out of a history of 3,500 years! In other words, for six-sevenths of its history Israel has been deprived of its freedom and for only one-seventh has it known the blessings of liberty. And yet daily in our evening prayers, when we call to mind the historic deliverance from the bondage of Egypt, we give thanks unto God, not for giving us a freedom which we since lost, but for bringing us forth to "everlasting freedom." And we conclude that magnificent passage with the blessing to God for our redemption, "Blessed art thou, O Lord, who hath redeemed Israel."

I have gone to some trouble to determine the approximate date when this formula was first introduced into our statutory prayers, and I find that whereas the text of the Prayer Book of R. Saadya Gaon which forms the basis of the critical edition published in 1941 has the words "And brought forth Israel from among them to freedom," a fragment in the Taylor-Shechter collection from the Cairo Geniza, preserved in Cambridge, has our text, "to *ever-*

*lasting* freedom." R. Saadya Gaon died just over a thousand years ago, and we can therefore assume that for the last thousand years this formula has been used.

Let us for a few moments imagine the recital of this formula during the last millennium. The Jews of France and Germany during the First and Second Crusades in 1096 and 1146, persecuted, hunted, exiled and decimated, burnt alive at the stake. At the whim of their cruel torturers, they yet piously recite their daily prayers and give thanks to God for bringing them out to "everlasting freedom" and for redeeming them. Expelled from England in 1290, from France in 1291, from Spain in 1492, their whole history in Germany and in Italy a miserable and tragic record of expulsion from one dukedom, of pogroms in another, of discrimination in a third. Imagine the Jews locked away night after night in the noisome and pestilential ghettos of Venice, where the ghetto was first instituted, and then in the other towns, rendering thanks unto God for bringing them forth to "everlasting freedom." Imagine the Jews cooped up in pales of settlement in Eastern Europe, their freedom of movement restricted, their occupations severely circumscribed, a helot class in the population, yet rendering thanks to God for the boon of "everlasting freedom." And lastly in our own time the seven million Jews subjected to the persecution of Hitler, forced to wear the Jew-badge, hunted, persecuted, and the vast majority of them destroyed, still singing a praise to God for their redemption and for the boon of "everlasting freedom." Did they pray with a lie on their lips? Did they utter a meaningless formula completely at variance with the stark, ugly facts of reality? They did not. They most certainly did not.

For with the exodus of the Jews from Egypt the Jewish people tasted the heady wine of freedom, and having tasted it, they never allowed the flavour thereof to dissipate. Planted in the Jew is the seed of freedom and centuries of bondage have never succeeded in eradicating it from his soul. Deep down in his being, overlaid by an overburden of infertile accumulation, that seed has remained potentially fertile and the effect of the celebration of Passover has been to irrigate it and keep it alive. It is because we were once free that we shall again be free; it was because we gave the message of freedom to the world, that the Jew ever stands in the vanguard of those movements whose aim is the ultimate freedom of the world.

How dearly has the Jewish people had to pay for its instinctive love of freedom! What untold sacrifices he has been called upon to bear! It was no wilful act of irrational spite which made the Jew the chief victim of that most formidable attempt in world history to enslave the world which we know by the name of Nazism, the doctrine of totalitarianism with its complete subjection of the freedom of the individual, with its suppression of freedom of thought, with its subordination of the divine spirit of man to the dictates of the State. Instinctively but correctly Hitler realised that the Jew by his very existence constituted the most clamant protest against the spirit which he tried to inculcate in the world. The slave mentality which is the essence of Nazism stood at the opposite pole of the unquenchable spirit of freedom which is the essence of the Jew, and although it cost us six million precious souls, no greater tribute was ever paid to the Jew than the fact that he was singled out as the especial victim of that doctrine.

And because through centuries of persecution and bondage the Jew kept alive that spirit of freedom, we have witnessed the phenomenon to which there is no parallel in world history, of a people, deprived of its freedom for nigh upon 2,000 years, harassed, persecuted, decimated and discriminated against, yet regaining its freedom, and emerging again to freedom. Because he kept alive that spirit of freedom he was able, as we have seen in recent months, to defy the pressure of a hostile world which would have denied it the possibility of providing these conditions which would assure its continued freedom until the justice of its cause was reluctantly conceded, at least in principle. In the words of our Rabbis, "That ear which heard from Mt. Sinai the words 'Unto me are the Children of Israel servants,' but not servants to my servants, which hearkens to the voice of bondage is doomed to everlasting shame." For we are a people who has known how to maintain an inner freedom even in bondage, and as a result we shall achieve the complete redemption for ourselves, and show the world the way to its attainment.

## THE NIGHT PRAYER

### השכיבנו ה׳ אלהינו לשלום והעמידנו מלכנו לחיים

*Cause us to lie down, O Lord our God, in peace, and raise us up, O our King unto life.*

(Evening Service.)

As I pointed out in my sermon on the structure of the evening service, there is one portion of the evening service which has no counterpart in the morning service. Whereas in the morning the reading of the Shema is preceded by two blessings and followed by one only, in the evening it is not only preceded by two blessings but is also followed by two blessings. The two preceding blessings in the morning, for the blessing of daily light and for the boon of the Torah correspond closely to the two preceeding blessings in the evening, for the evening twilight and the boon of the Torah. Similarly the blessing which follows the Shema in the morning is exactly the same as the one which follows the evening Shema, a blessing for the redemption of Israel. The additional blessing in the evening, however, finds no counterpart in the morning service, and when we read that beautiful and moving prayer, it is not easy to find a reason for it. Surely when in the evening we say "Cause us to lie down in peace, and raise us up to life . . . Be thou a shield about us, remove from us every enemy pestilence, sword, famine and sorrow . . . O shelter us beneath the shadow of thy wings, etc.," could we not equally pray in the morning for a day blessed by God? If there is, in the words of the Psalmist, "the terror by night," is there not equally "the arrow that flieth by day?" If there is "the pestilence that walketh in darkness," is there not equally "the plague that ravageth at noonday"? (Psalm xci). But if it is difficult to explain it logically, it is an easy matter to do so emotionally and psychologically.

There are two Psalms in the Book of Psalms which give beautiful expression to the thoughts which enter into the mind of the Psalmist when he contemplates the heavenly firmament and the marvels of creation which are revealed by that contemplation, and the most cursory reading of these Psalms reveals an entirely different mood in these two Psalms. The first is the Eighth Psalm and the mood is revealed in the words "When I look upon thy heavens, the work of thy fingers, the moon and the stars which thou hast ordained, what is man that thou art mindful of him, and the son of man that thou givest heed unto him?" (Psalm viii: 4/5). How different is that mood from that expressed in the Nineteenth Psalm: "The heavens declare the glory of God, and the firmament declareth his handiwork. Day unto day poureth forth speech and night unto night proclaimeth knowledge. . . . And the sun is as a bridegroom coming out of his chamber, and rejoiceth as a strong man to run his course." (Psalm xix: 2/3/6).

The former is the mood of what Milton calls "Il Penseroso," the mood of thoughtful contemplation of man's insignificance when measured against the vast infinity of God's work, the mood of realisation of man's frailty and utter dependence on God. How different is the mood of the other Psalm! It is "L'allegro." It is joy and gladness, the joy of the bridegroom emerging from the wedding canopy, the joy of the man in the full pride of his prime pitting his athletic prowess against his competitors, and presumably winning the race.

What is the difference between those two moods? The answer is obvious. The former is induced by the sight of the moon and the stars, the latter by the sight of the sun in all its glory. One represents the thoughts which come at night when silence prevails and the darkness is relieved only by the pale gleam of the moon and the fitful light of the stars, when man is overawed by the absence of light; the other is the joy which comes with the blessing of light.

One often reads of a person afflicted by blindness having the blessing of sight restored, or granted, to him, and one reads the impressions which the first sight of light makes upon him. But is it possible to imagine a person experiencing darkness for the first time in his life? Our Rabbis, who truly merit the name "those poets of religion" given to them by Jeremy Taylor, realised that there was one such instance in the Scriptural narrative. Adam was created during the day and when night fell at the close of that first day he experienced darkness for the first time. And they weave a beautiful Midrash round this idea. On the day of his creation he looked upon this world into which he had been placed. And he lifted up his head on high and saw the golden orb of the sun and felt the warmth of its radiance. And then he watched it traversing the expanse of the sky until it reached the horizon and slowly dipped beyond it. And in place of warmth there was cold, and in place of light there was darkness. What were his feelings at the onset of this phenomenon? What thoughts did it induce? And with beautiful and imaginative poetic insight they say that he exclaimed זוהי מיתה שנגזרה עלי מן השמים "This then is the death which has been decreed upon me from heaven." Light is life and darkness must be death, and if he never witnessed darkness no more had he witnessed death, and he equated the two. And there he sat cowering and in terror all that long night until at last the dawn came and he felt that he had walked through the valley of the shadow of death to life renewed.

Of the beauty of this Midrash there can be no question, and it should be linked with the equally moving one that when Cain slew Abel, Adam did not recognise the lifelessness of his son as death. But there is more than beauty in it. I believe that there is an element of truth in it—not in the fact that darkness is death but that man equates it somehow with death. Deep down in the soul of every person there is a streak of that primeval feeling which our Rabbis ascribe to Primal man at the onset of darkness. That feeling of terror of the dark which is characteristic of practically every child, exists to some extent in every individual. He feels a loneliness, an isolation, an insecurity which makes him turn to God as instinctively as a child in fear hides its face in its mother's apron.

And when to that darkness is added that mysterious state of suspended animation which is called sleep—which is so much like death; when in that sleep that even more mysterious phenomenon of the dream state comes with its vague intimations of another world, or another life, even when it is not accompanied by fearsome visions in which we find ourselves the helpless victims of circumstances beyond our control; it is under circumstances like these that Man feels that the buttresses of security which are around him when the sun is riding high in the heavens are being removed. He feels that his soul is parting company with its partner the body and returning for a while to its source. Is it not natural that under circumstances like that he addresses himself to God and commends to him his spirit, prays for protection and for the guarding of the Guardian of Israel who neither slumbers nor sleeps?

For this Hashkivenu prayer is the prayer בשכבך "when thou liest down," and to such an extent is it so that it is repeated, as you will see if you turn to page 293, in the special prayers before retiring to bed at night. And although it has no counterpart in the morning Shema, it does have its counterpart in the beautiful prayer "O my God, the soul which thou hast given me is pure," which forms part of the early morning service, that prayer which concludes "Blessed art thou O Lord who restoreth souls unto dead bodies." And he awakes in the morning and he feels the return of that soul. And all around him is light and bright and he feels ready and able to cope with the problems before him and after him. He feels ready for the race of life, ready to face whatever may come. God is in his heaven and all is well with the world, and by lying down in the peace of God he is able to rise to life renewed.

## THE SABBATH

ושמרו בני ישראל את השבת לעשות את השבת לדורותם ברית עולם

*And the Children of Israel shall keep the Sabbath. to observe the Sabbath throughout their generations, for an everlasting covenant.*

(Exodus xxxi: 16.)

After the statutory evening service which is identical for weekday, Sabbath and Festival, we read on Sabbaths and Festivals a special Scriptural passage giving the specific message of the Sabbath or the Festival. But whatever difficulty there might possibly be in finding a suitable passage for the Festivals, in selecting a passage to emphasise the institutions and the sanctity of the Sabbath, the liturgical selectors must have been faced with a veritable *embaras de richesse*. If I am not mistaken, the injunction of the Sabbath occurs about forty times in the Bible and there must be some special content to this passage to justify its selection. For instance, the fourth commandment readily suggests itself, as does the first mention of the Sabbath, the ויכולו prayer which is included in the Amidah. Why is this particular passage selected in preference to these two? And the answer is to be found in both context and in content, in the context in which this passage occurs, as well as in the importance of the passage itself.

First there comes the context, and a reference to this context shows that only half of the passage enjoining the observance of the Sabbath is recited. The passage comes immediately after the completion of the details given by God to Moses to erect the Sanctuary in the Wilderness. It reads: "And the Lord said unto Moses saying, Speak unto the Children of Israel saying, nevertheless ye shall keep my Sabbaths, for it is a sign between me and you throughout your generations, that ye may know that I am the Lord who sanctify you. . . . Six days shall work be done, but on the seventh day is a Sabbath of solemn rest, holy to the Lord." It is surely obvious, as our Rabbis point out, that the reference in these verses is a limited one, referring to the subject with which it is connected, the command to erect the sanctuary, and its purpose is to emphasise that even in the erection of the sanctuary the Sabbath had to be observed. Probably no undertaking was fulfilled by the children of Israel with such enthusiasm as the erection of the sanctuary. It is the only instance on record that the response to the appeal for contributions was so overwhelming that the command had to go forth through the camp of Israel that the collection was to stop. If in the words of the Rabbis when they were invited to give their gold for the Golden Calf, they gave, and when they were invited to give for the erection of the Sanctuary they gave, נתבעין לעגל ונותנין נתבעין למשכן ונותנין, their contributions to the Sanctuary came after those for the Golden Calf, and the enthusiasm and the generosity of their response went far to atone for that act of national apostasy.

Could there be a higher and more sacred purpose than the Sanctuary? That purpose is expressed succintly in the words ועשו לי מקדש ושכנתי בתוכם "They shall make for me a sanctuary that I shall dwell in their midst." And yet these verses come and insist that there *is* a higher sanctity than the Sanctuary and that it is the sanctity of the Sabbath אך את שבתותי תשמרו "Nevertheless ye shall observe my Sabbaths." The sanctity of the Sabbath overrides that of the Sanctuary.

And only then does the divine legislator turn from the

particular to the general. After the limited application of these words to the specific task of the erection of the Sanctuary come these verses which are read in the Friday evening service. "And the children of Israel shall keep the Sabbath to observe the Sabbath throughout their generations for an everlasting covenant." Surely its meaning is clear, that as was the injunction of the observance of the Sabbath on the particular occasion, so was its injunction for future generations. As in the erection of the Sanctuary no consideration, even the highest and most sacred, was permitted to override the Sabbath, in that spirit shall the Sabbath be observed in future generations. No plea that there are considerations of equal sanctity to the Sabbath can be accepted as an excuse for its non-observance; if the building of the Sanctuary cannot be accepted, what can? And the answer in Jewish law is that to all practical purposes the only consideration which takes precedence over the Sabbath is פקוח נפש saving of human life.

That is why the words "For it is a sign between me and your generations" is repeated in both halves of the passage. Could there be a more moving sign of the covenant between God and his people than the complete cessation of the work entailed in the erection of the Sanctuary? And should there not be the same sign to-day?

What has then happened to this glorious conception of the Sabbath, of a day so universally observed that, as I pointed out in my sermon on the Meaning of Ceremonial, it takes the place of Tephillin? What has happened to this sign?

To the outward observer, attending this Synagogue on Friday night, and seeing the throngs of worshippers who come week after week to welcome in the Sabbath, to sanctify it and extol it, it might well appear that the Sabbath still exerts its sway over us. But if that same observer were to take up his position outside the Synagogue and see the incredible sight of so many of these seemingly devout worshippers immediately lighting up their cigarettes almost within the precincts of the Synagogue before entering their cars; if he were later to take up his stand outside the cinemas later on in the evening, if to-morrow morning he would continue his investigations in the hairdressing saloons, the tea shops, the business areas of the city; if in the afternoon he were to visit the sporting clubs and see the activities, not of those to whom the Sabbath means nothing, but of those who, from 6-7 p.m., are here in Synagogue, he would have ample reason to reverse his opinion. How would he explain the hold of the Sabbath or its lack of hold on the outwardly faithful?

I was recently reading the biography of Mahatma Gandhi by one of his fervent and devoted followers, Stanley Jones, who was an American missionary in India. Although Jones was a devout Christian and Gandhi rejected Christianity, he regarded him in essence, in his thoughts, ideals and activities as a better Christian than those who professed and propagated the faith, and in analysing the superficial Christianity of its adherents in India he expressed the metaphor that they have been inoculated with a mild form of Christianity which rendered them immune to an attack of the real "disease"! And that is exactly what has happened to the Sabbath in South Africa. Were it to be entirely disregarded it might perhaps have been possible to infect you with its virus. But you have developed and perfected a serum which, after you have become injected with it, renders you immune to the Sabbath "disease." That serum is the mildest and easiest form of Sabbath observance, a weekly visit for one hour on Friday evening, and that is the beginning and end of it.

On the last word of that passage וינפש our Rabbis make a beautiful and poetic pun. They interpret the word as being two words וי נפש "Woe for the soul," and they explain that when the Sabbath comes every Jew is possessed of an "added soul" which comes down from heaven and enters the body ot the Jew who for those twenty-four hours is possessed of that נשמה יתירה that "added soul." And consequently God is deprived of that soul which comes down from heaven to earth and God, so to speak, is deprived of it. It is a fanciful and poetic thought but it is difficult to reconcile that added sanctity with God's grief. Alas and alas, it is not difficult to do so to-day when we consider the Sabbath as it is observed and as it ought to be observed. For to-day the Almighty looks down from heaven and sees what has become of the Holy Sabbath, of the virtual obliteration of the sign which it was supposed to erect between him and his people, and he exclaims אבדה נפש "Woe unto me, for the soul of the Sabbath has been lost," and במסתרים תבכה נפשי and in the hidden places of the Almighty that soul weeps and finds no consolation, for it wanders alone and there is none to give it a resting place.

# PASSOVER AND EASTER

## For the Intermediate Sabbath of Passover, coinciding with Good Friday

---

ומביא גואל לבני בניהם למען שמו באהבה

*And God in love will bring a redeemer to their children's children for his name's sake.*

(Amidah.)

In view of the coincidences of Passover and Good Friday, I break the continuity of this series in order to deal with a subject topical to this coincidence.

The first blessing of the Amidah speaks of God as the God of history. He is not only our God, but the God of our Fathers; he is the God of Abraham, the God of Isaac and the God of Jacob. It is the God who works out his Divine Purpose through the instrumentality of Man, and particularly through that branch of the human family who are the descendants, actual or spiritual, of Abraham. Each generation has added to the slow but ever increasing unfolding and revelation of the spirit of God. Isaac is not content with inheriting the God of Abraham; he makes him also the God of Isaac, and Jacob adds to that knowledge and awareness to the extent of making him the God of Jacob. It is in this way that the "God of our Fathers" becomes "Our God" as well. But that process of the gradual development of the world in the spirit of God until the whole of mankind will ultimately accept his Sovereignty has not yet been fulfilled. It will find its ultimate fulfilment only when the Redeemer comes and the Kingdom of God will be established upon earth.

We Jews believe with a passionate faith in the coming of the Messiah, in the ultimate redemption of mankind, in the final triumph of right and justice over wrong and evil. It is that faith which has sustained us through centuries and aeons of persecution and hardship. It is that faith which is embodied in the twelfth of the Thirteen Principles of Faith of Maimonides, that article of faith which, sung with fervent ardour by Hitler's victims when they went to their death, has become one of the battle cries of our people, and whose rendering by our Chief Cantor has earned it a deserved place in the classical music of our people.

But as passionately as we believe in the coming of the Redeemer, so passionately do we reject the belief that he has already come, particularly that he came 1,957 or 1,953 years ago. And that is why, when to-day the adherents of the dominant faith celebrate the Resurrection of the Messiah we still pray daily for his coming, an advent which still belongs to the distant future.

How have we suffered as a result of that rejection! The whole tragedy of Jewish history during the last two millennia, the odyssey of Jewish suffering is directly attributable to our adamant refusal to accept that belief, and I can think of no better way to justify it than to recount to you a famous incident of Jewish history.

In July of the year 1263 there took place in Barcelona, in Spain, the most famous of all these miserable and sorry disputations between Jews and Christians which are one of the unhappy episodes of the medieval history of the Jews. These disputations were not sought by the Jews. Their advocate was almost without exception an apostate Jew who, armed with a knowledge of his natal faith and filled with zeal for his adopted one, essayed to place the former at the disposal of the latter in the vain hope of proving the truths of Christianity to the obdurate Jews. In this instance it was an apostate who had adopted the name of Pablo Christiani, while the champion of the Jews was the famous Moses b. Nachman, Nachmanides, known to us as the "Ramban." One of the terms of reference of his disputation was just that point which is the subject of this sermon, whether the Messiah had already appeared. The Ramban conducted himself with fearless courage and superb dignity, and to this question he gave a striking answer. "You maintain," he said, "that the Messiah came 1,263 years ago. You have now had 1,263 years to put that theory to the pragmatic test of fact," and he made his telling point in the following words as quoted by Graetz: All the prophets had foretold that at the time of the Messiah a more elevated standard of morality would prevail among mankind, and especially that all war and bloodshed would cease. But since the appearance of Jesus the world had really become filled with violence and injustice. The Christians were considered to be the most warlike among the nations, that is to say, the people that shed most blood. Then turning to the king, Nachmanides said, "It behoves thee and thy knights, O King, to put an end to thy war-making, as the beginning of the Messianic era demands."

It can hardly be said that the seven hundred years which have elapsed since that striking and bold declaration have done other than reinforce the critique which it contains. Have we indeed been living in the Messianic age for nigh on two thousand years? Is there a sign of the Golden Age which he was to usher in? When there would be peace on earth and goodwill between men? When the nations of the world would "beat their swords into ploughshares and their spears into pruning hooks. Nation shall not lift up sword against nation neither shall they learn war any more"? Only yesterday, on the eve of Easter, a distinguished British General announced that in any future nuclear war, only the airfields would be defended, while the population would be left to their fate! And this nearly two thousand years after the presumed advent of the Messiah!

No! The progress of the world towards that blessed day if it is a sure, it is a slow and unsteady process. It does not even advance steadily; it suffers periods of setback and retrogression, one of which we are passing through to-day. But if it will not come to their "children," it will come to their "children's children." In the words of the Ani Ma'amin "even though he tarry, I will yet wait daily for his coming." It is that dissatisfaction with the present, coupled with a sure faith of an ultimate glorious future, which is the mainspring behind all our strivings. Once one believes that the Golden Age has come, the impetus and the stimulus towards improvement disappears. When the Romans saw in the age of Augustus the Golden Age which their poets had foretold, when Virgil sang of it as fact, he planted the seed for what was to become the Decline and Fall of the Roman Empire. We believe in the ultimate triumph of right; we deny that it rules in the world. And inspired by that faith we apply ourselves to the painful ascent up the mountain of the Lord. "Though he tarries, yet will he come." If we do not see it our children's children will see it, and until the process begun by the revelation of God to Abraham finds its fulfilment we shall continue to strive for its coming.

## THE EIGHTEEN WHICH ARE NINETEEN. ON THE AMIDAH.

"EVERYTHING depends upon luck, even a Sefer Torah in the Ark," says the old Jewish proverb, and that "Mazal," extending as it does to everything, includes even Jewish jokes. There are some stories which for some reason every Jew knows and one of them is the story of the Shofar. Its most popular version is that a dispute in Synagogue on Rosh Hashanah involving the blowing of the Shofar found its way to Court. When the witness referred to the Shofar, the judge asked what it is. The witness could only repeat that a Shofar is a Shofar until he was threatened with action for contempt of court. He then reluctantly explained that a Shofar is a trumpet. "Why couldn't you say so at once?" asked the judge testily, "instead of wasting the time of the Court?" "Because," answered the witness triumphantly, "a Shofar is *not* a trumpet. A Shofar is a *Shofar*."

I found myself thinking of this story when I thought of the serious subject of my sermon this evening, the Amidah. And I imagined to myself the following imaginary conversation between myself and one of my congregants:

"I am going to speak to-night about the Amidah."

"The Amidah? What is the Amidah?"

"Well, perhaps you know it better under the name of Shemoneh Esreh."

"Oh! Shemoneh Esreh? Then why don't you say Shemoneh Esreh? Why do you call it Amidah?"

"Because," I answer triumphantly, "the Shemoneh Esreh is *not* a Shemoneh Esreh, and hasn't been so for over 1,800 years."

Let me explain that apparently paradoxical statement. The words Shemoneh Esreh mean Eighteen, and is short for Shemoneh Esreh Berachot, "the Eighteen Benedictions." These Eighteen Benedictions constitute beyond question the oldest component of daily prayer, and in the Talmud the word "Tefillah," Prayer, applies to this portion of the liturgy alone. Its original formulation is ascribed in the Talmud to the Men of the Great Assembly, these anonymous architects of Judaism who carried on the work of Ezra the Scribe, who died in the fifth pre-Christian century, and whose activity covers two or three centuries. That original formulation was revised in the time of Rabban Gamaliel II about the year 100 of this era. In the course of that revision, however, the same Rabban Gamaliel took a fateful and drastic step which was fraught with the most fateful of consequences for the future of Judaism, and which is directly connected with the rise and spread of Christianity.

When Christianity first started it was a movement within the Jewish community itself. The founder of Christianity had explicitly stated that he came not to change a jot or tittle of the Law of Moses, that he came to fulfil and not to destroy. The only difference between the Jews and the Christians was that the latter believed that the Messiah, in whose coming both explicitly believed, had already come while the former denied that he was the Messiah. But in their adherence to the Law of Moses and in the observance of the ceremonial of Judaism they were completely at one. Sabbath, circumcision, and dietary laws were binding upon Christians as they were upon Jews, and admission to the new faith depended upon the acceptance of these principles. Many Gentiles, however, who were otherwise desirous of joining the new faith were reluctant to undergo circumcision and take upon themselves the burden of the observances and ritual of Judaism. Then it was that Peter declared that the dietary laws were no longer binding while Paul declared circumcision as non-obligatory upon Gentile converts to Christianity. Henceforth faith and not observance was to be regarded as the qualification for the new faith. That there was, during the first century, a widespread dissatisfaction with the prevailing paganism and polytheism and a desire to accept the One God of Israel, is amply attested, and when the one barrier to the acceptance of this faith, the regulations of Judaism, was removed, the new faith spread with unprecedented rapidity. Thousands and tens of thousands of Gentiles eagerly adopted the new faith, and the group of Jewish Christians, the "Evyonim," the "poor ones," became a small and insignificant minority in the vast body of Christians. Then it was that Rabban Gamaliel took the drastic step referred to. He realised that unless some steps were taken, the small Jewish community would be swamped by these Gentile Christians, that Judaism was in danger of disappearing. He thereupon instructed one of his disciples, Samuel the Younger, to compose an additional blessing to the existing eighteen, consisting of an imprecation against all "Minim," "Sectarians," among whom were included the Jewish Christians, which would have the effect of making it impossible for them to join in worship with the Jews and would exclude them from the Community of Israel (Berachot 28b). It was inserted before the blessing for the "righteous converts," those who had accepted the full faith of Israel, and the final separation of Christians from Judaism is to be dated from this fateful step by Rabban Gamaliel II at the end of the first century. That this was the purpose of the "Birkat Ha-Minim" is explicitly stated by such authorities as the eighth century author of the Halachot Gedolot (p. 27a) and the Mahzor Vitry. All attempts to explain it away belong to apologetics and not to facts.

With the complete separation of Christianity from Judaism, however, the object of this blessing was attained, and it might well have been excluded from the Amidah which would then have reverted to its original eighteen blessings. During the Middle Ages, however, a new danger arose which threatened the existence of the Jewish community, namely, slanderers, informers and traitors, "Mosrim" who instigated persecutions against their brethren, informed against them to the authorities, and imperilled their already insecure position. The danger of these informers was so great that as great an authority as R. Asher b. Yehiel unhesitatingly expresses his opinion that they should be put to death to prevent them bringing about the destruction of the community. Such a drastic step, mentioned also by Maimonides as a daily occurrence, could not, however, always be effected, and recourse was had to this blessing whose original purpose had already been fulfilled. The wording was changed from ולמינים "Against the sect-tarians" to ולמלשינים "Against the slanderers . . . and against all the enemies of thy people Israel," and so it has remained in our prayer books.

But even that epoch of malicious minded informers whose actions can undermine the security of the Jewish community is no longer the actual and ever-present danger that it was in the days of Jewish rightlessness, but the prayer still has its application to-day.

We stand this evening on the eve of the Day of Mourning, the day when we call to mind the victims of the most savage and ruthless act of genocide in world history, the cold-blooded doing to death of six million Jews as a part of the process of their complete extermination, the most awful example in history of man's inhumanity to man. What are the thoughts which should possess our minds at the contemplation of this act of horror? There are those, especially those whose kith and kin were so brutally done to death, who are still filled with thoughts of vengeance against the perpetrators of this foul deed—and who can find it in his heart to blame them? And those people can and no doubt do pray "Let all the wicked perish as in a moment . . . and the men of violence do thou uproot and crush, cast down and speedily humble," and that formula is found in some of the older versions of this prayer. But there are those who with the passage of time and the healing of wounds are able to rise to a higher level of ethics, to the Jewish level of ethics. They see the signs of contrition on the part of those responsible for this genocide; they think of the apparently sincere attempts to make amends in the way of Reparations, they think of the amazing and gratifying reaction in Germany to "The Diary of Anna Franks," they realise with Burke that "One cannot indict a whole nation" and from thoughts of the punishment of the sinners, they pray, in accordance with the true spirit of Judaism for the extirpation of sin;* that those guilty of these acts shall turn from their evil ways and live. And they, instead of praying "Let all the wicked perish," say "Let all wickedness perish," and instead of "Crush the violent," they say "Crush the dominion of violence" and that is the formula which is found in our prayer books to-day.

And so the prayer remains but its meaning and application are changed. From a prayer instituted in a moment of crisis to save Judaism, it became a prayer against those who would endanger the existence of the Jewish Communities in the Diaspora, and from that it has become a prayer which expresses the noblest of sentiments, a prayer for the abolition of wrong and injustice, that the sovereignty of God may rule supreme in the world.

* See Sermon 4, "Ye that hate evil."

# ORIGINAL VIRTUE—THE MERITS OF THE FATHERS

וזוכר חסדי אבות

*And* (*God*) *remembers the merits of the Patriarchs.*

(Amidah.)

In my last sermon I explained why I prefer the Sephardi name "Amidah," the "Standing Prayer" to the commonly accepted name "Shemoneh Esreh." In addition to the reason given in that sermon for that preference, namely that for nearly two thousand years the "Eighteen Benedictions" have been nineteen, there is the fact that only on weekdays is this large number of blessings included in the Amidah. On Sabbaths and Festivals, apart from the Musaph service of Rosh Hashanah, we recite only Seven Blessings in the Amidah. For the Amidah consists of both constant and variable elements. The constant element is represented by the three first and the three last blessings which are statutory and invariable for all Amidoth, while the intermediate blessings vary according to the occasion and the service. Only on weekdays are there thirteen. On the Sabbath there is but one, dealing with the sanctity of the day, and making a total of seven blessings.

It is surely therefore no exaggeration to suggest that these six blessings which are recited at least three times a day on each of the 365 days of the year, which are the oldest and most essential element of our prayers, represent the quintessence of Jewish prayer, the fundamental thoughts of Judaism in its approach to God. As such they are deserving of the most profound study, and it is my intention to devote a series of sermons in this general series to these concepts, in order that we may be the better able to appreciate these essential beliefs of Judaism. For when one has fixed formulae of prayer there always lurks the danger that our very familiarity with them breeds a mechanical repetition which is destructive of that "Kavvanah," that concentrated devotion which should accompany prayer.

To one of these concepts, the Messianic belief I have already devoted a sermon,* and one has already been delivered on the idea of the God of History, which is enshrined in the first paragraph,** and I therefore turn to a consideration of these words which occur in the first paragraph, to the effect that God "remembers the merits of the patriarchs."

What do we mean by חסדי אבות, translated as "the pious deeds of the patriarchs" as a result of which God will bring a redeemer to their "children's children"? It is another way of referring to one of the characteristic doctrines of Judaism, the doctrine of זכות אבות "the merit of the patriarchs," and for that phrase Rev. S. Levy of England coined a beautiful phrase in English, "Original Virtue." In contrast to the Christian doctrine of Original Sin, which is based on the assumption that there is in man a natural tendency to sin, that the sins of the fathers are visited upon the children, and that the act of disobedience of the first man, Adam, caused the Fall of Man from which all his descendants must suffer to the end of time, Judaism posits the completely opposing and contrasting ideas, that man has a natural tendency to virtue, that the virtues of the fathers are visited upon the children, and that certain acts of obedience and faith on the part of these fathers is held to the credit of their descendants.

---

* See Sermon 29, "Passover and Easter."

** See Sermon 14, "The God of History."

There is to my mind no better way of illustrating this spiritual concept than to bring a parallel from the world of material things. A man makes a success of his business and leaves a fortune to his children, with the result that they are able to live on this patrimony without having to toil themselves. That, transferred from the material to the spiritual sphere, is in a nutshell the concept of זכות אבות the merits of the fathers. The Patriarchs are regarded as having amassed such a huge fund of spiritual treasure that the increment of it is made available to their descendants. But the metaphor does not stop there. Does it mean that his descendants can sit back and live on the spiritual increment without having to lift their finger in order to toil in the world of the spirit and add to that patrimony? And on what terms was that fortune of the spirit left to their descendants? For one father—and I consider him a very foolish father—will leave his whole fortune to his children, making it possible for them to squander and dissipate it, and in the process completely ruin their moral fibre. Another, with more prescience, will invest his money and making it impossible for his descendants to touch the capital will make available only the interest. And between those two extremes there is the middle course whereby both capital and interest are made available so that over a period of time the capital is gradually liquidated until it is completely exhausted and the descendants are thrown back on their own resources. To which of these categories does the spiritual inheritance of Zechut Avoth belong?

The answer to that question is a fascinating one. Let it be said at once that the conception of Zechut Avoth is that of a limited patrimony. It does not and cannot mean that it is such that no amassing of spiritual treasure, no effort in the world of the spirit is necessary for the Jew. All it means is that as a result of the efforts of the patriarchs they are provided with a useful income which is not enough to live on, but which can be added to the fruits of one's own spiritual labours so that the sum total is increased. The doctrine that the Jew can sit back content in the knowledge, to change the metaphor, that the vineyard of the Lord has already been tended by his ancestors, and he can enjoy the fruit is nowhere found and is wholly unacceptable. That way weeds grow; that way, in the expressive words of Isaiah, the grapes that he hopes to enjoy become wild.

But as to the nature of that patrimony, whether it is a temporary or permanent investment, there is a difference of opinion in the Talmud. At what period was the Zechut Avoth terminated? asks the Talmud (T.B. Shabbat 55a). Rab expresses the opinion that it lasted until the time of Hosea, Samuel, that it did not last as long, but was exhausted in the time of Hazael; R. Joshua b. Levi gives the period of Elijah, while R. Johanan says that it lasted until the time of the pious King Hezekiah. The one thing common to all these views is that they all accept the theory that the fund of the merits of the fathers is not inexhaustible, and that at a certain period of Jewish history it was spent and henceforth the Jewish people were thrown on their own resources. Only, in one place, by an authority who cannot be compared with those four whom I have quoted, is the view expressed that the fund is a permanent and eternal one.* if the חסדי אבות is to be understood as זכות אבות ** it is upon this latter opinion that we rely.

And I tell you frankly that I much prefer the doctrine of the gradual exhaustion of the "merits of the patriarchs" to that of its eternal availability. Unconsciously we tend to rely overmuch upon the doctrine of the eternal availability of these merits, with the result that we fail to justify our Jewish heritage by our own efforts. When we are called upon to justify our existence, so to speak, we wax lyrical. "We Jews," we say, "gave the Bible to the world. We Jews have stood fast to our faith despite all blandishments. We Jews have given to the world an ethical code of conduct,

* See Tosafot in loc.

** Ibid.

we gave the world the message of God. We are the People of the Book, we have been called a God-intoxicated people," and so on. But when we begin to ask ourselves, who are those "we" to whom we refer in such vainglorious terms we must regretfully come to the conclusion that the "we" is not the present generation of Jews. It is *not* we who stand as the eternal witnesses of God, it is not we who have added to the spiritual treasures of mankind. When we make these assertions we are relying upon the doctrine of Zechut Avoth, we are taking the credit for what our ancestors and our forebears amassed. Were we but to accept the idea propounded by Rab and Samuel in Babylon, by R. Joshua b. Levi and R. Johanan in Palestine, that the fund of spiritual treasure amassed by our ancestors has been exhausted, it would constitute a challenge to us so to conduct our lives as to emulate their example, to begin anew the amassing of these treasures of the spirit for the benefit of our immortal souls and for the benefit of mankind as a whole.

# THE RESURRECTION OF THE DEAD

מכלכל חיים בחסד מחיה מתים ברחמים רבים

*Thou sustainest the living with lovingkindness, revivest the dead with great mercy.*

(Amidah.)

During the period of the Second Temple the Jewish Commonwealth was riven in twain by two of the opposing sects of the Pharisees and the Sadducees. The divisions between them invaded the religious, the political, the social and economic fields. Suffice it for the moment to explain that the Sadducees were the conservative, aristocratic party of privilege, nationalist in sentiment, their conception limited to this material world. As against them the Pharisees were the progressive, the plebeian party who insisted on the rights of the ordinary people, spiritual in sentiment and regarding the world, in the words of the Rabbis who were the spiritual descendants of the Pharisees, as a vestibule before the palace, the palace being the world to come.

One of the many contentious issues between these two parties was the belief in an after life, and in the resurrection of the dead. The Sadducees, who denied the very existence of any future life, naturally rejected the belief in resurrection. They appeared to be on solid ground in the rejection of this doctrine since, for reasons which one need not go into here, references to the dead in the Bible are few, vague and nebulous. The Pharisees on their part made the doctrine of the resurrection of the dead a fundamental belief of Judaism. They countered the lack of reference to this doctrine in the Bible by denying salvation to the person who maintained that the Bible has no reference to the doctrine of the resurrection of the dead (Mishnah Sanhedrin x: 1) and emphasised the importance of this belief by making it the subject of the second blessing of the Amidah.

Certainly since Maccabean times, as Dr. Hertz points out, "the pious have ever believed not only in the soul's survival of death and decay, but that, in God's unfathomable wisdom and in His own time, the body will be reunited with the soul" (Commentary on the Prayer Book p. 255). R. Elazar Ha-Kappar expressed the belief in the simplest of words: "They that are born are destined to die, and the dead to be brought to life again" (Aboth iv: 29) and another authority, Gabiha ben Pasissa, answers any incredulous objection with the equally simple comment, "If what never before existed can come into existence, why cannot that which once existed not exist again?"

Beyond the statement of faith in belief in his doctrine, however, it is almost impossible to go. I well remember, when I was a theological student, asking my saintly and learned father whether he could explain to me in some detail this doctrine of the resurrection of the dead. He answered me in words which I shall never forget. "Look," he said, "every Sabbath morning we say in our prayers, 'There is none to be compared unto thee, O Lord our God, in this world, neither is there any beside thee O our King, for the life of the world to come. There is none but thee, O our Redeemer, for the days of the Messiah, neither is there any like unto thee, O our Saviour, for the resurrection of the dead'." "You see," he continued, "that as against the phrase 'in this world' there are three contrary phrases, 'the world to come,' 'the days of the Messiah' and 'the resurrection of the dead.' No teacher of Judaism has ever propounded an authoritative or universally accepted doctrine on the exact connotation or relationship between these three mystic doctrines. Some maintain that the Messianic age belongs to this world, while others maintain that it belongs to the conception of the world to come. Similarly some equate the doctrine of the resurrection of the dead with the Messianic Age, and whether it will take place in this world or the next, depends upon whether the Messianic Age is of this world or the world to come. Until clarity is achieved on these difficult questions it is impossible to give an answer to your question."

When I first heard that answer I regarded it as almost an evasion of the question, but the more I have thought about it, the more it has borne in upon me that the very vagueness of that answer is in accordance with the essentially sane and healthy outlook of Judaism which has its feet planted firmly on earth, and which in consequnce frowns upon excessive and profitless speculation on these things which are inevitably beyond mortal ken. There is a verse in the Bible, הנסתרות לה׳ אלהינו והנגלות לנו ולבנינו עד עולם לעשות את כל דברי התורה הזאת

That verse is usually translated: "The secret things belong unto the Lord our God, but the things which are revealed belong unto us and to our children for ever, that we may do all the words of this Law" (Deut. xxix: 28). There is, however, a more attractive division of these words, which gives us the rendering "The secret things belong to our Lord as well as the revealed things. For us and for our children is the duty of carrying out all the words of the Law." Stated thus, the verse enshrines a profound truth. All things both hidden and revealed belong to God, and both can, so to speak, be safely left in his hands. The duty of the loyal Jew is to fulfil the Commandments of God, confident in the knowledge of their rightness and of their truth, of God's justice. Once one accepts that doctrine, the statement of the Talmud אין לך עסק בנסתרות "Thou hast no concern with the hidden things," becomes more than sage counsel, it becomes the guiding star of Jewish living. We have been shown the way that we should go and the things which we should do, and we do them and walk in that way sure in the knowledge that it is the way of the Lord which will lead us to the haven of our desires, and which will justify our pilgrimage on earth. What lies at the end of that road is hidden from us.

Whether, therefore, one accepts the belief, for which one could, if one wished, quote Talmudic authority that the doctrine of the resurrection of the dead implies that there will come about in the future the reunion of the soul with the body the dissolution between which took place on death, or whether we transmute and sublimate the doctrine as did Maimonides who wrote a special monograph on the subject in which he makes the doctrine of the resurrection of the dead merely a figurative expression for the doctrine of the immortality of the soul, explaining away all Talmudic statements to the contrary as mere figures of speech, is immaterial. What is important, is that it is a fundamental belief of Judaism that man is endowed with an immortal soul which is the element of the divine in him, that that part of his personality which is represented by the soul continues its separate existence after the dissolution of body and soul, that if "the dust returneth unto the earth as it was," "the spirit returneth unto God who gave it," that that soul will stand in judgment before God and answer for its way of life when upon earth. That in its essence is the doctrine which is central to the faith of the Jew. Life continues beyond the grave, and in that continuation the purpose of God is fulfilled and man comes into his own.

## HOLINESS IN ACTION

אתה קדוש ושמך קדוש וקדושים בכל יום יהללוך

*Thou art holy and thy name is holy, and the holy praise thee daily.*

(Amidah.)

MANY and manifold are the attributes which we ascribe to God. In the first paragraph of the Amidah we call him "great, mighty, revered, and most High," and the Talmud declares that the Men of the Great Synagogue forbade the tendency towards undue piling up of epithets, for, as we say in the Kaddish, "though he be high above all blessings and hymns, praises and consolations which are uttered in the world," or in the words of Rashi, " he is exalted over all the songs and all the praise of which man is capable. Whatever praise one utters concerning him, there is still more that can be added" (Rashi, Exodus vx: 1).

But of all these numerous and inexhaustible epithets, there is one which was favoured by the Rabbis above all others, namely, the epithet Kadosh "Holy," with the result that the name above all others which refers to God is הקדוש ברוך הוא. The Holy One, blessed be He. It is this epithet also which is used to describe God in the last of the first three blessings of the Amidah, "Thou art Kadosh and thy name is Kadosh," but to these words is added the sentence "and the Kedoshim praise thee."

Who are these "Kedoshim," these "Holy Ones" who praise God, and in what manner do they express that praise? S. Baer, the author of the famous prayer book "Avodat

Israel," puts forward a suggestion that the "Holy Ones" referred to here are the people of Israel, who were to be a "Holy Nation," but at the same time he expresses his preference for the usual interpretation that the " Holy Ones" are the angels who sing God's praise on high. But sometimes there are different interpretations which are not necessarily exclusive of one another, and that this is the case with regard to the "Kedoshim," the "Holy Ones" who praise God, is shown by the most popular wording of the introduction to the Kedushah which is said on those occasions when the Amidah is repeated, נקדש את שמך בעולם כשם שמקדישים אותו בשמי מרום "May we sanctify thy name in this world, even as they sanctify it in the highest heavens." If the angels are "Kedoshim" who sanctify God, so may we, who are, alas, far from being angels, also be Kedoshim who sanctify God, and by sanctifying God we praise him.

What constitutes this sanctity which man can share with the angels? In what manner is it expressed? By what virtues and way of life does Israel attain to the title of גוי קדוש, a holy nation?

The answer to that question is so different from what one might expect, that whenever so far I have rendered the Hebrew word "Kadosh" as "holy," I have felt a certain sense of incongruity. The word "holy" in English implies a super-piety, an utter unworldliness if not other-worldliness. It conjures up the thought of a person withdrawn from all the temptation, the passions, the lusts of life, giving himself over to mystic contemplation and self-purification. The word Kadosh in Hebrew, when applied to human beings as distinct from God or angels, bears an entirely different connotation. And in order to determine what is meant by human "Kedushah" one cannot do better than turn to that chapter of the Bible, the Nineteenth Chapter of Leviticus, which begins: "Speak unto the children of Israel and say unto them, Ye shall be Kedoshim, for I the Lord your God am Kadosh." True it is that the Rabbis comment קדושים תהיו — פרושים תהיו "Ye shall be holy" means "Ye shall be separated," but the separation does not consist, as is made abundantly clear, in a withdrawal from the world, but just the opposite. It implies a complete participation in every kind of worldly activity, in coming into contact with every temptation, in rubbing shoulders with men in every walk of life, with unscrupulous men in business, with people one dislikes in one's social contacts, with idolatrous practices in religion, and yet maintaining an inner purity and integrity because of the ethical standards which one upholds because of the awareness of the spirit of the Divine which is in man. Where the English proverb states that one cannot touch pitch without being defiled, the principle of human Kedushah demands that though one has to touch pitch one need not be defiled.

That noteworthy conclusion clearly emerges from a simple reading of that chapter. After that introductory verse there follows a list of laws which appear to bear no inner relationship whatsoever between one another. They include ritual laws, ceremonial laws, agricultural laws and business laws, laws regulating the ethical standard which should exist between man and his fellows, as well as laws regulating the duties of man to God. It includes, to quote Dr. Hertz, "reverence for parents, consideration for the needy, prompt payment of wages for reasonable hours of work, honourable dealing, no tale-bearing or malice, love of one's neighbour, and cordiality to the alien, equal justice to rich and poor, just measures and balances—together with abhorrence of everything unclean, irrational or heathen." All these constitute examples of holiness in practice, examples taken almost at random from the whole sphere of human conduct, and as Dr. Hertz rightly points out, "Holiness is thus attained not by flight from the world, nor by monk-like renunciation of human relationships of family or station, but by the spirit in which we fulfil the obligations of life in its simplest and commonest details."

And since that constitutes Kedushah, we get the concepts

of Kiddush Hashem, of the sanctification of God by the manner of our life, of which I have already spoken, and the title Kadosh given to the martyr. If living in the way of God represents Kedushah, its most sublime expression is in surrendering that life for God.

But if that represents human Kedushah, what connection has it with the Kedushah, the sanctity of God? Obviously when we say of God "Thou art Kadosh," it cannot be susceptible of the same interpretation. When applied to God it denotes "the sublime and overpowering majesty of God . . . His complete freedom from everything that makes man imperfect." And though it may be true, as Maimonides has pointed out, that when we apply an attribute to God, it differs both in essence and degree from its application to man, there must nevertheless still be a basis of comparison.

That comparison between the Kedushah of God and the Kedushah of man, is beautifully expressed by our Rabbis. It consists in their words of consciously basing one's actions upon our knowledge of God's attributes. "Just as I am holy, so shalt thou be holy. Just as he is loving, be thou loving; as he is merciful, be thou merciful; as he is long-suffering, be thou long-suffering. In the first chapter of the Bible God clothes the naked; in the last he buries Moses. He heals the sick, he frees the captives, he is compassionate to his enemies, he is merciful both to the living and the dead." Go thou and do likewise. These activities constitute the link between God and Man, and by them he reveals the existence of the spirit of the Divine which is implanted in him.

For there is only one alternative to being beast-like in one's conduct, and that is being God-like in one's conduct. Among beasts only the law of the jungle prevails, red in tooth and in claw. Can one imagine an animal leaving part of its prey to another animal before it has gorged its fill? Can one imagine sacrifice, consideration for others, ethical conduct on the part of a beast? When one sets aside a portion of one's field to the poor, when one suppresses the animal-like desire to revenge oneself on one's fellow-man, when one abstains from oppression, from theft, from lying, when one abstains from cheating in one's weights and measures when the opportunity to do so arises, when doing so would be to one's material advantage, what impulse is it in man which inspires him to refrain from them? It is the consciousness that man is more than an animal, that he is formed in the image of God. By integrity, uprightness, compassion and kindness, by honesty and separation from evil we become Kedoshim, exponents of the way of God. It is in that sense that every Jewish Congregation is called a "Kehillah Kedoshah," which means, not a "Community of Saints," but a community of people who in one way or another give expression in their daily lives to the uplifting spirit of God which is implanted in them, and by so doing they become of the Kedoshim who in action more than in words praise God.

# MIRACLES AND CREATION

ויכולו השמים והארץ וכל צבאם ויכל אלהים ביום השביעי מלאכתו אשר עשה וישבות ביום השביעי מכל מלאכתו אשר עשה.

*And the heavens and the earth were finished and all their host. And on the seventh day God had finished his work which he had made, and he rested on the seventh day from all his work which he had made.*

(Genesis ii: 1-2.)

About the year 250 B.C., an epoch-making event took place in the world of literature and in the world of the spirit. The Bible was translated from its original Hebrew into Greek.

Although scholars to-day are unanimously of the opinion that the purpose of the translators was an internal one, to provide the vast Jewish population of Alexandria, which had forgotten Hebrew, with a version of the Scriptures in the vernacular, the traditional explanation found both in the Talmud and in the Greek Letter of Aristeas, is that it was done at the command of the Egyptian King and Bibliophile, Ptolemy Philadelphus, who wished to include in his famous library a copy of the sacred Scriptures of the Jews.

The importance of this translation cannot be overestimated. Within the framework of Bible studies its importance lies in the fact that in many instances it reflects a Hebrew text which differs from the accepted Massoretic text. But it has its importance in the world of letters as well. It is the first instance in the whole of world literature of a translation of the thoughts of one people being made available to another people, with results almost incalculable for the future of world civilisation.

It is a fascinating story which is told in these two sources, and one which explains the title given to that epoch-making work, the Septuaginta, the "Seventy," short for "Septuaginta dua," "Seventy-two." It is to the effect that on the advice of his librarian the king sent the captain of his bodyguard and Aristeas to the High Priest Elazar in Jerusalem asking him to send seventy-two elders, learned both in Hebrew and Greek, to Alexandria in order to render this translation. After feasting them royally for three days, they were conducted to the Island of Pharos where they undertook the work. But the king, suspecting the possibility of collusion and falsification, whereby they would deliberately render a wrong translation in order not to reveal to the heathens the mysteries of Judaism, took a remarkable precaution. He held each one of them incommunicado, completely isolated from his fellow-translators, and each of the seventy-two had to make an independent translation. And lo and behold, not only were the seventy-two translations completely identical, but each and every one of the translators had deliberately mis-translated the same passages in order to avoid giving a wrong impression which might arise were a literal translation to be given!

And among these pious and deliberate mistranslations of the original text was this well-known verse which I have taken as my text this evening. What is there in that verse which, if taken literally, could give rise to a misconception? Just read it over and see if you can detect anything wrong! Even if you do, the circumstances do not allow you to raise your hands and show your perspicuity, so let me give the answer. It is the words ויכל אלהים ביום השביעי מלאכתו אשר עשה "And God completed on the *seventh* day the work which he had made." Does it not suggest, nay, say clearly, that God worked right into the Sabbath and did not complete his work until the Sabbath, and only then did he rest? And in order to avoid this misconception each and every one of the translators rendered the verse into Greek as though the Hebrew were ויכל אלהים ביום הששי מלאכתו אשר עשה וישבות ביום השביעי "And on the *sixth* day God completed the work which he had done and he rested on the seventh day."

And so they got out of the difficulty of explaining to the pagan Egyptians why the Bible, in the very verse which enjoins the observance of the Sabbath, suggests, so to speak, that God himself did not fully observe the first Sabbath! But to us who preserve the original text what is the answer? To that question there are two remarkable answers given in Rabbinical literature. If we maintain that in fact no work was done on the Sabbath, then there are one of two possibilities, either that it was, so to speak, a "Sabbath which was not really Sabbath," or else it was "work which in reality is no work." The first answer is based on the conception that although from one point of view it was the Sabbath, from another it was not, while the other depends on the idea that it was work which was no work. It is with the former that I wish to deal this evening, reserving the discussion on the second for next week.

The "Sabbath which is not Sabbath" is the בין השמשות the twilight, that period between sunset and the emergence of the stars which is neither day nor night, or both day and night, and it is to this, according to the first explanation, that "God's work on the seventh day" applies. It was during this period, so to speak, that the finishing touches were given to the act of Creation. And what were these finishing touches? Solemnly our Rabbis enumerate the "Ten things created on the eve of the Sabbath in the twilight," such as the mouth of the earth which opened up to swallow the rebellious Korach and his company, the mouth of the ass which spoke unto Balaam, etc. (Ethics v: 9). As Singer succinctly comments, "All phenomena that seemed to partake at once of the natural and supernatural were conceived as having had their origin in the interval between the close of the work of Creation and the commencement of the Sabbath," to which Dr. Hertz adds the comment, "in this way the Rabbis gave expression to their conception of the miraculous in the scheme of things. Miracles, they held, were not interruptions of Nature's laws: at Creation, God had provided for them in advance as part of the cosmic plan." And he concludes with the acute comment of Israel Zangwill, "The Fathers of the Mishna, who taught that Balaam's ass was created on the eve of the Sabbath, in the twilight, were not fantastic fools, but subtle philosophers, discovering the reign of universal law through the exceptions, the miracles that had to be created specially and were still a part of the order of the world, bound to appear in due time much as apparently erratic comets are."

And so in this roundabout way they express their opinion on one of the problems of philosophy and religion, the place which the supernatural has in the natural scheme of things, of the apparent defiance by God of the rules which he himself instituted for the ordered regulation of the world which he had created.

## THE POSITIVE ASPECT OF THE SABBATH

ויכל אלהים ביום השביעי מלאכתו אשר עשה וישבות ביום השביעי מכל מלאכתו אשר עשה.

*And God finished on the seventh day the work which he had made, and he rested on the seventh day from all his work which he had made.*

(Genesis ii: 2.)

THE problem of this verse has been fully explained in the sermon which I gave last week, the clear suggestion that it was on the Sabbath and not on the preceding day, the sixth day, that the work of Creation was completed. And as I pointed out, there are two answers given by the Rabbis to explain this paradox. The one is that the seventh day was not actually the seventh day, but בין השמשות the twilight between the sixth and the seventh, whereby an attempt is made to give an explanation of the place of miracles in the scheme of creation, as I pointed out in that sermon.

But even more acceptable, and more in keeping with the spirit and the wording of the verse is the solution of the problem which depends not in the theory of "the seventh day which was not really the seventh day," but on the theory that the "work" referred to was not really work! If such a thesis can be maintained, it would fit in beautifully with the words of the verse, "God finished his work on the seventh day, and God rested on the seventh day." In other words, that "work," whatever it was, was part of that "rest." Can such a thesis be maintained? Our Rabbis say that it can. ומה נברא בו לאחר ששבת What then, ask the Rabbis, was created after God rested? And they answer with four pregnant words, שאנן ונחת, שלוה והשקט Tranquillity and serenity, peace and quiet contentment (Gen. Rabba x: 12.) In that answer and in these four words there lies enshrined a whole cosmos, a whole world, the world of the spirit of the Jewish Sabbath. It is because that spirit has been so woefully misconstrued and misunderstood that the Sabbath fails to have the benign and blessed impact upon our lives which it ought to have, and if there is to be any improvement in the spirit of Sabbath observance, it will depend upon a true and undistorted appreciation of that spirit.

Were I to ask any gathering of Jews what is meant by keeping the Sabbath, I am convinced that ninety-nine out of a hundred would either quote the sentence of the Fourth Commandment, "Six days shalt thou labour and do all thy work, but the seventh is a Sabbath unto the Lord thy God. On it thou shalt do no work," or answer in accordance with its spirit. It is the day, they will answer, when one ceases from the gainful occupations on which one is engaged for six days of the week, with the result that inactivity takes the place of activity. Once one approaches the Sabbath from that point of view alone, the essence of the observance of the Sabbath becomes a completely negative one, and automatically and unthinkingly one associates it with a formidable and irksome list of "Thou shalt nots." On the Sabbath we must not do this, and we must not do that. We are forbidden to write and we are forbidden to play, we are forbidden to carry and we are forbidden to smoke. We cannot shop and do a hundred-and-one things. Thirty-nine heads of labour are enumerated and these "fathers," as they are called in the Talmud, beget such a proliferous progeny that their children run literally into hundreds if not thousands. Is it surprising, in view of this, that with almost monotonous uniformity non-Jews who stand outside the world of the Jewish Sabbath have described it as a day of oppressive gloom and irksome restrictions which make the old Puritan Sabbath shine in comparison with their appraisal of it?

And yet I would put this common conception of the Sabbath to a simple pragmatic test. Let us imagine a Jew who wishes to observe the Sabbath in accordance with this conception. When he finishes his work on Friday he goes home and spends the next 24 hours in a state of complete and masterful inactivity and passivity, spending it in eating and sleeping. Is there a single Jew who knows anything of the authentic spirit of the Sabbath who would for one moment concede that that Jew is observing the spirit of the Jewish Sabbath? Is there one who knows that spirit who does not find it expressed in the simple yet beautiful words of the refrain of the Sabbath hymn written by that great mystic Isaac Luria and found in our Prayer Book, יום זה לישראל אורה ושמחה שבת מנוחה This day is to Israel light and joy, a Sabbath of rest? And when there is no light and joy there is no Sabbath rest. In other words, in addition to the negative aspect of cessation from labour and the "Thou shalt not," there is the positive aspect of Sabbath joy and "Thou shalt." Is there a more beautiful way of expressing that profound truth than by saying that "something was created after God rested," that the very act of cessation from work involved a positive creation, and that creation was the spirit of tranquillity and serenity of peace and quiet contentment? The true observer of the "Sabbath unto the Lord" *creates* something by resting, as did God himself.

שאנן Tranquillity and ease. The throwing off of the burden of material cares which press down so heavily during the days of the week, that casting off of those burdens which is so beautifully symbolised by the emptying of one's pockets which a Rabbi called "One of the great laws of the Sabbath," the freedom from worldly cares, that is one of the positive creative aspects of the Sabbath which was made when God rested.

נחת the serenity of rest. Who does not know the meaning of נחת in its restricted sense, that word which expresses the quiet joy, the glow of satisfaction, the feeling of spiritual well-being which comes to a parent when he sees his child going in the way in which he would like him to go, in the way which brings him the esteem and respect of his fellow-men? Surely that נחת is more than the absence of "Verdruss," of pain and disappointment? Surely it is a positive feeling, even if it is intangible? And it is that spirit, transferred from the relation of parent to child to the Jew who is imbued with the spirit of the Sabbath which is conveyed by this positive aspect of the Sabbath which represents an act of creation.

Shalvah, the feeling of peace and wholeness of one's soul being attuned with the spirit of the world. The state of being at peace with others is expressed by the word Shalom, the infinitely greater spiritual state of being at peace *with oneself* is conveyed by the cognate word Shalvah. For the warring elements within oneself to lay down their arms and proclaim a truce of God for twenty-four hours every week, for all those tensions and stresses, those anxieties and inner turmoils which bedevil our lives during the working days to disappear, for inner harmony to take the place of disharmony, and melodious music that of the strident discords. All this and much more is meant by Shalvah, and again it is not a mere absence of inner strife but a positive creation which has its origin in the rest of the seventh day.

And lastly השקט which I have translated "The quiet of contentment." For all of us, I think, know the word שקט, the cry for silence, the appeal for the ceasing of noise, the silence which is imposed by command of someone else. And the difference between "Sheket" and "Hashket" is that the former is a command, while the latter is the causative form, "the causing, the coming into being of silence." It is the quietude which comes of itself from contentment, when all nature is stilled. It is the fulfilment of the remarkable statement of our Rabbis, "Were it not for the sound of the tumult of the city, we could hear the heavenly spheres revolving." And the sound of the tumult of the city is stilled, and the peace of God enters our souls, and something is created.

These are the things which by resting on the seventh day God actively created on the seventh day. These are the things which make the difference between the negative aspect of the mere cessation from work and the positive observance of the Sabbath, which makes it a day of light and joy. And that person who has experienced it and lived it can say with passion what the author of the Song of Songs says of love: "Many waters cannot quench it neither the floods overwhelm it. If a man would give all the wealth of his house instead of it, he would be utterly despised." (Canticles viii: 7.) For its price is far above rubies, and he who exchanges it for rubies may gain wealth but he has paid the price of his immortal soul.

## DIVINE GRACE

### וטהר לבנו לעבדך באמת

*And purify our heart to serve thee in truth.*

(Amidah.)

It would be difficult to find in our liturgy a better example of economy of words to express profound and fundamental ideas than these four simple and well-known Hebrew words which are included in the intermediate blessing of all Amidahs of Sabbath and Festivals. That this prayer for the purification of the heart in order that we may serve God in truth is said on these days of rest and not on weekdays is easily explained. We believe, as has already been indicated, that man is born into this world with a pure and innocent heart, free from all sin and evil, but that in his passage through life the pristine purity of that heart becomes contaminated and unclean through unworthy thoughts and actions. It is naturally during the week-days, the working days when man is engrossed in his pursuit of material wealth, that this process of spiritual contamination is most liable to take place. Mammon dethrones God, the מושב לצים the "seat of the scoffers" is substituted for the seat of learning and prayer, man succumbs more and more to the animal part of his being and the spiritual divine side becomes obfuscated and obscured. A layer of foreign matter forms over that pure heart, and detracts from the true service of God. And then there comes the Sabbath, with its diminution, if not the actual cessation, of these worldly cares. The tranquillity, the serenity, the peace and quiet contentment, which are the essential components of the Sabbath, come, and with it the prayer that these foreign accretions which have attached themselves during the week days be removed, that we may restore our hearts to their pristine purity, and thus dedicate ourselves once more to the service of God in truth.

There is, however, one aspect of this prayer and of many similar prayers which calls for some comment and explanation. The complete and unfettered freedom of man's will is one of the fundamental beliefs of Judaism. Without that belief, which Maimonides calls the very cornerstone of the Torah, the whole concept of both human and divine justice, of reward and retribution, becomes untenable. "Behold, I have set before thee life and death, blessing and curse, therefore choose . . ." (Deut. xxx: 19) is the basis of this thought. With such emphasis do the Rabbis insist upon this doctrine that they go so far as to maintain that it is the one thing in which the otherwise complete control of God over the destiny of man is limited. "Everything is in the hands of heaven, save for the fear of heaven," and man chooses his own way entirely of his own volition. Man alone can decide by his thoughts, his speech and his actions whether his heart shall be pure or impure; whether he shall follow the right path or the wrong. Man alone is the master of his soul and the captain of his destiny.

Yet despite this undoubted fact, continually in our prayers we turn to God and pray to him to do what Judaism believes is in the power of man, and not in the power of God, to do. "Purify our heart to serve thee in truth; "O my God, guard my tongue from evil, and my lips from speaking guile"; "O lead us not into sin or transgression, iniquity, temptation or disgrace; let not the evil inclination have sway over us; keep us far from a bad man or a bad companion; make us cleave to the good inclination and to good works; subdue our inclination so that it may submit itself unto thee"—these are but a few examples chosen almost at random which suggest unequivocally that God can purify our heart and not we; that God can prevent our tongue from speaking evil instead of man himself placing a bridle upon his tongue, that we are led by the hand of God, and not by our freedom of choice into sin or temptation or away from it, that eternal struggle that goes on within the heart of man, half-angel and half-brute, between the Yetzer Tov and the Yetzer Ra, between his better self and his ignoble passions, God and not man can decide which way this struggle shall go and what the outcome of the battle.

The resolving of that apparent inconsistency is provided by a profoundly true statement of our Rabbis expressed in four simple Hebrew words, הבא לטהר מסייעין אותו "He who undertakes the process of purification receives help from on high." A person sets himself a noble goal; he stands at the foot of a mountain and he looks up and scans the heights which he has to scale, the obstacles which he has to overcome, the anti-gravitational pull against which he will have to contend, and conscious though he is of the limitation of his physical powers, he determines to exert them to the utmost in order to reach the heights. He starts resolutely on his journey, and as long as he holds firmly to his intention of overcoming these obstacles, he finds that there flows into him an unexpected accretion of strength which infuses his muscles and hardens his will. It seems to him that this flow of energy comes to him from without, and in the sphere of the spirit it undoubtedly is so.

I came across the following profoundly true comment in a pamphlet entitled "The Ladder of Prayer" by Dr. Robert Gordis. "If the petition is concerned with the worshipper himself, and is *sincere,* its very expression sets its fulfilment into motion. The irascible father who prays for a better temper in dealing with his children, the untutored youth who prays for wisdom will, if the prayer issues from the depths of his soul, be answered. For the father will be inspired to forbearance, and the youth to greater zeal in his studies. . . . Obviously the prayer that cries out "O God, make me" receives a more direct answer than the one that begins "O God, give me," because in the former case all the factors that enter into the situation are ready at hand. "Cause us, O Lord, to lie down in peace, and raise us, O God, unto life," the beautiful evening prayer Hashkivenu pleads. When it is recited with true inwardness, the contentment and peace for which it prays are forthcoming." There is more than auto-suggestion in this process; there is a conscious flowing of divine Grace into man, giving him the added strength to resist his evil inclination, and free himself from its enslaving sway.

If only man had the moral courage to put this theory to the test! The formidable difficulties which he imagines would beset his path diminish in size; the mountains become molehills. If there is a pathetic Jewish proverb which says "May we never be put to the test of the limits of our endurance and suffering," it is equally true that we are afraid to put ourselves to the test of what conviction and the desire to do what we know is right, for we fear that the flesh is too weak for the willing spirit.

It is that challenge which the last of the prophets of the Bible, Malachi, boldly puts into the mouth of God. The returned exiles were backward in paying their dues of Maaser and Terumah, of Tithe and Heave Offering to the Temple. They could not afford it; times were bad, a succession of bad harvests had impoverished them. They saw no profit in serving God, and the prophet adjures them: "Bring ye all the tithes into the storehouse, that there may be meat in my house," and in answer to the unspoken question, "But how can we afford it?" he challenges them, ובחנוני נא בזאת "Put me to the test, saith the Lord of Hosts, if I will not open you the windows of heaven, and pour you out such a blessing that there will not be room enough to receive it" (Malachi iii: 10).

And the voice of God comes to us to-day as well, ובחנוני נא Put me to the test, and put yourselves to the test as well. Accept the challenge, take up the gauntlet. Make up your minds to purify your hearts to serve God in truth, and divine help will come to your aid. Make up your minds to guard your tongue from evil, and God will help you do so. In Sabbath and in Kashruth, in charity and in goodness, set your foot upon the path that you know is right. And the mountain will become a plain and the rough places a smooth paved highway. For when the first step is taken by man and "he *comes* to purify" then מסייעין אותו he becomes the recipient of God's assistance, overcoming his weakness, and his heart becomes purified to serve God in truth.

# THE SACRIFICIAL SYSTEM

רצה ה׳ אלהינו בעמך ישראל ובתפלתם והשב את העבודה לדביר ביתך... ותחזינה עינינו בשובך לציון ברחמים.

*Accept, O Lord our God, thy people Israel and their prayer, restore the service to the oracle of thy house . . . And let our eyes behold thy return in mercy to Zion.*

(Amidah.)

I TAKE as my text this evening the first of the last three blessings of the Amidah which, as I have pointed out, are statutory for all occasions on which the Amidah is recited.

The formula of this prayer, as it is found in our prayer book to-day, prays for the restoration of the sacrificial system, which automatically came to an end with the destruction of the Temple in the year 70. It is therefore obviously not the original formula, since that original formulation goes back to the Men of the Great Assembly who lived at least three centuries before that catastrophe. I hope to deal with that point next week, but it is surely necessary to deal with the difficult problem of the possibility of the restoration of the sacrificial system for which we pray not only in this passage but at every Musaph service.

Let it be said at once that the idea of offering up animals in sacrifice as part of an act of worship to God, is entirely repugnant to modern thought. It appears to be meaningless and superstitious where it is not downrightly cruel. It would appear to hark back to the most primitive ideas of mankind, and, as will be pointed out, such a view is not unknown to Judaism.

I doubt whether there is anyone else in this congregation who has had the experience which was mine, of witnessing animal sacrifices as I did when I was in India. I have referred to it in my book "Far East Mission," from which the following quotation is taken: "There was one thing in the Temple which made an incredible impression upon me. . . . I saw the ceremonial sacrifice of a kid, and I must confess that it severely shook my belief in the restoration of the sacrificial system and made me appreciate even more the remarkably modernist explanation of Maimonides in his famous "Guide to the Perplexed." I then proceeded to give a description of the decapitation of that unfortunate animal, and offered some comments to which reference will be made.

That modernistic view of Maimonides is to be found in the thirty-second chapter of the third section of the Moreh Nevuchim. It is so radical and startling that he admits "I know that you will at first thought reject the idea and find it strange," but he nevertheless maintains that it is correct. Briefly stated it is that the institution of the sacrificial system was nothing but a concession to the primitive instincts of the period in which it was instituted. "It is impossible," in the words of Maimonides, "to go suddenly from one extreme to another, it is therefore according to the nature of man impossible for him suddenly to discontinue everything to which he has been accustomed." The Children of Israel lived in a milieu and in a civilisation in which the only form of worship known was the sacrifice of animals in Temples of Idolatry. Had the Bible enjoined the complete cessation and dissociation from this form of worship, it would have imposed an impossible burden upon the people. It therefore permitted the continuation of this system, but it was purified in its performance, and limited to one single spot in the whole world, namely, the Temple in Jerusalem. "All these restrictions," concludes Maimonides, "served to limit this kind of worship and keep it within those bounds within which God did not think it necessary to abolish sacrificial service altogether. But prayer and supplication can be offered everywhere and by every person." The implications of this radical interpretation are enormous. It not only means that with the destruction of that single safety-valve for the release of the primitive emotions of the people, as Maimonides expresses it, the sacrificial system automatically ceased, and "prayer and supplication (which) can be offered everywhere and by every person" took its place. But what is more important is that this interpretation is surely an argument against the restoration of the sacrificial system for which we pray. It was something, again to quote Maimonides, which was not "commanded for its own sake, but only for the sake of some other thing, as if it was the only means which he employed for his primary object." Mankind has evolved other forms of worship, "prayer and supplication," and no longer feels the need to give expression to this form of worship. Why then do we still pray for its restoration?

The whole question of the Sacrificial Cult is the subject of a long and comprehensive essay which forms one of the additional Notes to Hertz's edition of the Pentateuch. It is not my intention to repeat, paraphrase, amend, or elaborate upon the arguments which are so persuasively put forward there, and whosoever is interested in it should refer to it.* All that I wish to do is to put forward two aspects, which arise from a consideration of this subject. To the first of them I made passing reference in the description to which I have referred, of the animal sacrifice which I witnessed. I was given to understand that this sacrificial meat is the only meat permitted to Hindus, who otherwise are strict vegetarians. It was this fact which led me to suggest that the only person who can without hypocrisy have a valid ethical objection to the sacrificial system as such is the strict vegetarian, who, disapproving of the

---

Pages 560/2.

slaughter of animals for food, and expressing his disapproval in practice, can equally object to its slaughter as an act of worship. The sight of the animal sacrifice which I saw was no more revolting than the sight of the despatch of animals at the abattoirs to provide us with our food. It is not a sight which I would recommend to a squeamish or sensitive person. We should not put ourselves in the position which has caused such justifiable criticism in England, that some of the most active members of the Society for the Prevention of Cruelty to Animals are enthusiastic fox-hunting men. They burn with righteous indignation at the thought of a poor hawker ill-treating a horse and the following Sunday they set a pack of dogs on to hunting a fox and savaging it, and then, proudly cutting off its tail, display it as a trophy. It is these same gentry who object equally to Shechitah, despite the fact that its humanitarianism has been abundantly proved. It is impossible for the carnivorous beef-eater to enjoy his steak, smack his lips over a juicy joint, demand the choicest cut from a prime animal for the satisfaction of his own physical appetites and yet recoil in horror from the thought of the slaughter of animals in service of God.

But that argument, valid though it may be, pales into utter insignificance in the light of the other, which is fundamental and central to the whole conception of Traditional Judaism. It is the doctrine of the inviolability of the Torah, which is one of the thirteen Principles of the Faith, the belief that it will never be abrogated. As soon as one begins to pick and choose among the Commandments of the Torah, one enters upon that slippery slope which leads to an abandonment of Judaism as a whole. In essence such a procedure involves the subjection of the infinite wisdom of God to the criterion of the finite wisdom of man. It pays God the doubtful compliment of saying approvingly of one law, "Now that one makes sense, and God knows what he is talking about," while of another it says disapprovingly, "I can't agree with God in this instance." It is subversive of the fundamental belief of the Jew concerning the Torah, that it represents the infinite wisdom of God which we accept in toto, both that which we understand and that which is beyond the grasp of our comprehension, that which is easy as well as that which is difficult, that which is pleasant as well as that which appears to be unpleasant. Whatever is in the Torah must have to the Jew an eternal validity. It is his bounden duty to try and understand it, but if he fails to do so, its verity and validity is not thereby affected.

Perhaps fortunately for us the question of the fulfilment of this prayer still belongs to what is called the הילכתא דמשיחא these laws whose operativeness depends upon circumstances which belong to the distant future, if and when the site of the Temple Mount is in our possession and the Temple is rebuilt. It is not the only question which will have to be solved then, but until that time our attitude must be the famous answer of Rabban Johanan b. Zakkai to his disciples: "I cannot answer your question, but thus saith the Holy One, blessed be He, I have made a statute, I have decreed a decree, 'tis not for us to think unfavourably of it."

# THE MODERNISATION OF PRAYERS

## והשב את העבודה לדביר ביתך

*And restore the service to the oracle of thine house.*
(Amidah.)

I WANT this evening to deal with another aspect of that same text as I took for my sermon last week. As I pointed out last week, this prayer for the restoration of the Temple Service with its sacrificial system is obviously not the original reading of this prayer, since the Amidah was originally formulated while the Temple still stood and the sacrificial system was in full operation. In point of fact we know what the formula was during Temple Times. According to Rashi (Berachot 11b.) the wording was: רצה ה׳ אלהינו עבודת עמך ישראל ואשי ישראל ותפלתם תקבל ברצון

"Accept, O Lord, the service of thy people Israel, and the fire offerings of Israel and their prayers accept thou in favour."

while the concluding blessing, instead of reading "Blessed art thou, O Lord, who restoreth thy divine Presence to Zion," read either ברוך אתה ה׳ המקבל עבודת עמו ישראל ברצון "Blessed art thou, O Lord, who receiveth the service of his people Israel in favour," or the formula which we still retain when the Priestly Blessing is recited ברוך אתה ה׳ שאותך לבדך ביראה נעבוד "Blessed art thou, O Lord, whom alone we serve in awe."

It is thus a fitting opportunity to consider a question which constantly crops up in discussion on our prayer book, the question of the alteration and modernisation of our prayers, to make them more in accord with what is vaguely called the "spirit of the times." From what has been said, it is obvious that the theory that under no circumstances may our prayers be altered is one that will not bear a moment's examination, but on the other hand, whosoever approaches this task, or even the consideration thereof, must hear the voice of God saying unto him, as it said unto Moses, "Remove thy shoe from off thy foot, for the place whereon thou standest is holy ground." It is only in a spirit of awe and reverence, with an awareness of the sanctity with which the generations have imbued the prayer book that this question can be considered.

A man builds a new house on virgin soil, in a place where no house has been before. After a few years he finds that the kitchen has been badly situated, or some new-fangled notion in building, which is the last word in modernity, comes to his notice which makes it possible not only to "keep up with the Joneses" but even to steal a march on them. Without compunction or hesitation the owner will order a wall to be demolished here, a new window put in there, a piece of built-in furniture scrapped and the latest creation put in its place.

But imagine also a person with a love for history and for tradition who becomes the proud owner of a house which has its historical associations. Every stone and brick in that ancient building is redolent with history; every nook and cranny could tell a tale. Were the owner of that house to desire to modernise it, remove a wall, rebuild a wing, or do any of these things which the other is free to do, he would rightly be accused of vandalism and philistinism. And there comes a stage in such an edifice when the question of its preservation becomes a national question, and it is declared an Historic Monument, and its owner is deprived of his legal rights to tamper with it or alter it according to his own whims. He may enjoy the use of it, but any alteration must have the approval of the authorities who are duly appointed as the custodians of the national treasures of the human spirit.

Let me carry this metaphor a stage further by giving you an interesting actual example. There is no more conservative religious body than the proud Sepharḍi Congregation of London. I am not certain whether their place of worship, the Bevis Marks Synagogue, has been declared a National Monument, but to the Jewish Community of England this noble edifice, over 250 years old, a direct link with the Marranos and the Resettlement under Cromwell, redolent with tradition, it certainly is. One of the glories of that Synagogue were the magnificent candelabras which were literally candelabras containing some hundreds of candles; the duty of lighting them took the beadle hours every Friday afternoon. For years and decades the Gentlemen of the Mahamad vigorously and vehemently resisted the proposals of the more progressive element of the Congregation to change over to electric light. It was felt that the traditional atmosphere of the sacred place of worship might thereby be deleteriously affected, but at last they were forced to succumb to the growing pressure and to the realities of the situation. But how did they effect the change? The ancient candelabra remained as they were, and they adorn the Synagogue to this day. But cunningly and with maximum concealment the electric wires were inserted into them. Literally the old was made to accommodate the new, and a compromise was found which was a concession both to the spirit of tradition and the undeniable needs of the time.

There is no greater National Monument of the Jewish People than its Prayer Book, and I hope that by now, when I have delivered over 40 sermons on one small section of it, you are able to appreciate to some extent its glorious architecture. If, when we visit a medieval cathedral, and realise that it took, in some cases, over 600 years to complete, this edifice of the spirit, this Temple in which God dwells, represents four times that period. Every word is a brick in that edifice, and every word is thrice hallowed. It is not for the individual to hack and change, to demolish and to rebuild according to the passing whims or fancies of the moment. Such changes can be approved only by the custodians of the treasures of the Jewish People. And when they are effected they are done, as was the case with Bevis Marks, in such a way that the old and the sacred is disturbed as little as possible, and the new carefully made to fit in with that which is accepted and hallowed. That is how our prayers, while retaining the basic formulae of the Talmud, still have their perennial application to-day.

Let me give you one example from our Prayer Book, in which the process of modernising the prayer has been done so deftly and cunningly that I am sure that it has passed almost unnoticed. There is a prayer on Sabbath morning, in Aramaic, called by its introductory words Yekum Purkan. It is a prayer for the religious and lay leaders of the Community of Babylon and mirrors the communal organisation during the pregnant and important period of Jewish history when the Babylonian Talmud was written and the Geonim flourished, the Exilarch, the heads of the famous academies of Sura and Pumbedita, the heads of the Kallah, the judges at the gates.

When the demand for bringing the Prayer Book up to date was voiced, the abolition of this prayer was strongly urged. There is no Exilarch in Babylon, it was cogently urged, the Yeshivahs of Sura and Pumbedita are no more; the famous Kallah has ceased to exist. What purpose can there be in retaining this prayer? And yet it was part of a historic monument. It mirrored a state of affairs which obtained during the most significant period of Jewish social and religious history; it was hallowed by being recited for a thousand years and more. It was like the candelabrum of Bevis Marks, and like that candelabrum it was treated! The prayer was retained, but deftly inserted in it, by the late Dr. Adler, if I mistake not, were the words ובכל ארעת גלותנא "And in all the lands of our dispersions." This addition immediately brought it up to date, made it applicable to

South Africa as to ancient Babylon, but the ancient structure was retained.

It is without malice or rancour that I compare this delicate and reverent process which retains the old while admitting the new, with the Reform Prayer Book. Without fear of contradiction it can be stated that since the first Reform Prayer Book was issued over a century ago, there have appeared at least a hundred different versions, each one a radical departure from its predecessor, each country producing a different formula. For their Prayer Book is like the modern house built according to the latest fashion—and fashions change with bewildering speed. There is no ancient tradition hallowed by age and the pious recitation of centuries. Convenience, expediency and comfort are the sole criteria. Pull down a wall here, introduce a new fad there, demolish the whole house and build a super modern glittering edifice in its place. Why not? It is no historic monument linking the glorious past with the present. "Let us be attractive," is the cry, "let us go one better than the Joneses."

And we enter into our House of Prayer which is the Siddur. Its ancient formulae are the portraits of our ancestors on the wall, its words are the stones which speak to us, its foundations are two thousand years old and more, and it still stands as an eternal refuge. And when we introduce a touch of modernity we do so with reverence and awe, and in such a way that the ancient structure still stands as it will stand for ever.

# THE PRAYER OF THANKSGIVING

## מודים אנחנו לך

*We give thanks unto thee.*

(Amidah.)

THE penultimate blessing of the Amidah, the middle of the three last blessings is called הודיה thanksgiving, a word which fully expresses its contents. It is "a singularly beautiful anthem of gratitude for God's manifold mercies to us." It gives expression to the thanksgiving that we feel for "our lives which are committed unto thy hand, and for our souls which are in thy charge, and for thy miracles which are daily with us."

But our thanksgiving to God is not confined to this daily prayer. The element of thanksgiving and praise is the most pervasive and characteristic element of our prayers. According to the Talmud, the Jew is enjoined to utter a minimum of 100 blessings daily, and the apparently difficult theological and psychological problem of how man can "bless" God by saying "Blessed art thou, O Lord," is simply resolved when we appreciate the fact that whatever the etymological meaning of the root "Barach" may be, the formula is simply a form of thanksgiving. We do not "bless" God for giving us our daily bread; we *thank* him. And so we thank him for giving us the Torah, for the wondrous structure of the human body, for the dawn which is heralded by cockcrow, for opening our eyes, for every little daily action. We thank him for food and we thank him for choosing us; we thank him for every pleasant fragrance, we thank him for renewing life. And impossible though it may be of realisation by the normal person, we are enjoined כשם שמברך על הטובה כך מברך על הרעה "*In exactly the same way* as we thank God for boons conferred, so should we thank him for evils which come upon us." And after apparently exhausting every epithet and expression of praise, we say in our Sabbath morning prayers, "For such is the duty of all creatures before thee, O Lord our God and God of our fathers, to thank, praise, laud, glorify, extol, honour, bless, exalt and acclaim thee, even beyond all the words of song and adoration of David."

When one considers the extent, both in length and in depth, of this thanksgiving to God, one is tempted to ask, "Is it all really necessary?" Does God indeed demand our thanks for every little act of kindness? And there have not been wanting those who have scorned this fulsome adulation as unworthy of modern man. They have painted a picture of God as some proud Oriental potentate sitting upon his throne and demanding a continuous and continual paean of praise and exaggerated flattery. "Thank you, your Majesty, for letting us breathe, thank you for letting us live," and if in a moment of cruelty which is characteristic of these Oriental potentates, the whim seizes him to flog or to torture his cringing, servile creatures, they are enjoined not to cease in that noisome and nauseating flattery and fulfilling the injunction "In exactly the same way as we thank God for boons conferred, we should thank him for evils which come upon us," they must still, quivering and trembling under the lash of his unreasoning anger, still stammer out a "thank you." "Thank you for the blows and thank you for the suffering."

No opinion could be more superficial or more mistaken. It completely misrepresents the impulse which lies behind this thanksgiving. Let me give you a trite, but I hope a telling, example. A few weeks ago I had occasion to visit a country community over a hundred miles from Johannesburg for the purpose of launching the I.U.A. campaign there. The journey took over two hours. I finished my address about 9.30 p.m. and then there took place that sometimes none too edifying but nevertheless essential adjunct of a campaign meeting, the persuasive cajoling of those present to make a satisfactory contribution. It was during the recent cold spell; the hall was unheated. The warmth which I had engendered in the course of my address was rapidly dissipating. I sat in increasing misery while the hands of the clock moved inexorably on to 10 p.m., 10.30 p.m. I turned to the chairman and pleaded with him, "It will be nearly 1 a.m. by the time I get home, even if I leave now. I have a heavy day before me to-morrow. There is nothing more for me to do here. Don't you think that I could go home?" "Oh, no! Rabbi," he said to me, "it's quite impossible. You must wait for the Vote of Thanks." "I don't want any vote of thanks," I said, "I am prepared to renounce it; I take it for granted." To which he made the effective retort: "Rabbi, you may not want a vote of thanks, but we feel that we should thank you, and we would be failing in our duty and in courtesy if it were omitted."

In that true and simple story there lies the answer to the question of whether God needs our thanks. God indeed does not need our thanks, but we feel the impelling need to pour out from a heart welling over with gratitude our thanksgiving to God! When men thank God and praise him, they are doing it not for his sake but for their own.

In a pamphlet on prayer to which I have had occasion to refer already, another example is given, and I cannot do better than quote the actual words.

"The process of rearing children offers an illuminating parallel. Why, in raising a child, do parents train him to say 'please' and 'thank you'? To be sure, the phrases are conventional, and are often pronounced in purely mechanical fashion. But what lies behind the convention and what gave it rise? Behind the ritual of etiquette stands a profound ethical sentiment. The purpose of these formulae of politeness is to remind the speaker that he has no real claim upon the service or the benefit conferred upon him, that it represents an undeserved blessing, an unexpected plus for which gratitude is due."*

It is indeed an illuminating parallel. In exactly the same way as a "thank you" can become and tends to become a conventional and purely mechanical formula, stripped and denuded of any inner meaning, so the repetition of prayers can become and tends to become an equally conventional and purely mechanical formula. But once the profound ethical sentiment which lies behind it is appreciated, that sentiment which is so rightly expressed in the idea that it is a reminder that the person expressing those thanks has no claim upon the services or benefit conferred it immediately becomes charged with deep meaning.

We have no claim upon God; we have no claim upon life. We have done nothing to God or for God which entitles us to the boon of life or of joy. They belong to רחמים and to חסדים, to acts of mercy and to acts of loving-kindness for which we are beholden, and for which we have not paid.

What a difference it would make to our lives if we could but grasp this simple and essential truth! It would change our lives completely both from the negative and the positive points of view. From the negative point of view, it would destroy all these railings and grousings, these petty annoyances, these dissatisfactions at what we consider the unkindness of fate when we do not get everything we want exactly in the way we want it. Were we to consider all a bounty we would not, to quote a well-known proverb, "Look a gift horse in the mouth." And from the positive point of view, how much would it add to our consciousness of the blessings we enjoy! We would cease to take them for granted, and our enjoyment of the simplest pleasures of

*Robert Gordis: The Ladder of Prayer.

life, the air we breathe, the sights we see, the food we eat, the fragrant odours that assail our nostrils would be heightened beyond measure. The things which happen and which are "every day with us" become, in the words of this prayer, "miracles," and we joyously welcome them as such.

I had occasion some weeks ago to make passing reference in a speech to a man who is a benefactor to the Community, although he was not present. He was informed of my reference and sent me a letter which I shall treasure to the end of my days. Let me read to you an extract from it:

"For all these things happened over 20 years ago and I am pleased and appreciative that you recall them, on such a happy occasion. The Lord has been good to me, the Lord is good to me.

"The wife celebrates her 81st birthday this month, in good health and still able to look after me and my comfort, whilst I reached my 88th birthday anniversary yesterday, also in comparatively good health. Of course neither of us is able to do any more work, but it is not required of us.

"Our family consists of 22 souls now, all enjoying good health, of whom 17 live here in Cape Town, and we meet every Friday night at our house—a very happy state of affairs, for we enjoy the company of our children and most of our grandchildren who visit us frequently.

"The Lord has given me everything I want. He has given me more and I am deeply grateful to Him for these gifts and am glad to be able to report so well to you.

"Thank you for the occasion you have given to me to make this report. The Lord has given me every blessing that I could have asked Him for—He has given me more—and I am constantly grateful to Him for these blessings."

There is mirrored the beauty of a soul which has learned to thank God; that is the state of mind which the spirit of thanksgiving engenders. And our Rabbis, realising that thanksgiving is essential not to the giver but to the recipient declare with truth that in the Messianic age "All sacrifices will be abolished, but the sacrifice of thanksgiving will remain for ever."

# INDIVIDUAL AND UNIVERSAL PEACE

שלום רב על ישראל עמך תשים לעולם

*Grant abundant peace unto Israel thy people for ever.*

(Amidah.)

THE last blessing of the Amidah is the prayer for peace. The wording differs in the morning prayer on the one hand and in the afternoon and evening on the other, but it is a change only in wording; the contents are identical, and they sum up the one overwhelming social passion of the Jew, the passion for peace.

That the Amidah, the prayer par excellence of the Jewish liturgy should conclude with this prayer for peace is entirely in line with Jewish thought. It is related of the famous Roman statesman, the elder Cato, that so convinced was he that the existence of Carthage represented a continuous and ominous threat to the very existence of Rome, that he finished every single speech that he made in the Roman Senate, no matter what the topic under discussion was, with the words "Delenda est Carthago"—"Carthage must be destroyed."

In exactly the same manner, but with what a revealing wealth of difference in outlook, whatever prayer the Jew recites, no matter what its content is, he is impelled to conclude it with a prayer for peace. The Amidah ends with a prayer for peace; the individual prayer which follows in the silent reading of the Amidah ends with a similar prayer. The Kaddish ends with the same formula, as does the Grace After Meals. The collection of Scriptural verses which form an addendum to that Grace concludes with the verse "The Lord shall give strength to his people; the Lord will bless his people with peace." It forms the last word of the Priestly Blessing. When the Jew greets his fellow he does so with the word Shalom; when he bids him farewell it is with the same warm word. In short, it is the distinctive word of the Hebrew language, and with it the Jew gives expression to the most passionate of his longings.

The immortal passage, "They shall beat their swords into ploughshares and their spears into pruning hooks. Nation shall not lift up sword against nation, neither shall they learn war any more," is found in both Isaiah and in Micah, and the coincidence has given rise to much discussion among Biblical scholars as to which of these prophets is the actual author of that noble sentiment, and which one borrowed it from the other. To me the whole discussion is an academic one. Micah said it and Isaiah said it, but in saying it they were but expressing the deepest feeling of every single Jew throughout the ages. It is not Isaiah or Micah who is its originator; it is the Jewish people as a whole.

One of the outstanding characteristics of our Rabbis is that they emphasise the value of the cardinal virtues of Judaism by making the heroes of the Scriptural narrative the prototypes of these virtues in action. Abraham represents hospitality, Moses justice, and the paragon of the ideal of peace is Aaron.

"Be of the disciples of Aaron," says Hillel, "loving peace and pursuing peace; loving God's creatures and thereby bringing them near to the Torah" (Aboth i: 12). When, however, we analyse the picture which our Rabbis paint of Aaron the Peacemaker, there is one noteworthy fact which emerges. Consistently, and as far as I am aware without exception, the Rabbis confine themselves, in their appreciative appraisal of the peace-loving proclivities of Aaron, the prototype of peace, to one single aspect of the practice of that sublime virtue. I cannot think of a single instance where the pursuit of peace is in the direction of peace between nation and nation, of the glorious ideal of international peace, of that vision of an Isaiah or a Micah. It is a much more homely picture that they depict, one painted on a much smaller canvas and what the thoughtless may consider to be in much more drab colours. It is the homely virtue of peace "between man and his neighbour, between brother and brother, between husband and wife." They even go as far as to suggest that in the pursuit of that ideal Aaron was not averse from telling a white lie, and lovingly they describe that when he heard that two men had quarrelled, he would go to the one and tell him, quite wrongly, that his enemy had expressed to him his contrition for the wrong he had inflicted upon him, and his desire for a reconciliation. He would then go to the other and tell him the same story, and thus having paved the way for bringing about peace, would retire into the background while the seed which he had planted germinated, sprouted and produced its goodly fruit.

One might be tempted to think that in thus confining themselves to this comparatively insignificant aspect of that great and overwhelming ideal of peace the Rabbis were devoid of vision. One might legitimately ask what bearing this aspect of domestic bliss has upon the great problems of peace and war which are agitating the minds of all thoughtful men at this moment. What has the question whether a home is a haven of connubial and domestic bliss or whether the husband and wife are continually quarrelling with one another to do with the burning question of whether the world is to be blown to nothingness by the H-bomb? What has the consideration whether Mr. Cohen has quarrelled with Mr. Levy and refuses to speak to him to do with the urgent topical problem of whether the tremendous energy released by nuclear fission is to be used for destructive ends or for constructive progress? Surely it is the question whether, in the words of Isaiah, "they shall beat their swords into ploughshares and their spears into pruning hooks" shall prevail, or whether it shall be the opposite described by Joel: "Prepare war! Wake up the mighty men, let all the men of war draw near; let them come up. Beat your ploughshares into swords and your pruning hooks into spears" (Joel iv: 9/10) that is the real problem of peace and war, of good and evil, of destruction or construction?

I was brought up in Scotland, which is the land of my birth, and I can tell you that all the traditional jokes which are based upon the reputed niggardliness and even miserliness of the Scot have a certain factual basis in that thrift and carefulness were taught to us in school as one of the cardinal virtues. We were told stories to illustrate the positive value of thrift, and these stories were crystallised in proverbs which we had to learn, such proverbs as "Waste not, want not," "A stitch in times saves nine," and so on. And one of these proverbs was "Look after the pennies and the pounds will look after themselves." It seems to me that that proverb has a much wider application than its immediate one of husbanding one's financial resources. It expresses a profound truth which applies to every sphere of one's thoughts and conduct. It suggests that however great may be the temptation to look to the big things, to the ultimate consummation of ideals in their widest sphere, the only sure way to effect that consummation is by concentrating on the small and the insignificant aspects of it which are usually ignored. Domestic peace, harmony between brothers, amity between man and his fellow-man may be the "pennies" of the ideal of peace, and the glorious vision of the Utopian age of Universal Peace the "pounds," but if we could but learn to look after these pennies the pounds would look after themselves. For peace is an attitude of mind; it is a disposition. The man who is quarrelsome at home is a quarrelsome person, and a multitude of quarrelsome persons make a quarrelsome people. A man who nurses a senseless grudge against his fellow and refuses to become reconciled with him engenders a state of mind which rends the society in which he mixes in twain and like the stone thrown into the pond it causes ripples which spread in ever wider concentric circles until the last is beyond the vision of one's eyes. And conversely a harmonious attitude and a peaceful community is the basis of a peaceful world.

I could command your universal assent and enthusiastic approbation by preaching the evils of war and thundering from this pulpit that the hydrogen bomb tests must be stopped, but the practical effect of that sermon will be nil. But if I say, what I am going to say, that here in this Synagogue there sit two brothers who can hardly be induced to speak a civil word to one another, that if one says black the other says white; and if I appeal to them to drop this senseless animosity and patch up their differences; if I point out that in the right-hand side of the Synagogue there is a man who declares that he would not touch a certain person on the left with the traditional bargepole; and I tell them that this attitude is unjustified, I am doing something which, if they would but hearken to me, would imperceptibly, but none the less really, bring nearer the ideal of peace.

When I was in Margate last week I was told that the Rabbi of Durban had to cancel a proposed visit to the handful of Jews in that seaside resort because half of them refused to assemble in one house if the other half were there, and vice versa. And because of that there is not a vestige of communal life there. It is these "pennies" of the ideal of peace that each and every one of us can carefully look after, and the result will be that an atmosphere of harmony and goodwill will be created whose influence will begin to seep through and permeate an ever-widening circle.

No! Our Rabbis knew what they were about when they concentrated their attention on these "pennies." For peace is one and indivisible, and when God blesses husband and wife, or brother and brother, or man and his fellow-man with peace, there comes about the next stage that "God blesses his people with peace" and a combination of peaceful peoples brings about a peaceful world.

From peace, peace to the near, comes peace, peace to the far, and thus alone does healing come to a world which is sick with strife and dissension. Let us indeed look after these pennies, and the pounds will look after themselves. Then only will "nation not life up sword against nation, neither shall they learn war any more."

## INDIVIDUAL AND CONGREGATIONAL PRAYER

### ON אלהי נצור

TRADITIONAL Judaism requires man to recite his prayers thrice daily, "evening, morning and afternoon," and as I have pointed out in my sermon on the Amidah, it is the Amidah which constitutes prayer proper and which is referred to in the Talmud by the expressive name of "Tephillah," "Prayer." There is, however, one difference between the Amidah of the morning and afternoon and that of the evening. The morning and afternoon Amidah is repeated by the Cantor whereas the evening Amidah is not. I do not desire to go into the historical and liturgical reasons for this difference; my reason for mentioning it is that those who confine their attendance to Synagogue to Friday evening, and who come, as the majority of the Congregation does, after Mincha, miss one noteworthy fact, namely, that the beautiful prayer beginning "O my God, guard my tongue from evil and my lips from speaking guile," with which the Amidah ends, is not said by the Chazan when he repeats the Amidah. If you will compare this prayer with the rest of the Amidah, however, you will see one striking difference between it which goes a long way, if not the whole way, towards explaining the reason. Whereas the Amidah proper is consistently couched in the plural, from the beginning "Our God and God of our fathers," to the end, "Grant peace to us," this prayer is in the singular. "O *my* God, guard *my* tongue from evil, and *my* lips from speaking guile."

The reason for the change is a simple one. The Amidah constitutes *Congregational* prayer and it is a *sine qua non* of Congregational prayer that it is couched in the plural. The Jew in the congregation does not pray for himself alone; he prays for himself and for his brethren. He thinks of himself as a member of the community and his supplications and petitions are for the community of which he is a member, whether that specific request applies to him or not. Thus where Jeremiah says רפאני ה׳ וארפא הושיעני ואושע "Heal me O Lord, and I shall be healed, save me and I shall be saved," the author of the Amidah renders the verse in the plural: "Heal us O Lord, and we shall be healed, save us and we shall be saved." And if he feels the brotherhood of Israel, though he be himself brimming over with rude health and full of bodily vigour, he will pray for the sick and the afflicted of Israel with the same fervour as he would for himself. He may have had such success in his business that he has "never had such a good year," yet if he feels that association with his fellows which is of the essence of the meaning of the word Congregation, he will pray fervently, "Bless, O Lord, for us this year . . . and bless our years like the good years." It is that conception alone, for instance, which justifies the alphabetical and double alphabetical list of sins which constitutes the confession on Yom Kippur. The individual Jew who prays may never have been guilty of the particular sin which he enunciates but as long as there is one member of the Community to whom this sin can be attributed he says, "Forgive us for this sin which we have committed." And so he identifies himself with the Community and he shares their corporate responsibilities and corporate supplications.

This prayer at the end, however, belongs to the category of individual prayers. As to the reason therefor I hope to speak next week, but since it is an individual prayer it is couched in the singular, and since it is only the Congregational part of the Amidah which is repeated by the Chazan, it is omitted in that repetition. The inclusion of this individual prayer in the liturgy shows an appreciation of the need for that kind of prayer, and the very silence of its omission in the repetition speaks more eloquently than words. It says to the Congregation, so to speak, "This is none of your business; it is a matter between me and my Maker."

And if there was a justification for organised religion and for Congregational prayer which is its most emphatic expression, it lies in the fact that individual prayer has almost ceased to exist. We have forgotten how to pray, unless that prayer is organised for us. In our approach to God we have become like children who have to be spoon-fed, because unless the words are put in our mouths we will starve spiritually. This prayer is not the only example of private prayer. After the Amidah at the morning and afternoon prayers there is a prayer called "Tahanun," "Supplications." In the prayer books Psalm vi is prescribed to be read, and the fact that it is, like this prayer, a psalm couched in the singular, gives us a clue to the reason for its selection. For this psalm should be called "A suggested prayer for silent meditation." It is at this point of the service that the worshipper is supposed to disregard the congregational aspect of prayer and devote his thoughts to personal petitions. He is supposed to make the ceremonial gesture of נפילת אפים of "falling on his face" and, lowering his head on to his arm, make his individual communion with God. The very physical effect of this posture surely renders it impossible to read printed words in this position, and in addition to the physical aspect there is surely also the symbolic act of withdrawal when one, so to speak, cuts oneself off momentarily from the Congregation, and communes silently and individually with God, pouring out one's heart to him.

A few months ago I received a letter from the Chief Rabbi in London informing me that a revision of Singer's Prayer Book was contemplated and asking me for any suggestions which I might have. I was tempted to suggest that before אלהי נצור and Tahanun the rubric be added: "Silent meditation. The following passage can be read as an alternative." For reasons quite unconnected with the point which I am making, I did not do so; but had I done it, and had my suggestion been accepted, would it have made any difference to the worshippers? How many would seize the opportunity, within the framework of the statutory prayers, of offering up the spontaneous outpouring of their hearts?

I speak with some feeling on this subject because of a most stimulating experience which I had a few weeks ago. I spoke to the Oxford Youth Group on the History of the Synagogue, and rarely have I had a more intellectually and spiritually satisfying evening. I would wish that those Jeremiahs who speak so gloomily about our youth and the decline of religion among them had been present at this gathering of some 50 adolescents and youths, mostly University students, and not only seen the rapt attention with which they listened to what could hardly be called a popular subject, but also heard the flood of pertinent questions about the Synagogue and its services which were poured out on me.

Among these questions, all serious and to the point, were the questions of the retention of Hebrew as the medium of prayer, and how one could possibly avoid the danger of mechanical rendering of set and stereotyped prayer. As I pointed out to them, these criticisms and these difficulties apply only to Congregational Prayer, in which, as I hoped I convinced them, the advantages of the retention of Hebrew and fixed formulae outweigh the disadvantages which attach to them. But when it comes to individual prayer and silent meditation there is no prohibition whatsoever against the person who wishes to pray addressing himself to God in whatever language he can best express himself and in whatever terms he finds most suitable.

I quoted the beautiful and moving story told at the beginning of the Sefer Chassidim of the pious and narrow-minded Chassid who overheard an ignorant and illiterate cowherd, filled with passionate love of God, exclaiming to God: "O Lord, I love you so much, that if you had a herd of cattle I would tend them for you free of charge." The Chassid peremptorily ordered him to cease from this — to him— blasphemous prayer, and taught him to recite the statutory blessings, the Shema and the Amidah, on condition that he desisted from this daily prayer which was his wont. And in a dream there appeared a vision to this Chassid, and said to him, "If you will not go back at once to that cowherd and tell him to revert to his original prayer, evil will befall you, for you have robbed me of one who was worthy of the world to come — for the all-Merciful desires only the heart."*

That beautiful tale surely expresses the complete freedom of the form and content of the prayer which the individual Jew can offer up to God. Yet is there one of us who in thanksgiving or in tribulation can find the words to give expression to the thoughts which are in his heart?

And until the Jew can learn to do so, until he can learn to blaze his own trail through the maze which separates him from his Father in Heaven, there is but one highroad which he can follow which can lead him to the Gates of Prayer which are ever open, and this is the road which has been cut out and paved by successive generations of God-intoxicated souls who made that road which is the statutory Prayer Book.

---

* Sefer Chassidim. Berlin 1811 p.6, para. 6.

## THE EVIL TONGUE

**אלהי נצור לשוני מרע ושפתי מדבר מרמה ולמקללי נפשי תדום ונפשי כעפר לכל תהיה**

*O my God, guard my tongue from evil*
*And my lips from speaking deceit.*
*And to such as curse me let my soul be dumb,*
*Yea, let my soul be as the dust to all.*

(Amidah: Silent Prayer.)

A REPORT appeared in the Press recently about a problem which has arisen in the Belgian Congo which has developed into a veritable national emergency. Apparently there is an attractive purple flower which some people introduced into their gardens in order to beautify them and render them more attractive. They were completely unaware that the plant was a particularly noxious weed which spreads like wildfire, causing widespread devastation. The weed has invaded the Congo River and has spread with such incredible rapidity and taken such deep roots that it has clogged up the whole of that mighty river and rendered it unnavigable. It fouls the propellers of the ships, it threatens to suffocate the fish. Anxious conferences are being held at the highest level how to deal with it. Tens of millions of pounds have been allocated to the task, and yet they are doubtful whether the drastic steps contemplated will be successful. The whole economic life of a large section of the Community is threatened. I wonder what the thoughts are in the minds of those garden-lovers who so innocently introduced that weed.

Those thoughts entered my mind when I considered the subject of the social evil which I am making the theme of my sermon to-day and which is indicated in my text. For I believe that social evils follow the same course. I do not believe—I would not like to believe—that those responsible for their introduction are animated by an active, positive malice. I believe that they introduce them innocently in order to adorn their otherwise prosaic conversation. A touch of colour, a bloom of brightness is all that they are after, but they do not realise that they are thereby introducing a noxious weed which must spread like wildfire, choking the well-springs of our social life and our relations with our fellow-men, vitiating and poisoning the atmosphere which we breathe, causing havoc and devastation. But if I have forgotten the name of that noxious weed of the Congo, I have not forgotten that of our social life. For of these noxious weeds the most toxic and the most dangerous is that evil which is reflected in my text. It is the evil of לשון הרע, of gossip and slander, of tale-bearing and tittle-tattle, of backbiting and defamation.

"O my God, guard my tongue from evil
And my lips from speaking deceit.
And to such as curse me let my soul be dumb,
Yea, let my soul be to all as the dust."

These simple yet poignant words are worthy of a detailed analysis.

When I was in Jerusalem a few years ago, I heard a delightful story from Dr. Judah Kaufman, whose visit to this country thirteen years ago is so vividly remembered. It was about a Mitnagid whose sole ideal was that his son should acquire as much knowledge of the Torah as possible. The son however became attracted to Chassidism, which tends to stress the emotional and the ethical aspect of Judaism more than the academic, and under its influence he ran away from home and spent six months with a Chassidic Rebbe, after which he returned home. "Well," said his father sneeringly, "and what did you *learn* in these six months?" "Father," answered the son, "I learned the meaning of the verse ואהבת לרעך כמוך "Thou shalt love thy neighbour as thyself." "What?" said the father, "in six months you only learnt one verse which any child in Cheder knows." "But, father," answered the lad calmly, "I learnt a new translation." "A new translation?" asked the father, "what other translation can there be than "Thou shalt love thy neighbour as thyself?" "Father," he answered, "for the six months I was with the Rebbe I learnt to translate it '*I* shall love *my* neighbour as myself.'"

The implications of that delightful story are simple and yet far-reaching. We are all of us prone and eager, ready and uninhibited, to say to the other fellow in everything which appertains to the sphere of morals and ethics, of right thinking and right doing, "Thou shalt" and "Thou shalt not." We are equally indisposed and reluctant to say to ourselves "I shall" and "I shall not." We overlook and disregard the wise counsel of our Rabbis on the verse הוכח תוכיח את אמיתך ולא יהיה בך חטא הוכח את עצמך ואחר כך הוכח אחרים "If you would be free from sin reprove yourself before you reprove others."

And that is exactly what Mar Bar Ravina, the author of this beautiful prayer did to the opening words of this prayer. For its origin is to be found in the 24th Psalm, in which the Psalmist declares: "Who is the man who delightest in life and loveth length of days that he may see good?" and answers: "Guard *thy* tongue from evil, and *thy* lips from speaking deceit," with its corollary that lips that speak evil bring in their train death instead of life, days which become hateful and burdensome instead of days full of good and of love. And Mar Bar Ravina changes the person from the second to the first, as did the son of the Mitnagid in that tale, and renders it "Guard *my* tongue from evil, and *my* lips from speaking deceit."

But that does not exhaust the analysis of that verse. Is it not remarkable that when the authors and architects of our beautiful liturgy sought for a theme which every single

Jew shall recite as a personal, individual prayer after every Amidah, three times a day, they should have chosen this theme? Does it not suggest that they realised that there is hardly a person who is not in some way guilty of it, that we all have to pray for divine help in overcoming our proneness to it and falling into its clutches?

That view is strongly reinforced by a remarkable article which appeared recently in The Star. In the magazine of St. George's Cathedral, Cape Town, the question was posed whether one can spend a whole day without criticising anybody. It suggested that people try the experiment and they would be surprised at the tremendous amount of self-discipline involved. A reporter of the Cape Argus thereupon decided to put it to the test and selected as his guinea-pigs three people, a University student, a prominent business man and a housewife. The student said: "I didn't manage to get through the day without criticising. I was astonished and disgusted at the number of times I caught myself on the edge of criticism. The experiment has shown me to what a shocking extent my circle talks about people." The business man confessed that he had to exercise a great amount of self-control, and the housewife, while denying that she herself was guilty of it, added: "But I was driving in the evening with two old ladies and I noticed that their conversation consisted almost entirely of criticising other people." (The Star, 17/8/1957).

But I have not finished with my analysis. It prays for guidance and divine help not only for the *perpetrator* of that evil, but equally for the *victim* of it. For if all of us are guilty of it, we all equally become its victims. I have translated the words which follow as they appear in the Prayer Book "And those that curse me." But true though it is that קללה means a curse, and true though it is that the persistent victim of it feels that he is lying under the burden of a curse, in general the translation is too strong. There is an equally acceptable and truer rendering for

ולמקללי and that is "Those that cheapen me." Every person holds his reputation, his good name, his integrity, his standing with his fellow-men, dear. He is jealous of the good opinion people hold of him. He regards himself as having some "value" and the effect of לשון הרע is to cheapen that value and diminish that self-respect, to reduce the image of the divine in which each man is formed.

What shall we do against this pernicious cheapening? Shall one protest violently against it? Shall one take drastic steps to vindicate one's honour and good name? Shall one cry from the housetops that it is not true? Surely each and every one of these is a natural reaction but alas, one must come to the gloomy conclusion that they are of no avail. There is but one way of dealing with that cheapening of one's dignity. However much it goes against the grain, however much one's soul cries out for vengeance and for restitution one is enjoined but to turn to God and say "God, give me the moral strength to ignore it. God let my soul be as the dust." And the juxtaposition of these two verses induces the salutary and sobering thought: "Perhaps it is because I myself have not guarded my tongue against evil that I have become the victim of the evil tongue of others."

Every language teaches this essential lesson that the only way to deal with that evil is to treat it with contempt. When I was a child in Scotland I was taught the proverb "Sticks and stones 'll break your bones but names 'll never hurt ye." When I learnt Latin I learnt the disdainful proverb: "Dicunt? Quid Dicunt? Dicant"—"They say, what do they say? Let them say!" When I became familiar with Yiddish I found it expressed with almost vulgar pungency: "Sollen die hint billen!" And in English the same thought is expressed more elegantly, "The dogs bark, the caravan moves on!"

But only in our prayers is the thought of the victim combined with the thought of the perpetrator. Only after one has said "O my God, guard my tongue from evil and my lips from speaking deceit," when one's conscience has been cleared of guilt, can one say "O God, let me learn to ignore it from others."

Oh that evil tongue, that evil tongue! God guard me against it, both as perpetrator and as victim.

## ABBREVIATED PRAYERS

*He with his word was a shield to our forefathers, and by his bidding will quicken the dead; the Holy God, like unto him there is none, who giveth rest to his people on his holy Sabbath day.*

(Friday Evening Service.)

WHEN I was in North Africa as a Chaplain during the last World War, I came across three exotic Jewish Communities about which I wrote and lectured extensively at the time. One was the remarkable Community of the Jews on the island of Djerba, which contained only two towns, both of which had a population which consisted only of Jews, not a single non-Jew residing in them. The second was the Community of the Troglodytes, the subterranean cave-dwellers of Tigruna, and the third the mountain Jews of the district of Jefren. The one characteristic common to these otherwise distinct and separate Communities was that time seemed to have stood still with them for two thousand years, with the result that many customs mentioned in the Talmud, which no longer obtain in any other Communities in the Jewish world still held their sway with them and were the norm of their lives.

It is to one of these customs appertaining to the fleet-footed mountain Jews of Jefren that I wish to refer. There were three villages which the Jews shared with the local Berbers, and in each of them their Synagogue was not situated in the village at all, but stood imposing and isolated in the middle of fields at a considerable distance from their habitations.

When I asked them the reason for this unusual fact they could not answer me, except by telling me that it had always been their custom. And in point of fact this peculiar custom dates back to the Talmud, according to Rashi, and is the reason for the addition of this prayer, Magen Avot, which is the subject of my sermon this evening.

Those of you who have been attending the Synagogue regularly and have been following this series of sermons on the Friday evening service will by now be aware of the fact that the Friday evening Amidah consists of seven blessings, the first three and the last three statutory and unchanging for all versions of the Amidah and the middle one having the Sabbath as its theme. If you will study this prayer carefully you will see that it is nothing more or less than a precis and a digest of the Amidah which has just been recited, each phrase giving the essential thought of a blessing. Thus "shield to our forefathers" corresponds to the first blessing "shield of Abraham"; "by his bidding will quicken the dead" corresponds to the second blessing, "Blessed art thou who quickenest the dead;" "The Holy God" to האל הקדוש and "who giveth rest to his people on the Sabbath day" to the central Sabbath blessing.

It is not the only example in our Prayer Book of what I may somewhat irreverently call "potted prayers." If you will turn to page 55 you will see a similarly abbreviated form of the weekday Amidah which, however, abbreviates only the thirteen intermediate blessings, while on page 286 there occurs a shorter form of the Grace After Meals. Whereas, however, these two shortened prayers were instituted to be said when time was lacking for the recital of the full form, this shortened form of the Friday evening Amidah, paradoxical though it may sound, was instituted because there was too much time, which had to be filled up!

According to Rashi* the reason for its introduction was as follows. During the period of the Talmud the Syna-

*T.B. Sabbath 24b.

gogues were, as I found them in the mountain villages of Jefren, in the fields. The normal day of labourers was from sunrise to sunset, and when they finished their work during the week it was too late for them to come to Synagogue to read the evening service with the Congregation and they used to read it individually at home. On Friday evenings, however, they desired to come to Synagogue in order to join in congregational prayer. Working as they did until sunset it took them some time to get to the Synagogue, and as often as not they arrived after the statutory service was over. As a result there were two provisions which had to be made. These latecomers could not be left alone in Synagogue because of the dangers which might attend them walking alone in the dark from the rural Synagogue to the village, and their desire for congregational service had to be met. As you know, the evening Amidah is the only one which is not repeated and therefore a happy solution was found which solved all three difficulties. The Congregation delayed its departure from the Synagogue and this abbreviated form of the Amidah was evolved which was said by the whole congregation, those who had already read the statutory service and those workmen who had come too late, and all left the Synagogue together, winding their way in company to the village, and, according to the beautiful legend, accompanied by the Angels of Peace who accompany Man from Synagogue to home on Friday night.

It is an excellent example of the manner in which our Prayer Book, representing as it does the gradual organic development of over two millennia, enshrines within it, like a fly caught in amber millions of years ago, fascinating glimpses of a past which is no more. The Synagogue in the fields, the labourers in pre-Trade Union days working till sunset, their desire to attend service at least on Friday night, the steps taken to make it possible for latecomers to join in service, and the sense of communal responsibility which caused arrangements to be made that they should not be exposed to danger by having to walk home alone.

All these considerations apply, as has been said, to a past which is no more, and their interest, however great, is merely historical. There is, however, one further aspect which has a wider importance and which is well worth consideration. It is obvious from what has been said that with the recital of this condensed and abbreviated form of the Amidah these latecomers had fulfilled their obligation of Sabbath prayer, without having recited the statutory Amidah. And in accordance with this the Machzor Vitry lays it down in the name of Rav Moses Gaon that "If an individual did not manage to recite the Amidah, as long as he listens to Magen Avot recited by the Cantor from beginning to end, and answers Amen, he has fulfilled his obligation."*

The implications of this Din are important. It clearly suggests that the accepted formulae of our statutory prayers represent the broad highway which leads man to his Father in Heaven. But that does not mean that there are no byways and sidetracks whereby, when the main road is blocked and unusable, the same journey cannot be made. One does not usually take a sidetrack; it is used only in emergencies; the going is harder and slower, but it can lead man to his destination. It is not the words which matter as much as the heart which expresses those words. It is because the heart of man is normally inarticulate to find the correct words to express these thoughts which he wishes to pour out to establish communion with God that they have been provided for him. A short prayer sincerely expressed can pierce the barrier which separates man from God and reach the foot of the Throne of Glory much more than a long prayer which may degenerate into a meaningless formula. The Midrash points out that the five monosyllabic Hebrew words uttered by Moses when he prayed for the recovery of his sister Miriam from the dread disease of leprosy, El Na R'fa Na la, were as acceptable before

*Vitry 105 and 156.

God as the forty days and the forty nights that he spent in prayer to avert the evil decree from the children of Israel after their sin with the Golden Calf. The sincere answer amen to a blessing constitutes in Jewish law the absolute equivalent of having actually recited the blessing.

There is a beautiful story told of a Chassidic Rabbi whose learning was equalled by his piety and the ecstatic devotion with which he used to recite his prayers. Aware not only of the meaning of each word of the prayers, but of their profound and mystical implications, he would recite his prayers lovingly and meticulously, stressing each word, omitting nothing. He was regarded as a model and pattern of prayerful devotion and Kavvanah. And one night there appeared to him a vision which said that however acceptable his prayers were before the Almighty, those of a certain poor cobbler in the village were even more acceptable. The Rabbi was amazed; as far as he was aware the man was so completely illiterate that he could not even read Hebrew, much less understand the prayers. He took the earliest opportunity of paying him a visit and concealing himself, waited for the cobbler to recite his prayers. Ultimately the cobbler put down his awl and reaching up to a shelf took from it a grimy piece of paper and pored over it. The Rabbi strained his ears and to his utter astonishment heard him slowly and lovingly recite—the Hebrew alphabet—Alef! Beth! Gimel! Daleth! and so on. When he had come to Tav he lifted up his eyes towards Heaven and said, "Ribono Shel Olam! That is all the Hebrew I was ever taught. But out of these letters all the saints and scholars have formed the words with which to praise and bless thee. Who is able better to form these letters into the words which my heart wishes to say but is unable to do so, than Thou? Oh, Ribono Shel Olam! Take these letters from me and turn them into those words of praise and thanksgiving which I would like to utter to thee." And lovingly and passionately kissing the piece of paper, he restored it to the shelf!

For whether we recite our prayers dutifully from the first word to the last; whether circumstances permit us only to recite a précis, in essence, as our Rabbis so aptly and beautifully point out, prayer is "the service of the heart" and more than our words רחמנא ליבא בעי the All-Merciful desires that heart.

## LIGHT AND SALVATION*

**ה׳ אורי וישעי ממי אירא ה׳ מעוז חיי ממי אפחד.**

*The Lord is my light and my salvation, whom shall I fear?*
*The Lord is the stronghold of my life, of whom shall I be afraid?*

(Psalm xxvii: 1.)

IF you will look at the back page of Singer's Prayer Book you will see there an index to the Psalms which occur in the Siddur. Of the 150 Psalms in the Book of Psalms, no fewer than 72, and part of a seventy-third, almost half, are to be found there, of which twelve occur twice. These Psalms can be divided into two categories, those which form part of the statutory prayers and are recited daily or on every Shabbat and Festival, and those which are recited on special occasions. That division underlines the wondrous qualities of that most wonderful of all Books of the Bible. For the Psalms give permanent and exquisite expression to two aspects of the spiritual emotions of man in his quest for God, the normal and the special. By the "normal" I mean those thoughts which reflect the emotions of a person when he is not under the stress of any particular or extraordinary occurrence, when his mind is at rest, except in its restless desire to establish communion with God, the source of life, the daily thoughts, the permanent experiences of the human heart, while by "special" I mean those emotions

* For the month of Ellul.

which are excited by unusual occurrences, sickness and sorrow, joy and exultation, despair and death. In short there is no occasion in human life for which the Psalms do not find their matchless expression. To quote from the Introduction to the late Dr. Cohen's Soncino edition of the Psalms:—

> "They are essentially human documents. They reflect life in its varied aspects as it was experienced by members of the Israelite community. In particular, the hardships of existence are faithfully mirrored: the struggles of the godly to remain faithful to their ideals in the face of oppression; the disturbing doubts created in their hearts by the triumph of evil-doers; the stern fight of the sinner for the victory of his better self; the conquest of despair by resolute faith in the righteousness of God.
>
> " Such experiences are not limited to one people or one age; they are recurrent and world-wide. Hence the unfading appeal of the Psalms. They echo the thought and feeling, the aspiration and yearning, of countless men and women in every era. In their matchless phrases the human soul has for tens of centuries found an outlet in its own struggle from the depths to reach the heights. "To weary travellers of every condition and every period of history, the Psalms have been rivers of refreshment and wells of consolation. They alone have known no limitations to a particular age, country, or form of faith (Prothero). To all seekers of God they remain a grateful aid to their quest."

Every occasion has therefore its appropriate Psalm, and as you will see from the rubric to this Psalm, it has been selected for recital during the whole month of Ellul and through to Hoshanah Rabba. In other words it is the Psalm which gives expression to our thoughts, or what should be our thoughts, as the impact of the forthcoming High Festivals, the days of Reconciliation and Repentance, of Atonement and Return begins to make itself felt. And the mood inspired by that Psalm should continue with us right through that period until the traditional final moment of judgment on Hoshanah Rabba. That mood is succinctly expressed by the Midrash, which explains: "The Lord is my light" on Rosh Hashanah, "and my salvation" on Yom Kippur.

What then is the message and the burden of this Psalm? To me the answer to this question is bound up with an incident of my student life. I was a student of the Yeshivath Etz Chaim in London, and until the day to which I am about to refer, the curriculum of studies was entirely limited to the acquisition of a knowledge of "Gemora with Tosafoth." No provision whatsoever was made for knowledge in the ethics and morals of Judaism. And then a distinguished Rabbi, the late Rabbi Aaron Bakst, then of Lomza, who was destined to become one of Hitler's Martyrs, was appointed Rosh Yeshivah, and he instituted a new departure — for the London Yeshivah. It was what I believe is called in Yeshiva a "Schmuez," a "causerie," a religious ethical talk on some topical theme.

His first such talk was during the month of Ellul and he took this Psalm as his text. I shall always remember his remarkable introduction: "There is nothing more bankrupt than the plaudits and acclaim of the multitude. Let us take as an example Lloyd George," he began. He then proceeded to give a vivid description of the manner in which the British Premier had stepped into the breach at the most critical period of the First World War when it looked as though all was lost, and by dint of his energy, courage and indomitable spirit had overcome all obstacles and turned what looked like certain defeat into a glorious victory. How enthusiastically was he acclaimed! What hero-worship was accorded him at the time! And then no sooner was the war over than he was discarded and thrown overboard like so much useless and unwanted rubbish. What thoughts must have entered his mind at this base ingratitude and thanklessness! How he must have realised the hollowness and the emptiness, the fleeting nature, if not the insincerity, of all that fulsome flattery. It may have been sincere at the time, but it exploded like a burst balloon.

And from the parallel he turned to the text of the Psalm. David the beloved of God and of Men, David who from a hunted fugitive became the most powerful king of Israel, first of Judah, then of the whole kingdom. David who consolidated the kingdom both internally by his remarkable organisation of the kingdom and externally by his successive conquests of the Philistines, of Edom and Moab and Ammon, David the sweet singer of Israel, one of whose outstanding characteristics was his ability to evoke the affection, love and admiration of all with whom he came into contact, and yet at the end of his life he is surrounded by intrigue, the rebellion of his sons, the cursing of Shimei ben Gera, the ruthlessness of Joab. And he reviews the results of his life; he compares the days when the women sang joyously, "Saul hath slain his thousands and David his tens of thousands" with the present, "when evildoers come upon me to eat my flesh." And even although "they stumbled and fell," he comes to the sad realisation that the fruits of victory are Dead Sea Fruits, and that the taste of victory has turned to ashes in his mouth, and he declares, "One thing have I asked of the Lord, that will I seek after, that I may dwell in the house of the Lord all the days of my life, to behold the graciousness of the Lord and to meditate in his temple." All earthly joys are nothing and material achievements are vain, and he concludes: "Wait for the Lord; be strong and let thy heart take courage, yea, wait thou for the Lord."

Scholars may take leave to doubt the accuracy of that interpretation. They may point out that the Septuagint, the ancient Greek version of the Bible which sometimes preserves an older text than the Massoretic, adds, after the words "to David," the words "before he was anointed," and that therefore the passionate desire for peace and tranquillity reflects the period of peril and not that of security. But does not that interpretation exactly interpret the mood with which the period through which we are passing, when this Psalm is recited, should inspire us? What benefits have we from all our worldly successes, from our victories, our achievements, our progress? Do not these days say unto us, in the words of R. Jacob in the Ethics of the Fathers, "Better is one hour of repentance and good deeds in this world than the whole life of the world to come, and better is one hour of blissfulness of spirit in the world to come than the whole life of this world" (iv: 22)? Do they not say to us "What shall it profit a man if he gain the whole world and lose his soul?" And these days come to restore the soul to the place it should have in our being, to bring light where otherwise there is darkness, and salvation instead of damnation. Does not the tranquillity and the serenity of spirit which comes to that person who is at peace with himself and at peace with God outweigh all temporal successes? It is to these questions that Ellul and Tishri give their emphatic and affirmative answer, when we dwell in the house of the Lord, behold his graciousness and meditate in his Temple.

# KADDISH AND KOL NIDREI

THE fortuitous fact that this sermon on the Kaddish is being delivered on Shabbat Shuvah, the Sabbath before Yom Kippur, has suggested to me a comparison between two prayers, the Kaddish and the Kol Nidrei.

On the face of it, and in point of actual fact, there appears to be not the remotest basis for such a comparison. Kaddish is a prayer, an exultant expression of praise to God who is beyond all human praise; Kol Nidrei is a legal formula of absolution from vows in which the Name of God is not even mentioned. Kaddish is the most "Vochedik" of prayers. If I mistake not, in its various forms it is recited at least ten times every day of the year, and the Jew who cannot say Kaddish is regarded as the nearest thing to an apostate. The recital of Kol Nidrei, albeit it is thrice repeated, is limited to one single occasion of the year and as "Vochedik" as is Kaddish, so is the Kol Nidrei the "Holy of Holies" of our liturgy.

Yet despite these obvious differences there are two points of comparison. The first is that neither of these prayers is couched in the language of prayer, Hebrew, but in its cognate sister-language, Aramaic. That fact is not unconnected with the second and the main point of comparison. Aramaic was the vernacular, the language of the people at the time that these prayers were composed, and the Rabbis of the time, as have the Rabbis in nearly all generations, fought against the natural tendency for prayers to be offered in the vernacular, in favour of the retention of Hebrew as the sole language of prayer, as the common link between the various communities in the far-flung Diaspora. One of the peculiar weapons in this struggle was a statement in the name of R. Johanan to the effect that "He who recites his prayers in Aramaic will receive no assistance from the Ministering Angels, for they do not understand Aramaic" (Shabb. 12a; Sotah 33a). I am sure that he would have liked to have said that the Almighty does not understand Aramaic, but since such a statement was clearly inadmissible, since one could not ascribe ignorance to God, he was obliged to attribute this ignorance to the angels!

It is obvious therefore that the retention of prayers in Aramaic is in itself tantamount to evidence that these prayers maintained an affectionate and tenacious hold upon the sentiments and emotions of the people to such an extent that they were powerful enough to overcome the opposition of the great scholars whose writ and authority otherwise reigned supreme. They represent the powerlessness of authority, however undisputed it may be, upon the determined united will of "Amcha," the common people, and no one with a knowledge of the laws of prayer can fail to be impressed by the legislative force of the words נהגו העולם "The people have adopted the custom." And that custom becomes law even if it is in conflict with the letter of the Din.

That theory is more than vindicated by the pragmatic test. It cannot be denied that even to-day the word Kaddish makes a more direct emotional appeal to the Jew than the word Shema, that the words Kol Nidrei convey infinitely more to him than do the words Shemoneh Esreh, though no one with a knowledge of the value and importance of our prayers would for one moment entertain the idea that the Kaddish can compare with the Shema or the Kol Nidrei with Shemoneh Esreh. In other words the Kaddish and the Kol Nidrei are the most popular portions of our prayers. That popularity has had its different effect upon each of those prayers. In the case of Kol Nidrei it succeeded in assuring its retention in the teeth of the most formidable opposition. Theological considerations combined with public policy to urge its abolition. The theological claims were pressed at the time of its introduction. Some of the Geonim, the undisputed spiritual heads of the Jewish people at the time, vigorously opposed its introduction and its recitation in our prayers. As a formula for the absolution of vows it is meaningless and of no effect. The people rebelled with a passive disobedience against the order for its removal, and the people won. Much more serious was the second consideration. No sooner did it become an integral part of the Yom Kippur Eve service than it became the subject of a sustained, malicious and libellous attack by anti-Semites that the word of the Jew could not be trusted since he had absolved himself from all his vows on the previous Yom Kippur. For centuries the Jews and Kol Nidrei were made the victims of this sustained attack. Expediency surely demanded that a largely meaningless formula should be abolished. Yet I would like to see the Jew who would not rise in indignant revolt against such an impious suggestion. Kol Nidrei remains the Holy of Holies of the Jew.

The popularity of Kaddish has affected it in an entirely different manner. Nine hundred and ninety-nine Jews out of a thousand will tell you with a certainty which brooks of no doubt or questioning that the Kaddish is the prayer of filial piety which is recited by mourners, and especially children during the year following the death of their parents and on the anniversary of that death. That aspect of Kaddish has so completely overshadowed all the others that a popular name in Yiddish for one's son is "Mein Kaddish'l," and yet it is the only aspect of Kaddish for which there is no mention in the Talmud and the justification for which is doubtful and vague. The Kaddish is liturgically justified on two occasions only. It was originally instituted to be recited in the House of Study after the completion of daily study in the form of the Kaddish D'Rabbanan, "The Scholar's Kaddish." It also finds its place in the service in the form of Half-Kaddish and full

Kaddish. Where it marks the end of a section of the Service, the Half-Kaddish is said. Where it marks the end of a complete service, such as Shacharit or Musaph, the whole Kaddish is recited. As such the contents of the Kaddish are self-understood. It consists of a glorification of God and the Messianic hope of his future reign in the world. It is a prayer of great antiquity and is undoubtedly reflected in what is called in the Christian religion "The Lord's Prayer."

> Our Father who art in Heaven,
> Hallowed be thy Name.
> Thy kingdom come;
> Thy will be done,

is to all intents and purposes a literal translation of the first verse of the Kaddish.

It is when one comes to consider the association of this prayer with the dead that the problem arises. One searches in it in vain for a single reference to death or to the Hereafter, and Talmudic literature is entirely silent on any connection between the recital of this prayer and mourning. You will probably be surprised, if not pained, to hear that the first reference to any such association is found in a late legend with the name of R. Akiba but in a work which has no authority. It is to the effect that Rabbi Akiba once met a ghost. And that ghost was groaning under a load of firewood which he was carrying on his back. The ghost told him that he was a Jew who had died and had not only been condemned to the fires of hell, but even had to prepare for himself the fire of his own torment. He told R. Akiba that there was but one hope for him. He had left behind an infant son, and if that son could only be taught to say the Kaddish so that the Congregation could respond "May God's great name be praised for ever" he would achieve salvation. Rabbi Akiba sought out the child and found that his mother had remarried a non-Jew and had not even had this child circumcised. Rabbi Akiba took him under his charge, taught him the Kaddish and a heavenly message came to him that his father had been granted salvation!

It is upon that frail and rickety foundation that the whole elaborate, complicated, magnificent superstructure of the Kaddish and all that is connected with it is built. And it is here that brain and heart, intellect and emotion, logic and instinct part company. As in the case of Kol Nidrei, all the learned arguments in the world which can prove that the sanctity attaching to this prayer is based upon a misconception, is theologically untenable, has little authority or sanction, are like so much ineffective beating of wings upon an impregnable fortress. Brain and intellect and logic say one thing and heart and emotion and instinct say another, and in matters of faith and religion it is the latter that always wins. The people has decided. There is one way for a Jew to build a bridge to join heaven and earth, one way for the child to give expression to his feelings of sorrow and of filial piety when those who brought him into the world have gone to their eternal rest, and that is by saying Kaddish. And the knowledge that it is being said, that one is not forgotten, but still remembered, indeed brings peace and solace to the souls of the dead, as the souls of those who are forgotten are tortured. Irrespective of the history of the prayer or the stages of its development is the fact that Kaddish reigns supreme as the prayer of filial piety and affection.

It is from this point that one commences to rationalise the prayer and interpret it to apply to this purpose. Nor is it a difficult task. It is the prayer of complete submission to the will of God even when He has brought sorrow and tribulation upon us. It says in the famous words of Job: "The Lord gave and the Lord hath taken away, Blessed be the name of the Lord." Yitgadal Veyitkadash Shmeih Rabba. "May the Great Name of the Lord be sanctified and magnified. May the Father of Peace bring peace to our stricken hearts." Amen.

## YA'ALEH VEYAVO

I TAKE as my theme this evening, the intermediate Sabbath of Succoth, that well-known addition to the Amidah as well as to the Grace After Meals, which is recited on the Three Pilgrim Festivals and on the New Moon and which is known, like most prayers, by its first distinctive introductory words, as Ya'aleh Veyavo.

It has acutely been said that "the best translation is a lie," and in that observation there lies a deep truth, a truth which is excellently illustrated by the story told in the Talmud of the translation of the Bible into Greek, which is known as the Septuagint, to which I have already referred in a previous sermon* According to that legend, all the translators without exception made the same alterations in the original text when they rendered the Bible into Greek, and the first example given is that unanimously they translated the first three words of the Hebrew Bible as אלהים ברא בראשית instead of בראשית ברא אלהים. The reason given for this apparent falsification of the text is that were the words to be translated literally into Greek it would convey the idea that a primal god called Bereshith created Elohim! That simple example underlines the impossibility of accurate translation, since the concept conveyed by a word or a phrase in one language is not necessarily the same as the concept conveyed by the literal translation of these words in another language. Grammar and syntax differ in different languages, making a literal translation impossible or misleading.

---

* See Sermon No. 34: "Miracles."

As a matter of fact the statement that the best translation is a lie is found in the Talmud itself. One of the institutions of Judaism in olden times was the Meturgeman, the translator who during the Reading of the Torah translated the Sidra verse by verse, or three verses at a time, from the original Hebrew in which it was read into the vernacular, Aramaic. Yet despite the fact that Aramaic and Hebrew are cognate languages, one gets the paradoxical statement in the Talmud in the name of R. Judah: "He who translates a verse of the Bible literally is a liar, and he who embellishes the translation is a scorner and blasphemer." (Kiddushin 59a.)

One can only say "Pity the poor translator"; but if that censure applies in translating from Hebrew to Aramaic, how much more so does it apply when translating from an Oriental language into a Western language like English! With the best will in the world, with the most perfect knowledge of both languages, it is not always possible to convey the spirit of one language into the other.

I want this evening to give but one example to illustrate my point. It is in the heaping up of epithets and verbs of almost equal meaning which is so characteristic of Hebrew yet, when translated literally into English, sounds meretricious, artificial, or even silly. In Hebrew it has the effect of raising one's emotions to a crescendo, in English it produces an effect of bathos and anti-climax. When one says in Hebrew יתברך וישתבח ויתפאר ויתרומם ויתנשא ויתהדר ויתעלה ויתהלל it raises the emotions to bursting point of exaltation and praise, when one reads the attempt of Singer to find an exact equivalent of these words, "Blessed, praised, and glorified, exalted, extolled and honoured, magnified and lauded," it becomes almost meaningless and certainly unimpressive.

On the face of it the introductory words of the prayer which we are discussing this evening belongs to the same category of epithets piled up, and it is interesting that whereas with the eight verbs of the Kaddish which I have quoted Singer manfully attempts to find an equivalent in English to each of the near synonyms, in his translation of Ya'aleh Veyavo he apparently abandons the attempt and satisfies himself with three verbs to convey what he thinks is the sense of the seven Hebrew words. His translation reads: "May our remembrance rise, come and be accepted before thee." In other words he translates "Ya'aleh," "yavo" and "yeratzeh," and leaves the other four untranslated. Although I am open to correction, it is the only example that I have noticed of Singer abandoning the severely literal translation whereby, as we have seen in the Kaddish, an equivalent in English is sought for each Hebrew word, and by doing so, he has, to my mind, missed the whole point of the multiplication of verbs.

For this prayer is recited on the three Pilgrim Festivals, on the three Festivals of the year when in ancient times, when the Temple stood in all its glory on the Temple Mount, the throngs of the faithful from every country within measurable distance of the Holy Land wended their way to Jerusalem to celebrate the Festival in joy and gladness. And with regard to that pilgrimage there comes the Biblical injunction: "They shall not appear before my Presence empty-handed. Each one according to the gift of his hand according to the blessing of the Lord which the Lord thy God hath given thee." They came to the Temple laden with gifts which they presented to the Temple.

Let us place ourselves in the position of a Festival pilgrim bringing his freewill gifts to the Temple. He stands at the foot of the fifteen steps leading from the courtyard of the Temple to the holy edifice itself ready to place it upon the altar, and let us imagine a herald, or an announcer, or a master of ceremonies regulating the flow of the procession so that it advances in regular order: "Let the pilgrim ascend the steps," he says, or in Hebrew "Ya'aleh"! The pilgrim solemnly ascends and when he reaches the top the command comes, "Yavo," "Let him draw near," and so he stands at the entrance to the place of the altar. "Let him appear" is the next stage, and by that he stands in the presence of the priest, his gift in his hand, ready to offer it. "Let the gift be accepted," says the priest, "Yeratzeh," and it is placed upon the altar. "Let him be heard" and the pilgrim makes his declaration, his affirmation of faith. "Let his gift be recorded," "Yipaked"; and lastly "Yizacher," "May his offering to God be remembered in his favour."

Is it not obvious now that this multiplication of verbs is not a mere verbal piling of Pelion on Ossa, but an attempt to reproduce the seven stages whereby the pilgrim proceeds from the foot of the steps of the Temple to deliver his festive gift and its acceptance in his favour?

But the Temple has been destroyed and is no more. We can no longer fulfil the Biblical command to offer up our material gifts to God on these Festivals. But we approach him in the same way and offer up—what? זכרוננו ופקדוננו etc. "Our remembrance and our visitation." "May we ascend the steps which lead to thy presence, come forward to the gates of mercy, approach them and wait to be admitted to thy presence. And once in thy presence may our offering be accepted, recorded and remembered in our favour."

If I am right in the interpretation, and I believe that I am, it gives an entirely new meaning and an infinitely deeper import to this well-known prayer. For if זכרוננו ופקדוננו are the substitutes for gifts which our ancestors brought to the Temple, it should be translated not "*Thy* remembrance of *us*," but "*Our* remembrance of *thee*." How much more meaning is thus added to the prayer! "Almighty God," we say, "our ancestors, when the Temple stood, brought you their gifts. But we can only bring the fact that as the Festival comes we remember thee." And there follow the four main ideals which the Jew has ever to keep in the forefront of his mind, especially on Festive occasions. First comes "the remembrance of our fathers," the Patriarchs Abraham, Isaac and Jacob, by whose faith Judaism was established; then comes "the remembrance of Messiah," the passionate belief in the ultimate triumph of right and justice, no matter how unpromising the omens may be at the moment. Thirdly comes "the remembrance of Jerusalem," the undying hope of Israel's restoration to its land, and lastly "the remembrance of all thy people the house of Israel," the doctrine of the brotherhood and unity of Israel. These things we offer up to Thee as our festive offerings. And as we bring those things to mind, be Thou, O Merciful God, mindful of us. Remember us, O Lord our God, for our well-being, remember us for blessing and save us unto life." And to the extent that we offer up the offering of our remembrance, God will remember us for life and for peace, for mercy and for grace.

## KIDDUSH IN THE SYNAGOGUE

As will be clear from what I said in my sermon on the Kaddish, this doxology originally marked the conclusion of the service. Everything which therefore follows the Kaddish Titkabbal represents later additions to the service. In the case of the Friday evening service these additions consist of Kiddush, Alenu and Yigdal, and it is to those portions of the service that the remaining sermons in this series, which have now been continuing for more than a year, will be devoted.

The recitation of Kiddush in the Synagogue poses a difficulty of Din, of Jewish religious law. For the law has been laid down אין קדוש אלא במקום סעודה Kiddush may be recited only where the subsequent meal takes place. For the Kiddush represents the sanctification of that meal, and the idea underlying it is fundamental to our conception of Judaism. Judaism does not believe in the dichotomy of man insofar as the service of God is concerned. True it believes that man consists of two opposing elements, of which we shall read the beautiful description in the first Sedra of the Torah to-morrow, body and soul. Man was created out of the dust of the earth, but into that earthly material God breathed the Nishmath Chaim, the spirit of life. Man is therefore both animal and divine. He shares with the animal all the physical appetites of eating and drinking and procreation, as of evacuation, but in addition to that there has been implanted in him a soul, and everything which is meant by soul, that spiritual unease which is called conscience, a desire for spiritual fulfilment, a striving for self-improvement. He is נפש חיה both נפש and חיה both soul and beast, and these two elements within him sometimes war with one another.

Such a conception of man and his spiritual struggles is, I believe, common to all religions, but the unique contribution of Judaism is the doctrine that one can serve God as passionately and sincerely with the animal side of one's nature as with the spiritual. כל עצמותי תאמרנה ה׳ מי כמוך "All my bones shall declare, O Lord, who is like unto thee," declares the Psalmist, and "all my bones" includes the physical side of Man as well as his spiritual. It has always been a matter of regret to me that a foolish convention and a false modesty has prevented me from drawing attention to one of the most beautiful of prayers in our whole liturgy which you will find on page 4 of the Prayer Book, and is actually the prayer which has to be recited when one has evacuated the waste matter from one's body, and a similar convention prevents me from referring at length to an even more beautiful prayer instituted prior to the consummation of one's marriage.

But fortunately that convention does not apply to the intake and the consumption of food. According to the well-known passage in the Ethics of the Fathers (iii: 4), the one and the same meal can constitute either "the sacrifices of dead idols," or "the table of the Omnipresent." The difference does not consist, as might be supposed, in whether the meal is kasher or not—although the considerations which I put forward apply equally to the dietary laws. It consists in whether, to quote the interpretation given to the words of the proof-verse, "the All-Present is in their thoughts" or not. When the spirit of God broods over the meal, the satisfactin of one's physical appetites becomes an act of service at the altar of the Lord, as acceptable as a service at the altar of the Temple. Where that thought is not present, the vigorous verse "for all their tables are full of vomit and filthiness" applies.

How are these thoughts induced? The author of the Mishnah suggests that it can come through speaking words of Torah at table, and of the truth of it there can be no question. But it can be equally induced by Kiddush and Zemiroth, by Grace Before and Grace After Meals. The Kiddush, as its name implies, sanctifies that meal and gives it spiritual content. One eats, so to speak, in the service of God.

That explanation suffices surely to justify the regulation that אין קדוש אלא במקום סעודה that Kiddush can be recited only where the meal is eaten. What place has it then in the Synagogue Service! According to this rule its recitation apart from a meal can be compared to making a blessing over wine without drinking the wine, which constitutes a ברכה לבטלה a blessing uttered for nothing, which in the last resort infringes the prohibition against taking the Name of the Lord in vain!

The answer to that question is a simple one. In Babylon and during the Middle Ages the Kiddush in Synagogues was in fact an introduction to a meal. Attached to the Synagogue was sleeping accommodation for wayfarers who happened to find themselves in the Community over the Sabbath. Naturally not only lodging but board was also provided and it was for them that the Kiddush was recited. It is for that reason that the Kiddush is not recited on Seder night. For on Seder night private hospitality took the place of communal hospitality. The Seder was no Seder unless the invitation כל דכפין ייתי ויכול "Whosoever is hungry let him come and eat" was fulfilled. There were no guests in the communal inn which was included in the Synagogue complex of buildings.

When in later centuries the Synagogues ceased to play that role there were not found wanting literal halachists who demanded the abolition of the Kiddush since it no longer conformed to the rule, but both the spiritual leaders and the members of the community resisted the demand, and it has remained, though its legal basis is wanting.

Needless to say, the reason which one sometimes hears that its recital in Synagogue is in order that those who do not make Kiddush at home may hear it is quite absurd. It is a sad commentary on the decline of religious observance that such a reason should be put forward, and I hope that there are none in this congregation to whom it applies.

Thus it is that in the Kiddush, as in the Magen Avot, we have enshrined a precious relic of a past which no longer obtains, but unlike the Magen Avot, it is a past which in a modified form shows encouraging signs of being revived in the future.

The conception of the Synagogue as merely a "Beth Tefillah" as a place of worship which is opened for religious worship and closed at the conclusion of the service is foreign and alien to the spirit of Judaism. It is one of the results of what one might call religious assimilation whereby in our forms and modes of worship we ape Christian custom. The accepted name of the Synagogue is Bet K'nesset, which means House of Assembly. To the Jew the Synagogue was the centre of the social as well as the religious life of the Community. Here he foregathered for all matters affecting his life. It was club and inn, it was meeting place and the place where all communal announcements were made. It was even his Parliament. And it is interesting that the word Knesset has been adopted for the name of Israel's Parliament.

When therefore we note with gratification the increasing tendency to transform the Synagogue from a Beth Tefillah to a Community Centre, where all religious, educational, social and philanthropic activities shall take place, it does not represent an innovation but a reversal of the original conception of the Synagogue. And of that fact the recital of Kiddush in the Synagogue is a constant reminder.

## ALENU AND THE CENSOR

I WISH to devote two sermons to that most beautiful of prayers, the Alenu, with which every service nowadays concludes. It is, as Abrahams says in his invaluable Companion to the Authorised Daily Prayer Book, which is now unfortunately out of print, "A notable instance of the transference to daily use of a prayer designed for a special occasion."

That special occasion was the Musaph service of Rosh Hashanah. That Musaph service is unique in that it includes within it thirty Scriptural verses which are called respectively, by virtue of their contents, מלכיות זכרונות and שופרות, ten verses in which God is referred to as King, ten in which he is referred to as "remembering" and ten whose subject is the sounding of the Shofar. Each of these sets of ten verses is preceded by a beautiful introduction and followed by an equally beautiful prayer. The whole composition is ascribed to Rab, the great founder of Talmudic studies in Babylon, and the father of the Babylonian Talmud, who lived in the first half of the third century. If you will refer to the Musaph service of Rosh Hashanah you will see that the Alenu prayer is nothing more or less than the Introduction to the Malchiyoth, including as its concluding verses the first two of the ten Scriptural verses which give this prayer its name, verses in which God is referred to as Sovereign of the Universe.

In the text which we have in our Prayer Books, however, there is a verse missing from the original. If you will read the first paragraph carefully, you will notice a peculiar hiatus. As it appears in our Prayer Books, it reads: "It is our duty to praise the Lord in all things . . . since he hath not made us like the nations of other lands, and hath not placed us like other families of the earth, since he hath not assigned unto us a portion as unto them, nor a lot as unto all their multitude. While we bend the knee and offer worship and thanks before the supreme King of Kings, the Holy One, blessed be He." It should appear obvious that there is something missing between the first verse and the second, that the contrast between the worship of the heathens and the worship of the Jews is left unexpressed. And in point of fact the original text, which is still included in the Sephardic Prayer Book, was: "For they bow down to vanity and emptiness and pray to a god that cannot save," upon which the antithesis "While we bend the knee and offer worship and thanks before the supreme King of Kings, etc.," follows naturally.

Incredible though it may sound, from the time that this Alenu prayer became part of the Daily Service, the accusation was levelled against it that the "Nations of the World" who are referred to as "bowing down to vanity and emptiness" were not heathen idolators but—Christians! In 1399 an apostate Jew called Pesach, who on baptism adopted the name of Peter, carried this outrageous accusation a stage further by maintaining that there was actually in it a veiled reference to the Founder of Christianity himself! How so? The numerical equivalent of the word וריק "And emptiness" is 316, which corresponds to the numerical equivalent of ישו, the Hebrew name for Jesus. Nor was the position eased by the peculiarly obnoxious habit, based upon the fact that the word translated "emptiness" can also mean "ordure," of spitting at the mention of the word!*

In vain the leading Rabbis of the 14th to the 18th century protested against this baseless and absurd accusation. Just over 400 years ago, for instance, Manasseh ben Israel,

* It is a remarkable example of the persistence of custom even after its reason has long ceased to obtain, that this custom persisted for centuries after the offending phrase had been expunged from the prayer.

in his famous Vindiciae Judaeorum, published in 1656, devoted a whole chapter of this work to a defence of this accusation, but it was all in vain. As late as 1777 a certain Professor Kypke, government inspector of the Konigsberg Synagogue, wrote a memorandum to the German Government repeating the allegation. Moses Mendelssohn wrote a counter-memorandum refuting the allegation, but all in vain. The Prussian Government issued an order that these words were to be omitted from the Prayer, and the Jews bowed to the decree. From that comparatively recent time the Alenu in the Ashkenazi rite omits these offending but by no means offensive words, whereas in the Sephardi rite they still obtain.

And so in our Prayer Book we have enshrined, embedded like a fossil remain, still another aspect of the life of the Jews in the Middle Ages, when the literature and even, as we see, the prayers, of the Jews were subjected to the heavy and malicious hand of the censor, lest, God forbid, the Jew might say something in his prayers, or study something in his sacred writings, which was not acceptable to the dominant faith. Anyone interested in pursuing this interesting subject further can be referred to the article on censorship in the Jewish Encyclopedia, but confining myself as I am to the Prayer Book, I wish to refer to a remarkable instance where the malevolent activity of the censor has had the effect of adding one of the most beautiful and impressive portions to our Sabbath Service! The Kedushah which is recited whenever the Amidah is repeated consists essentially of three passages of the Bible with suitable introductions. These passages are the Trishagion, the "Holy, Holy, Holy is the Lord of Hosts" from Isaiah, the "Blessed be the Glory of the Lord from His place" from Ezekiel, and "The Lord shall reign for ever, thy God, O Zion, unto all generations, Halleluyah" from Psalms. The Kedushah of Musaph, however, contains an addition which has become one of the most beautiful portions of our Service, but which has nothing whatsoever to do with the

Kedushah, which is the Sanctification of God by the angelic choir. It is the Declaration of the Faith of the Jew in the oneness of God, Shema Yisrael, and it concludes with the words "I am the Lord your God." As will readily be recognised, these two passages are the opening and closing verses of the three paragraphs of the Shema which forms an essential part of the Morning Service.

There was a period and a place in Jewish history when the Jews were actually forbidden by the Government to recite the Shema! It was in the Byzantine Empire during the sixth century, when the declaration of the Unity of God was regarded as a blatant attack upon the doctrine of the Trinity. It was not only the Jews who were forbidden to recite the Shema. Action was also taken against the Syrian Christians who, while accepting the Divinity of Jesus, denied the Trinity, and it is stated that it was their persecution by the Government authorities on these grounds in the seventh century which paved the way for their acceptance in the following century of Islam with its insistence on a pure monotheism. The decree against the recital of the Shema, however, was actually enforced by the appointment of Government inspectors who were posted in the Synagogues and were ordered to remain there during Shacharit in order to ensure that the Jewish worshippers did not offend the susceptibilities of the Christians by saying "Hear, O Israel, the Lord our God, the Lord is One." And there they remained until Shacharit was concluded, when they left. Whereupon the Chazanim introduced the custom of including the first sentence and the last of the Shema into the Kedushah of Musaph, and by the time the fatuous decree prohibiting the recital of the Shema was repealed, it had already become an integral part of the Kedushah, beloved by the people and therefore retained by them.

Thus it has come about that the impious attempts of our enemies to prevent us from worshipping God in our own way have not only left their permanent mark upon our

Prayer Books, but have in the end result brought about an intensification of our glorification of the One True God. For if on the one hand it has had the result of excluding from the original version of Alenu the sentence "For they bow down to vanity and emptiness and pray to a god that saveth not," on the other hand it has resulted in the most dramatic and meaningful proclamation of the undying faith of the Jew, when the attendance at Synagogue is at its maximum, and during the holiest portion of the service, when the congregation is standing, the Chazan and choir combine with the congregation in proclaiming "Hear, O Israel, the Lord our God, the Lord is One. One is our God; He is our Father, He is our King, He is our Saviour. And He of His mercy will let us hear a second time, in the presence of all living, His promise "To be to you for a God."

Thus do we turn the tables upon those who would have set up a barrier between Israel and their Father in Heaven. May we continue proudly and even defiantly to proclaim our faith in the One True God, the God of Israel.

# ALENU

A SUPERFICIAL reading of the Alenu prayer would inevitably lead one to believe that the two paragraphs of which it is composed were written by different authors with strikingly different outlooks upon Judaism. In the first paragraph the doctrine of Jewish particularism, of the concept of the Jews as the Chosen People, is stressed with an emphasis to which there is no parallel in the whole of our liturgy. It does not only say "Thou hast chosen us from all peoples," but in vigorous language it contrasts the worship of the true God by the Jews with the worship of emptiness and vanity by the Gentiles. It thanks God for making us different from them and our portion not as theirs.

But if in the first paragraph the doctrine of Jewish exclusiveness and election is stressed as in no other prayer, in the second paragraph we have an expression of universalism which also has no parallel in our liturgy for its breadth of outlook and for its concern with the salvation of the world as a whole. In it we pray for the acceptance of the sovereignty of God by every one of God's creatures, for the blessed day when "all the children of flesh will call upon thy Name," when "all the inhabitants of the world will perceive and know that unto thee every knee must bow, every tongue swear. . . . Let them all accept the yoke of thy kingdom and do thou reign over them speedily and for ever and ever."

Not only do we know, however, that both these portions are by one author, Rav, the famous founder of Talmudic studies in Babylon in the third century, but, as was pointed out last week, they are part of one and the same prayer, the Introduction to the Malchiyot which form part of the Musaph Service of Rosh Hashanah.

Not only so, but whatever incongruity may be felt by the modern reader of the prayer, it was certainly not felt by the author. The two words which introduce the second paragraph, על כן "therefore," surely presume that the second paragraph represents the *consequences* of the first; that the connection between the doctrine of Israel the Chosen People and the ultimate perfection of the world is the connection of cause and effect. *Because* we were placed in the position we were, *therefore* there is a hope of the world as a whole ultimately coming to accept the sovereignty of God.

That and that alone is the true conception of the much criticised theory of the Chosen People. It is a subject which has been treated so exhaustively that I do not intend to refer to it except in the briefest of terms. We believe that we were chosen to be the standard bearers of the Torah, of the revealed word of God, in order to bring the world ultimately to acknowledge the existence and sovereignty of God, and we believe that that selection, far from imposing special privileges upon the Jewish people, only places upon them added and heavy responsibilities. The classic utterance of Amos, "Only you have I known of all the families of the earth, therefore will I punish you for all your iniquities" (Amos iii: 2) expresses that idea for all time. And we believe that we are the Suffering Servant of the 53rd chapter of Isaiah, who suffer in the name of God, but whose reward shall be the ultimate acceptance of the knowledge of God by Mankind as a whole.

It is purely coincidental, but nonetheless instructive, that this sermon is being delivered on the Sabbath of Lech Lecha, the portion of the Scriptures which opens with the call of God to Abram, with which Jewish history begins. We read there that Abram and Sarah proceeded to the Promised Land with "the souls that they had gotten in

Haran" (xii: 5) and the interpretation of our Rabbis that it refers to those whom Abram and Sarah converted, "Abram converting the men and Sarah the women," is well known. Of that "conversion" there can be no doubt. The whole Scriptural record of Abram's life is studded with references to an awareness of God on the part of all those with whom he comes into contact, until at the end of his life he is able to refer to God as "the God of Heaven and the God of Earth" (xxiv: 3), whereas, when he received his call, He was but "God of Heaven" (v: 7).*

But nowhere is there any suggestion that that conversion was to Judaism, if we may so term the "charge, the Commandments, the statutes and the laws" (xxvi: 5) which he was commanded. The doctrine which he received was destined to be transmitted only by his lineal descendants until the family developed into a nation. In what then did that "conversion" consist? As already indicated, and succinctly expressed by Rashi, it was merely in the acknowledgment of the existence of God and his sovereignty in the world, and I have already devoted a sermon to the fact that we Jews do not believe that the salvation of the world depends upon the acceptance of Judaism.*

It also happens that last week I dealt with the savage treatment of Jewish religious literature by the censors, and confining myself as I did to two passages of our Prayer Book, I made only passing reference to their activities with other branches of religious literature. One of these passages is the magnificent last chapter of Maimonides' classic Mishneh Torah in which, in words of unforgettable beauty, he portrays the Messianic age when

> "In that era there will be neither famine nor war, neither jealousy nor strife. Blessings will be abundant, comforts within the reach of us all. The one preoccupation of the whole world will be to know

See Sermon No. 3, pp. 10 et seq.

> the Lord. Hence Israelites will be very wise, they will know the things that are now concealed and will attain an understanding of their Creator to the utmost capacity of the human mind, as it is written: For the earth shall be full of the knowledge of the Lord, as the waters cover the sea." (Isa. xi: 9.)

In the original text Maimonides includes a remarkable reference to the role which Christianity and Islam, the two ungrateful daughters of Judaism, are destined to play in bringing this about, and this passage was excised by the censor. After criticising the founder of Christianity, in that "All the Prophets affirmed that the Messiah would redeem Israel, save them, gather their dispersed, and confirm the commandments. But he caused Israel to be destroyed by the sword, their remnant to be dispersed and humiliated. He was instrumental in changing the Torah and causing the world to err and serve another beside God," he makes the following remarkable statement:

> "But it is beyond the human mind to fathom the designs of the Creator; for our ways are not His ways, neither are our thoughts His thoughts. All these matters relating to Jesus of Nazareth and the Ishmaelite (Mohammed) who came after him, only served to clear the way for King Messiah, to prepare the whole world to worship God with one accord, as it is written: For then I will turn to the peoples a pure language, that they may all call upon the name of the Lord to serve Him with one consent (Zeph. 3: 9). Thus the messianic hope, the Torah, and the commandments have become familiar topics—topics of conversation (among the inhabitants) of the far isles and many peoples, uncircumcised of heart and flesh. They are discussing these matters and the commandments of the Torah. Some say "Those commandments were true but have lost their validity and are no longer binding," others declare that they had an

> esoteric meaning and were not intended to be taken literally; that the Messiah has already come and revealed their occult significance. But when the true King Messiah will appear and succeed, be exalted and lifted up, they will forthwith recant and realize that they have inherited naught but lies from their fathers, that their prophets and forebears led them astray."

That is the ideal which Judaism sets before itself and which is the message of the beautiful prayer Alenu. We hold on tenaciously and faithfully to the Torah, and we give our daily thanks to God for making us its bearers, despite all the persecution, suffering, travail and sorrow which it has brought upon us. For as a result of our faith and our adherence to its details the knowledge of God will spread in the world, and that knowledge, imperfect and incomplete at first, will gradually become purified, until that blessed day when "The Lord will be King over the whole earth, in that day will the Lord be One and His Name One."

## YIGDAL—THE WORDS

THE first Mishnah of the tenth chapter of the tractate Sanhedrin reads "All Israelites have a share in the world to come, as it is said 'And the people shall be all righteous; they shall inherit the land for ever, the branch of my planting, the work of my hands that I may be glorified.'" This quotation from the Mishnah, as you will see by reference to page 184, is quoted in the Prayer Book as an introduction to the reading of each of the six chapters of the Ethics of the Fathers, and as it stands it sounds a very comforting doctrine. It suggests that because we are Jews we all possess, so to speak, reserved seats in Paradise, and each of us can claim that right. But alas, the Mishnah does not stop there. It continues: "And these are they that have no share in the world to come" and proceeds to enumerate certain heretical beliefs acceptance of which deny the Jew the pre-emptive right to the world to come which otherwise he could claim. When we take these two halves of the Mishnah together, it is an entirely different doctrine which is thus propounded. It says that each Jew has within him the seed of immortality, the potentiality of projecting his existence beyond the grave, but he can, by his conduct or false beliefs, lose this boon. It is a reflection of the belief to which I have so often referred of the intrinsic and natural goodness of man which, however, he can warp and corrupt.

When, however, in the twelfth century that greatest luminary of Medieval Judaism, Moses ben Maimon, known as the Rambam, came to write the first of his trilogy of epoch-making works, his Commentary on the Mishnah, he took this Mishnah as the basis upon which to propound a view which was distinctly original and novel, and which to a definite extent runs counter to one of the cherished popular beliefs of Judaism. That belief is expressed in the well-known statement ישראל אע״פ שחטא ישראל הוא Even if the Jew sins he remains a Jew, that there is no power in the world to deny the person who is born a Jew of his birthright. He may be a sinful Jew, a heretical Jew, a renegade Jew, but Jew he remains. So powerful is this conception that it is part of Jewish law to the extent that even an apostate Jew is regarded legally as still belonging to the Community.

Against this view Maimonides puts forward an idea which is entirely original. Accepting the phrase "They have no portion of the world to come" as synonymous with "They thereby cease to be regarded as Jews," for the first time in the history of Jewish thought (with the exception of the Alexandrian Jewish philosopher, Philo, who is outside the current of the development of Jewish thought) he propounds the idea that there are principles of Judaism which are fundamental to the faith, the non-acceptance of which deprive the born Jew of his right to "the world to come," that is, that he has thereby renounced Judaism.

The view of Maimonides and his formulation by no means went uncontested. On the one hand there were those who, in accordance with the view that "the Jew even though he sins, is still a Jew," denied that Judaism possessed any dogmas at all, and the clearest expression of this view is given by Moses Mendelssohn, who put forward the thesis that Judaism posits freedom of thought and conformity in action. On the other hand there were those who denied that of the divine law it is not possible for man to differentiate between the important and the unimportant, the fundamental and the secondary. Is there a greater authority in Judaism than R. Judah Ha-Nasi, the compiler of the Mishnah, and did he not say "Be as heedful of a light precept as of a grave one, for thou knowest not the grant of reward for each precept"? (Ethics ii: 1.) And lastly there were those who while accepting the principle of dogmas in Judaism queried the accuracy or validity of the enumeration of Maimonides. To that question, for instance, the last Jewish philosopher of Spain, R. Joseph Albo, in the fifteenth century devoted his famous work Ikkarim (Principles) in which he maintained that Maimonides had regarded as principles what were in fact derivatives, and maintained that there were but three dogmas in Judaism, belief in God, in revelation and in divine retribution. An excellent review of the subject can be found in the Annotated Prayer Book, pp. 248/9. Nevertheless, despite the might and logic of these objections, the unquestioned Talmudic authority of Maimonides caused his formulation to be accepted throughout the Jewish world as the fundamental creed of Judaism.

This formulation has found its place in our Prayer Book in two versions, one in prose and one in metrical form. The prose version is to be found on page 89 of Singer's Prayer Book, each of the principles being introduced with the words אני מאמין באמונה שלמה "I believe with a perfect faith." It should be pointed out, however, that this formula is not due to Maimonides. In recent years since the holocaust of the Jews in Europe, the twelfth of these thirteen principles, the belief of the coming of the Messiah has been immortalised as the song of faith of the victims of the extermination camp and crematoria as they went to their death, and the version of our Chief Cantor has received world-wide recognition.

The metrical version is Yigdal. It consists of thirteen lines, each one of which is a formulation in poetry of one of the thirteen principles, while the Sefardi version adds a fourteenth line stating specifically: "These thirteen are the principles of the faith." It is an interesting exercise to compare each principle in the prose version with its equivalent poetic version and to see how beautifully the author has succeeded in conveying in a few words the principle of faith. According to Samuel David Luzatto its author was Daniel b. Judah, Dayyan of Rome in the 15th century. He spent eight years improving and perfecting it until it was completed in 1404.

In the seventeenth century the author of the liturgical work, Yosef Ometz, refers to the custom prevalent in Germany in his day of reading it after every service. In the course of time it was limited to the Sabbath and Festival evening service.

Among those who objected to Maimonides' formulation of principles were the Cabbalists who maintained that each and every one of the traditional 613 commandments of the Torah is tantamount to an article of faith. As a result the Chassidim, who were so greatly influenced by the Cabbala, do not sing this hymn at the end of the service.

That is the origin and history of the text of this popular hymn. Next week I shall tell you the remarkable story of its popular melody.

## YIGDAL—THE MELODY

A FEW weeks ago I was approached by a certain organisation with an unusual request. At a local girls' high school, which has a large number of Jewish pupils, the headmistress had had printed a hymn book which was to be used by the whole school at assembly. The organisation which approached me was anxious to know whether all the hymns were suitable for Jewish girls and asked me to "vet" the volume as the headmistress had gladly undertaken not to have such hymns as were not acceptable to the Jewish girls. I went through it carefully, and it is only fair to state that an honest and praiseworthy attempt had been made to select only such hymns as were non-denominational in content and as such could not offend the religious susceptibilities of Jews. Of the 148 hymns in the hymnal there were only five to which I could take exception, and of those five, one was headed "T. Olivers, 1725-1799. Hebrew Melody." And thereby hangs the tale which is the subject of my sermon this evening.

There is a famous short story by Peretz called "The Gilgul of a Niggun" or "The Transmigration of a Melody" which describes how a melody which originated in the ecstasy of a Chassidic Rabbi degenerated into a popular tune sung in a public bar. And I want to-night to tell you the entertaining story of the "Gilgul" of another Jewish melody, that of Yigdal, which is sung on Friday night, a "Gilgul" whereby it has found its way into—the Hymn Book of the Methodist Church!

In the year 1767 the Great Synagogue of London acquired the services of a new Chazan, Myer Lyon. He was engaged at a salary of £40.0.0 per annum, but five years later the finances of the Synagogue were in such a parlous state that the salaries of all officials were reduced, and that of the Chazan was lowered to £32.0.0 per annum. His voice, however, was one of surpassing sweetness, and visitors, both Jews and non-Jews, used to visit the Synagogue in order to enjoy his singing. His fame as a singer spread, and under the name of Leoni he became a well-known opera singer at Covent Garden, where he sang every night, except Friday nights and Festivals. Whether it was because of his religious beliefs, or whether because he was "otherwise engaged" in Synagogue, I do not know. However, he subsequently relinquished his position as Chazan of the Great Synagogue and became joint manager of an English opera house in Dublin. He later decided to return to his sacred calling and was appointed Chazan to the Ashkenazi Congregation of Kingston, Jamaica, being the first qualified Chazan in the English Colonies. There he died in 1796.

Myer Lyon was the composer of the melody Yigdal which we sing on Friday evenings, and which has become traditional in English Synagogues. But it is not only in English Synagogues that that melody can be heard!

In 1770 the Rev. Charles Wesley, the hymn-writer, and brother to the Rev. John Wesley, the founder of the Wesleyan Methodist Church, together with Thomas Olivers, another Wesleyan Minister, attended a service in the Great Synagogue, in order to hear this famous Chazan. In his journal Charles Wesley has the following flattering reference to this memorable visit: "I was desirous to hear Mr. Leoni sing at the Jewish Synagogue . . . I never indeed saw a Jewish Congregation behave so decently. Indeed, the place itself is so solemn that it might strike an awe upon those who have any thought of God." It is not, however, with Charles Wesley's reaction to the service, but with Olivers' that we are here concerned. There is a long article on this divine in the Dictionary of National Biography which gives an impressive list of his many publications, one of which is "Hymn to the God of Abraham," to which is added the comment: "It is upon this hymn, now to be found in nearly all collections, that Olivers' fame chiefly rests." It is this hymn which is included in the local school hymnal to which I have referred and its origin is the direct result of that memorable visit to the Great Synagogue in 1770. Olivers was so impressed by the beauty of this melody that he asked Lyon's permission to use it for a hymn. Lyon, or Leoni as he was known in the world of opera, granted his request and gave him a copy of the melody which Olivers immediately used, and in the house of a certain John Bakewell, in Westminster, he sat down and wrote this hymn beginning

The God of Abraham praise
Who reigns enthroned above
Ancient of everlasting days
And God of love.
Jehovah Great I am
By earth and heaven confessed,
I bow and bless the sacred name
For ever blessed.*

It is in the third verse that the Christological reference which caused me to exclude it is to be found.

The hymn became an immediate success. In two years eight editions were reprinted and by 1779 a thirtieth edition had been reached. Olivers paid generous tribute to the author of the melody, and in the Methodist Hymn Book it is indexed as "Leoni" after the name of its Chazan-author and "Yigdal" after the name of the hymn.

A reference to that hymn will show that its contents have little if any affinity with the contents of Yigdal, about which I spoke last week, and that all that Olivers took

* The version here given is different from that found in some hymnals.

was the melody and the metre which he adapted to his own words, and its only connection with Yigdal and Jewish worship is in its name "Leoni" or "Yigdal" and in its melody.

In the twentieth century editions of the Methodist Hymn Book, however, there is another hymn which is also called Leoni, and is, of course, sung to the same melody. This hymn differs entirely from the original Leoni hymn written by Thomas Olivers in 1770. It is actually a *translation* in metre of Yigdal, and the translation is ascribed to a Rabbi Max Landsberg who died in Rochester, U.S.A., in 1928. When, many years ago, while still in England, I came across this curiosity, I wrote to the Rev. F. Luke Wiseman, B.A., D.D., an authority on the Methodist Hymn Book, and he informed me that this hymn "is frequently used" in their church services. I wonder whether those congregations, when they sing this hymn, to the melody composed by a London Chazan in 1770, are aware that they are giving expression to those principles which the greatest authority in Medieval Judaism, Maimonides, formulated as the creed of loyalty to Judaism!

But whether they are aware of it or not, the remarkable fact cannot be gainsaid that the Thirteen Principles of the Jewish Faith, the Ani Ma'amin of Judaism, formulated in the twelfth century by Maimonides, on the basis of a Mishnah compiled in the Second Century, rendered in metrical version according to the strict rules of Neo-Hebrew poetry which borrowed the metre from Arabic poetry, by Daniel b. Judah Dayyan of Rome in the fifteenth century, and translated into English by Rabbi Max Landsberg of the United States in the twentieth century, is sung to the inspiring melody of an English Chazan of the eighteenth century in the Methodist churches!

This phenomenon is all the more remarkable when we consider the extreme paucity of hymns in our liturgy. The only parts of our Sabbath service which can be called hymns are Lecha Dodi, Yigdal, Adon Olam and En Celohenu, and that one of these four, and that the most specifically Jewish in content, should find its way by two roads into a Church hymnal is nothing short of astonishing. Are we not entitled to give it the title of Peretz' short story, "The Gilgul of a Melody," as well as "The Gilgul of a Hymn"?

## THE SERMON

יהיו לרצון אמרי פי והגיון לבי לפניך ה׳ צורי וגואלי

*May the words of my mouth and the meditation of my heart be acceptable before Thee, O Lord, my Rock and my Redeemer.*

(Psalm xix: 15.)

I COMMENCED this unique series of sermons with the verse "O Lord, open thou my lips, and my mouth shall declare thy praise" (Psalm li: 17), which is the introductory verse of the Amidah, and I bring the series to an end with this verse from the nineteenth Psalm with which we conclude the Amidah. It is the silent prayer which I always recite to myself as I enter the pulpit, a prayer that my thoughts and words be acceptable, not to the congregation, which is a secondary consideration, but to God whose will I try to interpret. But despite that, the success of a sermon can be gauged only by the effect it has upon the congregation, and on reviewing this interesting experiment in preaching, I must say that I am more than gratified by the success which has attended it. But how can one accurately or even approximately gauge the success of a sermon or a series of sermons? In making this claim of success I refer only to the sustained and remarkable attendance in Synagogue during the year that this series has been delivered, and to the rustling sound of hundreds of pages being turned over when I indicated where the text is to be found in the Prayer Book. These I confess are purely empirical and rule of thumb tests, but, although the sermon cannot be properly regarded as part of the traditional Friday night service, I am presuming to conclude this series by speaking of the effect of the sermon itself.

At the Labour Party Congress recently held in London, a resolution was proposed in favour of the abolition of hydrogen-bomb tests by England. It seemed as though the resolution stood a fair chance of being passed, in which case it would presumably have become the official policy of the Labour Party, when opposition came to it from a most unexpected quarter, and that opposition served to decide the issue in favour of the defeat, or the withdrawal of the resolution. Aneurin Bevan, who belongs to the left wing of the Labour Party and who might therefore be regarded as closest in sympathy to Communist Russia, which has consistently urged the abolition of these tests, to the general surprise of all those present vigorously opposed the resolution, and in what the "Sunday Times" called "a typically brilliant flash of imagery," told the Congress that if Britain were to abolish the hydrogen bomb unilaterally "you would send your Foreign Secretary naked into the conference chamber, only able to preach sermons."

This "brilliant flash of imagery" depends upon the belief, of course, of the utter futility of a sermon as a means of influencing opinion, and no doubt Mr. Bevan, considering the very real effect which his speech had in deciding the fate of the resolution against which he was speaking, could not possibly have included in his disparaging reference to a sermon the oratorical fireworks of which he is such a master. In his belief that לא המדרש עיקר אלא המעשה "It is not words that are important, but actions"—the "words" being the sermon and the "action" the effect of an H.-bomb with a power of 10 million tons of T.N.T.—he surely confined himself to pulpit utterances.

That is one extreme of the views entertained of the possible efficacy of a sermon. The other extreme can best be described by an anecdote. Some years ago when Israel stood in a position of almost complete and certainly unsplendid isolation at UNO, when both the West led by America and the East under the leadership of Russia were courting the Afro-Asian bloc by supporting them in their implacable hostility to the State of Israel, I had a conversation with a highly placed official in the Government of Israel. I told him that Mr. Abba Eban was one of the most brilliant orators in the world and that when he spoke at UNO the hall normally filled up. But, I added, Israel was making a characteristic Jewish mistake in imagining that diplomatic victories are won by verbal *tours de force*. It is in the corridors and over a drink, in understandings and "deals" that these victories are gained. To my pleased surprise he agreed with me and said "It reminds me of Rabbi X." I asked him to explain, which he did. Whenever Israel is faced by a crisis of any magnitude, he said, the Rabbi in question announces that he will make it the topic of his sermon on the following Sabbath. Entering the pulpit he delivers himself of a fiery fulmination, at the conclusion of which he rubs his hands in satisfaction and declares, "Well, that's settled that!"

These two examples represent the two extremes of the value and potential efficacy of the sermon, the one taking it as the metaphor of utter and complete futility, the other as the panacea for all evils. And needless to say the truth lies somewhere between those two extremes, though he would indeed be foolhardy who would attempt to pinpoint with accuracy the exact point between those two extremes of futility and usefulness at which the sermon can be placed. There are times when the preacher himself, in a moment of gloomy introspection, when he considers how, week in and week out, Sabbath after Sabbath and year after year, delivers himself of the best of which he is humanly capable, exhorting, admonishing, expounding and instructing, and yet he sees no sign of any improvement in the religious loyalties or moral standards of his flock, is filled with the utmost pessimism, and inclines to the opinion of an Aneurin Bevan. There are others when he feels that he has captured the soul of his hearers, opened up to them new spiritual horizons and brought about a change of direction in their lives, that he feels that perhaps it has been worthwhile. The sermon has both a transmitting and a receiving end. If it fails it may well be due to a faulty transmitter, who is the preacher, which has blurred or distorted the message or not delivered it with sufficient clarity. But there is equally the possibility that the fault lies at the receiving end. The receiving apparatus, which is the hearer, may not be properly tuned in, and it even happens that the person at the receiving end switches off the apparatus completely !

It is worthwhile to pursue this metaphor a little further. Each and every one of us has his favourite programme on the wireless, which depends upon the character and education of the hearer. The person who wishes to keep abreast of affairs will listen to the news, the sporting fan to the sports commentary. Those who have no sense of musical appreciation will enjoy jazz and remain completely uninterested in a symphony concert. The music lover will eagerly scan the programme to know when classical music can be heard, and faithfully tunes in to it. But imagine a person who comes into a room where the wireless is turned on and he has no possibility of turning it off. He cannot exercise physical selectivity, but he can and does exercise mental selectivity. He does not attune his mind to listen to the programme in which he is not interested and allows the sound to pass over his head. It is when the programme is after his own heart that he attunes his mind and absorbs it. And yet, even in his unreceptive moments he is in a different position to the person who has switched off the apparatus. Unconsciously his mind can become arrested by a phrase, a bar of music, an item of news, and he absorbs something which he would not of his own volition have done.

So it is with the congregation who are on the receiving end of the sermon. There is the sermon which represents the programme which the hearer likes *a priori*. The preacher expresses an idea which puts into words the inchoate thoughts of the hearer, and it meets with his instant and unreserved approval. I had an experience with regard to that recently which caused me considerable amusement. Some months ago a controversy raged in the Press about the desirability and moral rightness of lotteries. A reference to the casting of lots in the Sidra decided me to give the Jewish view of lotteries, in which I expressed my opinion that not only did Jewish ethics see nothing wrong in a lottery but that since in Jewish theology nothing was regarded as purely fortuitous chance, there might even be something divine in it. It was the lightest of sermons, but everyone in the congregation who held a ticket for the Rhodesian or Irish sweepstake was delighted, and one congregant congratulated me expansively on "the best sermon I had ever given"!

Then there is what I might term the "news" sermon. It is the sermon which is essentially instructive and expository. To the person who wishes to increase his knowledge of Judaism the sermon will make its instant and sustained appeal; the one to whom Judaism is but a religious exercise will be quite uninterested. But, of course, there are exciting items of news which attract the attention of everyone, and when the preacher takes as his theme some topical event which looms large on the mental horizon he gets an almost complete attention.

But lastly there is the sermon which deals with a subject with which his congregation is not in agreement. The controversial sermon, the sermon which deals with a prevalent social evil, which attempts to jerk the mind of the hearer out of his mood of smug, self-satisfied complacency with himself, which urges the adoption of a higher moral, ethical or religious standard, which exhorts, admonishes, reproves and sometimes castigates. The listener does not want to hear it; he sets up a barrier of mental rejection. It is in this type of sermon that the preacher experiences his greatest sense of frustration. What boots it, he says to himself, all this expenditure of energy, all this admonition and exhortation? Where does it lead? Do not his words flow over the head of his audience like the wireless programme to which a listener listens willy-nilly? Where is the "Tachlis"? Where the results? And then in his mood of despondency there comes evidence that it is not all in vain as he thought. A phrase settles in the mind of his hearer, a thought germinates and takes root, an idea is born. The word of God, an ethical attribute, forces its way through the barrier of indifference and rejection and slowly and almost invisibly begins to affect the persons to whom they are addressed. The soul is led to God, the earthly gives way to that which is pure and true, and imperceptibly the religious climate of the congregation is improved. The seed is not all cast in vain. Here and there it finds fertile soil in which to take root.

That has been my hope in this series of sermons as it has been in all my sermons. It is my prayer that they have had the effect which I expressed as a hope in the foreword of my first published volume of sermons to "serve as a powerful impetus to Jewish faith and loyalty and as an effective inspiration to noble living."

# EVENING SERVICE FOR SABBATH

*On Chanukah and Purim the following is added:—*

We thank thee also for the miracles, for the redemption, for the mighty deeds and saving acts, wrought by thee, as well as for the wars which thou didst wage for our fathers in days of old, at this season.

*On Chanukah.*

In the days of the Hasmonean, Mattathias son of Johannan, the High Priest, and his sons, when the iniquitous power of Greese rose up against thy people Israel to make them forgetful of thy Law, and to force them to transgress the statutes of thy will, then didst thou in thine abundant mercy rise up for them in the midst of their trouble; thou didst plead their cause, thou didst judge their suit, thou didst avenge their wrong; thou deliveredst the strong into the hands of the weak, the many into the hands of the few, the impure into the hands of the pure, the wicked into the hands of the righteous, and the arrogant into the hands of them that occupied themselves with thy Law: for thyself thou didst make a great and holy name in the world, and for thy people Israel thou didst work a great deliverance and redemption as at this day. And thereupon thy children came into the oracle of thy house, cleansed thy temple, purified thy sanctuary, kindled lights in thy holy courts, and appointed these eight days of Chanukah in order to give thanks and praises unto thy great name.

*On Purim.*

In the days of Mordecai and Esther, in Shushan the capital, when the wicked Haman rose up against them, and sought to destroy, to slay and make to perish all the Jews, both young and old, little children and women, on one day, on the thirteenth day of the twelfth month, which is the month of Adar, and to take the spoil of them for a prey,—then didst thou in thine abundant mercy bring his counsel to nought, didst frustrate his design, and return his recompense upon his own head; and they hanged him and his sons upon the gallows.

*On* חֲנֻכָּה *and* פּוּרִים *the following is added :—*

עַל הַנִּסִּים וְעַל הַפֻּרְקָן וְעַל הַגְּבוּרוֹת וְעַל הַתְּשׁוּעוֹת וְעַל הַמִּלְחָמוֹת שֶׁעָשִׂיתָ לַאֲבוֹתֵינוּ בַּיָּמִים הָהֵם בַּזְּמַן הַזֶּה :

*On* חֲנֻכָּה.

בִּימֵי מַתִּתְיָהוּ בֶּן־יוֹחָנָן כֹּהֵן גָּדוֹל חַשְׁמוֹנַאי וּבָנָיו כְּשֶׁעָמְדָה מַלְכוּת יָוָן הָרְשָׁעָה עַל־עַמְּךָ יִשְׂרָאֵל לְהַשְׁכִּיחָם תּוֹרָתֶךָ וּלְהַעֲבִירָם מֵחֻקֵּי רְצוֹנֶךָ · וְאַתָּה בְּרַחֲמֶיךָ הָרַבִּים עָמַדְתָּ לָהֶם בְּעֵת צָרָתָם · רַבְתָּ אֶת־רִיבָם דַּנְתָּ אֶת־דִּינָם נָקַמְתָּ אֶת־נִקְמָתָם · מָסַרְתָּ גִבּוֹרִים בְּיַד חַלָּשִׁים וְרַבִּים בְּיַד מְעַטִּים וּטְמֵאִים בְּיַד טְהוֹרִים וּרְשָׁעִים בְּיַד צַדִּיקִים וְזֵדִים בְּיַד עוֹסְקֵי תוֹרָתֶךָ · וּלְךָ עָשִׂיתָ שֵׁם גָּדוֹל וְקָדוֹשׁ בְּעוֹלָמֶךָ וּלְעַמְּךָ יִשְׂרָאֵל עָשִׂיתָ תְּשׁוּעָה גְדוֹלָה וּפֻרְקָן כְּהַיּוֹם הַזֶּה · וְאַחַר כֵּן בָּאוּ בָנֶיךָ לִדְבִיר בֵּיתֶךָ וּפִנּוּ אֶת־הֵיכָלֶךָ וְטִהֲרוּ אֶת־מִקְדָּשֶׁךָ וְהִדְלִיקוּ נֵרוֹת בְּחַצְרוֹת קָדְשֶׁךָ · וְקָבְעוּ שְׁמוֹנַת יְמֵי חֲנֻכָּה אֵלּוּ לְהוֹדוֹת וּלְהַלֵּל לְשִׁמְךָ הַגָּדוֹל :

*On* פּוּרִים.

בִּימֵי מָרְדְּכַי וְאֶסְתֵּר בְּשׁוּשַׁן הַבִּירָה כְּשֶׁעָמַד עֲלֵיהֶם הָמָן הָרָשָׁע · בִּקֵּשׁ לְהַשְׁמִיד לַהֲרוֹג וּלְאַבֵּד אֶת־כָּל־הַיְּהוּדִים מִנַּעַר וְעַד זָקֵן טַף וְנָשִׁים בְּיוֹם אֶחָד בִּשְׁלוֹשָׁה־עָשָׂר לְחֹדֶשׁ שְׁנֵים־עָשָׂר הוּא־חֹדֶשׁ אֲדָר וּשְׁלָלָם לָבוֹז · וְאַתָּה בְּרַחֲמֶיךָ הָרַבִּים הֵפַרְתָּ אֶת־עֲצָתוֹ וְקִלְקַלְתָּ אֶת־מַחֲשַׁבְתּוֹ וַהֲשֵׁבוֹתָ גְּמוּלוֹ בְּרֹאשׁוֹ וְתָלוּ אֹתוֹ וְאֶת־בָּנָיו עַל־הָעֵץ :

*On New Moon and the Intermediate Days of Passover and Tabernacles the following to "merciful God and King" is added:—*

Our God and God of our fathers! May our remembrance rise, come and be accepted before thee, with the remembrance of our fathers, of Messiah the son of David thy servant, of Jerusalem the holy city, and of all thy people the house of Israel, bringing deliverance and well-being, grace, lovingkindness and mercy, life and peace on this day of

*On New Moon say—*

the New Moon.

*On Passover—*

the Feast of Unleavened Bread.

*On Tabernacles—*

the Feast of Tabernacles.

Remember us, O Lord our God, thereon for our well-being; be mindful of us for blessing, and save us unto life: by thy promise of salvation and mercy, spare us and be gracious unto us: have mercy upon us and save us; for our eyes are bent upon thee, because thou art a gracious and merciful God and King.

*On* רֹאשׁ חֹדֶשׁ *and* חוֹל הַמּוֹעֵד *of* פֶּסַח *and of* סֻכּוֹת, *the following to* וְרַחוּם אָתָּה *is added :*

אֱלֹהֵינוּ וֵאלֹהֵי אֲבוֹתֵינוּ · יַעֲלֶה וְיָבֹא וְיַגִּיעַ וְיֵרָאֶה וְיֵרָצֶה וְיִשָּׁמַע וְיִפָּקֵד וְיִזָּכֵר זִכְרוֹנֵנוּ וּפִקְדוֹנֵנוּ · וְזִכְרוֹן אֲבוֹתֵינוּ · וְזִכְרוֹן מָשִׁיחַ בֶּן דָּוִד עַבְדֶּךָ · וְזִכְרוֹן יְרוּשָׁלַיִם עִיר קָדְשֶׁךָ · וְזִכְרוֹן כָּל עַמְּךָ בֵּית יִשְׂרָאֵל לְפָנֶיךָ · לִפְלֵיטָה וּלְטוֹבָה וּלְחֵן וּלְחֶסֶד וּלְרַחֲמִים וּלְחַיִּים וּלְשָׁלוֹם בְּיוֹם

| *On* רֹאשׁ חֹדֶשׁ *say*— | *On* פֶּסַח— | *On* סֻכּוֹת— |
|---|---|---|
| רֹאשׁ הַחֹדֶשׁ | חַג הַמַּצּוֹת | חַג הַסֻּכּוֹת |

הַזֶּה · זָכְרֵנוּ יְיָ אֱלֹהֵינוּ בּוֹ לְטוֹבָה · וּפָקְדֵנוּ בוֹ לִבְרָכָה · וְהוֹשִׁיעֵנוּ בוֹ לְחַיִּים · וּבִדְבַר יְשׁוּעָה וְרַחֲמִים חוּס וְחָנֵּנוּ וְרַחֵם עָלֵינוּ וְהוֹשִׁיעֵנוּ · כִּי אֵלֶיךָ עֵינֵינוּ · כִּי אֵל מֶלֶךְ חַנּוּן וְרַחוּם אָתָּה :

4. He was before anything that hath been created—even the first: but his existence had no beginning.

5. Behold he is the Lord of the universe: to every creature he teacheth his greatness and his sovereignty.

6. The rich gift of his prophecy he gave unto the men of his choice, in whom he gloried.

7. There hath never yet arisen in Israel a prophet like unto Moses, one who hath beheld his similitude.

8. The Law of truth God gave unto his people by the hand of his prophet, who was faithful in his house.

9. God will not alter nor change his Law to everlasting for any other.

10. He watcheth and knoweth our secret thoughts: he beholdeth the end of a thing before it existeth.

11. He bestoweth lovingkindness upon a man according to his work; he giveth to the wicked evil according to his wickedness.

12. He will send our anointed at the end of days, to redeem them that wait for the end—his salvation.

13. In the abundance of his lovingkindness God will quicken the dead. Blessed for evermore be his glorious name.

---

*On the Eve of Sabbaths and of Holydays it is customary for Parents, either at the conclusion of the Service in Synagogue, or upon reaching their Home, to pronounce the following benediction upon their Children:—*

*To Sons say:—*

God make thee as Ephraim and Manasseh.

*To Daughters say:—*

God make thee as Sarah, Rebekah, Rachael and Leah.

*To Sons and Daughters:—*

The Lord bless thee, and keep thee: the Lord make his face to shine upon thee, and be gracious unto thee: the Lord turn his face unto thee, and give thee peace.

קַדְמוֹן לְכָל־דָּבָר אֲשֶׁר נִבְרָא ׃ רִאשׁוֹן וְאֵין רֵאשִׁית לְרֵאשִׁיתוֹ ׃

הִנּוֹ אֲדוֹן עוֹלָם ׃ לְכָל־נוֹצָר יוֹרֶה גְדֻלָּתוֹ וּמַלְכוּתוֹ ׃

שֶׁפַע נְבוּאָתוֹ נְתָנוֹ אֶל־אַנְשֵׁי סְגֻלָּתוֹ וְתִפְאַרְתּוֹ ׃

לֹא קָם בְּיִשְׂרָאֵל כְּמֹשֶׁה עוֹד נָבִיא ׃ וּמַבִּיט אֶת־תְּמוּנָתוֹ ׃

תּוֹרַת אֱמֶת נָתַן לְעַמּוֹ אֵל ׃ עַל יַד נְבִיאוֹ נֶאֱמַן בֵּיתוֹ ׃

לֹא יַחֲלִיף הָאֵל וְלֹא יָמִיר דָּתוֹ לְעוֹלָמִים לְזוּלָתוֹ ׃

צוֹפֶה וְיוֹדֵעַ סְתָרֵינוּ ׃ מַבִּיט לְסוֹף דָּבָר בְּקַדְמָתוֹ ׃

גּוֹמֵל לְאִישׁ חֶסֶד כְּמִפְעָלוֹ ׃ נוֹתֵן לְרָשָׁע רָע כְּרִשְׁעָתוֹ ׃

יִשְׁלַח לְקֵץ יָמִין מְשִׁיחֵנוּ ׃ לִפְדּוֹת מְחַכֵּי קֵץ יְשׁוּעָתוֹ ׃

מֵתִים יְחַיֶּה אֵל בְּרֹב חַסְדּוֹ ׃ בָּרוּךְ עֲדֵי עַד שֵׁם תְּהִלָּתוֹ ׃

*When a Festival or one of the Intermediate Days of a Festival falls on Sabbath, the Inauguration Service commences with* מִזְמוֹר שִׁיר, *p. 112.*

### תהלים צ׳ה

לְכוּ נְרַנְּנָה לַייָ נָרִיעָה לְצוּר יִשְׁעֵנוּ: נְקַדְּמָה פָנָיו בְּתוֹדָה בִּזְמִרוֹת נָרִיעַ לוֹ: כִּי אֵל גָּדוֹל יְיָ וּמֶלֶךְ גָּדוֹל עַל־כָּל־אֱלֹהִים: אֲשֶׁר בְּיָדוֹ מֶחְקְרֵי־אָרֶץ וְתוֹעֲפוֹת הָרִים לוֹ: אֲשֶׁר־לוֹ הַיָּם וְהוּא עָשָׂהוּ וְיַבֶּשֶׁת יָדָיו יָצָרוּ: בֹּאוּ נִשְׁתַּחֲוֶה וְנִכְרָעָה נִבְרְכָה לִפְנֵי־יְיָ עֹשֵׂנוּ: כִּי הוּא אֱלֹהֵינוּ וַאֲנַחְנוּ עַם מַרְעִיתוֹ וְצֹאן יָדוֹ הַיּוֹם אִם־בְּקֹלוֹ תִשְׁמָעוּ: אַל־תַּקְשׁוּ לְבַבְכֶם כִּמְרִיבָה כְּיוֹם מַסָּה בַּמִּדְבָּר: אֲשֶׁר נִסּוּנִי אֲבוֹתֵיכֶם בְּחָנוּנִי גַּם־רָאוּ פָעֳלִי: אַרְבָּעִים שָׁנָה אָקוּט בְּדוֹר וָאֹמַר עַם תֹּעֵי לֵבָב הֵם וְהֵם לֹא־יָדְעוּ דְרָכָי: אֲשֶׁר־נִשְׁבַּעְתִּי בְאַפִּי אִם־יְבֹאוּן אֶל־מְנוּחָתִי:

### תהלים צ׳ו

שִׁירוּ לַייָ שִׁיר חָדָשׁ שִׁירוּ לַייָ כָּל־הָאָרֶץ: שִׁירוּ לַייָ בָּרְכוּ שְׁמוֹ בַּשְּׂרוּ מִיּוֹם־לְיוֹם יְשׁוּעָתוֹ: סַפְּרוּ בַגּוֹיִם כְּבוֹדוֹ

## Psalm xcv.

*When a Festival or one of the Intermediate Days of a Festival falls on Sabbath, the Inauguration Service commences with "A Psalm, a Song, etc.," p. 112.*

O come, let us exult before the Lord: let us shout for joy to the rock of our salvation. Let us come before his presence with thanksgiving: let us shout for joy unto him with psalms. For the Lord is a great God, and a great king above all gods. In his hand are the deep places of the earth; the heights of the mountains are his also. The sea is his and he made it; and his hands formed the dry land. O come, let us worship and bow down; let us kneel before the Lord our Maker. For he is our God, and we are the people of his pasture, and the sheep of his hand. To-day, O that ye would hearken to his voice! Harden not your hearts as at Meribah, as in the day of Massah in the wilderness: when your fathers tempted me, and proved me, although they had seen my work. Forty years long was I wearied with that generation, and said, It is a people that do err in their heart, and they have not known my ways. Wherefore I sware in my wrath, that they should not enter into my rest.

## Psalm xcvi.

O sing unto the Lord a new song: sing unto the Lord, all the earth. Sing unto the Lord, bless his name: proclaim his salvation from day to day. Recount his glory among

בְּכָל־הָעַמִּים נִפְלְאוֹתָיו: כִּי גָדוֹל יְיָ וּמְהֻלָּל מְאֹד נוֹרָא הוּא עַל־כָּל־אֱלֹהִים: כִּי כָּל־אֱלֹהֵי הָעַמִּים אֱלִילִים וַיְיָ שָׁמַיִם עָשָׂה: הוֹד־וְהָדָר לְפָנָיו עֹז וְתִפְאֶרֶת בְּמִקְדָּשׁוֹ: הָבוּ לַייָ מִשְׁפְּחוֹת עַמִּים הָבוּ לַייָ כָּבוֹד וָעֹז: הָבוּ לַייָ כְּבוֹד שְׁמוֹ שְׂאוּ־מִנְחָה וּבֹאוּ לְחַצְרוֹתָיו: הִשְׁתַּחֲווּ לַייָ בְּהַדְרַת־קֹדֶשׁ חִילוּ מִפָּנָיו כָּל־הָאָרֶץ: אִמְרוּ בַגּוֹיִם יְיָ מָלָךְ אַף־תִּכּוֹן תֵּבֵל בַּל־תִּמּוֹט יָדִין עַמִּים בְּמֵישָׁרִים: יִשְׂמְחוּ הַשָּׁמַיִם וְתָגֵל הָאָרֶץ יִרְעַם הַיָּם וּמְלֹאוֹ: יַעֲלֹז שָׂדַי וְכָל־אֲשֶׁר־בּוֹ אָז יְרַנְּנוּ כָּל־עֲצֵי־יָעַר: לִפְנֵי יְיָ כִּי בָא כִּי בָא לִשְׁפֹּט הָאָרֶץ יִשְׁפֹּט־תֵּבֵל בְּצֶדֶק וְעַמִּים בֶּאֱמוּנָתוֹ:

### תהלים צ״ז

יְיָ מָלָךְ תָּגֵל הָאָרֶץ יִשְׂמְחוּ אִיִּים רַבִּים: עָנָן וַעֲרָפֶל סְבִיבָיו צֶדֶק וּמִשְׁפָּט מְכוֹן כִּסְאוֹ: אֵשׁ לְפָנָיו תֵּלֵךְ וּתְלַהֵט סָבִיב צָרָיו: הֵאִירוּ בְרָקָיו תֵּבֵל רָאֲתָה וַתָּחֵל הָאָרֶץ: הָרִים כַּדּוֹנַג נָמַסּוּ מִלִּפְנֵי יְיָ מִלִּפְנֵי אֲדוֹן כָּל־הָאָרֶץ: הִגִּידוּ הַשָּׁמַיִם צִדְקוֹ וְרָאוּ כָל־הָעַמִּים כְּבוֹדוֹ: יֵבֹשׁוּ כָּל־עֹבְדֵי פֶסֶל הַמִּתְהַלְלִים בָּאֱלִילִים הִשְׁתַּחֲווּ־לוֹ כָּל־אֱלֹהִים: שָׁמְעָה וַתִּשְׂמַח צִיּוֹן וַתָּגֵלְנָה בְּנוֹת יְהוּדָה לְמַעַן מִשְׁפָּטֶיךָ יְיָ: כִּי־אַתָּה יְיָ עֶלְיוֹן עַל־כָּל־הָאָרֶץ מְאֹד

the nations, his wondrous works among all the peoples. For great is the Lord, and exceedingly to be praised: he is to be revered above all gods. For all the gods of the peoples are things of nought: but the Lord made the heavens. Splendour and majesty are before him: strength and beauty are in his sanctuary. Give unto the Lord, ye families of the peoples, give unto the Lord glory and strength. Give unto the Lord the glory due unto his name: take an offering, and come into his courts. O worship the Lord in the beauty of holiness; tremble before him, all the earth. Say among the nations, the Lord reigneth: the world also is set firm that it cannot be moved: he shall judge the peoples with equity. Let the heavens rejoice, and let the earth be glad; let the sea roar, and the fulness thereof: let the plain triumph and all that is therein; yea, let all the trees of the forest exult before the Lord, for he cometh; for he cometh to judge the earth: he will judge the world with righteousness, and the peoples in his faithfulness.

## Psalm xcvii.

The Lord reigneth; let the earth be glad; let the many coast-lands rejoice. Clouds and darkness are round about him: righteousness and justice are the foundation of his throne. A fire goeth before him, and burneth up his adversaries round about. His lightnings illumine the world: the earth seeth and trembleth. The mountains melt like wax before the Lord, before the Lord of the whole earth. The heavens declare his righteousness, and all the peoples behold his glory. Ashamed are all they that serve graven images, that make their boast of things of nought: worship him, all ye gods. Zion heareth and rejoiceth, and the daughters of Judah are glad, because of thy judgments, O Lord. For thou, Lord, art most high above all the earth:

נַעֲלֵיתָ עַל־כָּל־אֱלֹהִים׃ אֹהֲבֵי יְיָ שִׂנְאוּ רָע שֹׁמֵר נַפְשׁוֹת חֲסִידָיו מִיַּד רְשָׁעִים יַצִּילֵם׃ אוֹר זָרֻעַ לַצַּדִּיק וּלְיִשְׁרֵי־לֵב שִׂמְחָה׃ שִׂמְחוּ צַדִּיקִים בַּייָ וְהוֹדוּ לְזֵכֶר קָדְשׁוֹ׃

### תהלים צ״ח

מִזְמוֹר שִׁירוּ לַייָ שִׁיר חָדָשׁ כִּי־נִפְלָאוֹת עָשָׂה הוֹשִׁיעָה־לּוֹ יְמִינוֹ וּזְרוֹעַ קָדְשׁוֹ׃ הוֹדִיעַ יְיָ יְשׁוּעָתוֹ לְעֵינֵי הַגּוֹיִם גִּלָּה צִדְקָתוֹ׃ זָכַר חַסְדּוֹ וֶאֱמוּנָתוֹ לְבֵית יִשְׂרָאֵל רָאוּ כָל־אַפְסֵי־אָרֶץ אֵת יְשׁוּעַת אֱלֹהֵינוּ׃ הָרִיעוּ לַייָ כָּל־הָאָרֶץ פִּצְחוּ וְרַנְּנוּ וְזַמֵּרוּ׃ זַמְּרוּ לַייָ בְּכִנּוֹר בְּכִנּוֹר וְקוֹל זִמְרָה׃ בַּחֲצֹצְרוֹת וְקוֹל שׁוֹפָר הָרִיעוּ לִפְנֵי הַמֶּלֶךְ יְיָ׃ יִרְעַם הַיָּם וּמְלֹאוֹ תֵּבֵל וְיֹשְׁבֵי בָהּ׃ נְהָרוֹת יִמְחֲאוּ־כָף יַחַד הָרִים יְרַנֵּנוּ׃ לִפְנֵי יְיָ כִּי בָא לִשְׁפֹּט הָאָרֶץ יִשְׁפֹּט־תֵּבֵל בְּצֶדֶק וְעַמִּים בְּמֵישָׁרִים׃

### תהלים צ״ט

יְיָ מָלָךְ יִרְגְּזוּ עַמִּים יֹשֵׁב כְּרוּבִים תָּנוּט הָאָרֶץ׃ יְיָ בְּצִיּוֹן גָּדוֹל וְרָם הוּא עַל־כָּל־הָעַמִּים׃ יוֹדוּ שִׁמְךָ גָּדוֹל וְנוֹרָא קָדוֹשׁ הוּא׃ וְעֹז מֶלֶךְ מִשְׁפָּט אָהֵב אַתָּה כּוֹנַנְתָּ מֵישָׁרִים מִשְׁפָּט וּצְדָקָה בְּיַעֲקֹב אַתָּה עָשִׂיתָ׃ רוֹמְמוּ יְיָ אֱלֹהֵינוּ וְהִשְׁתַּחֲווּ לַהֲדֹם רַגְלָיו קָדוֹשׁ הוּא׃ מֹשֶׁה

thou are exalted far above all gods. O ye that love the Lord, hate evil; he preserveth the souls of his loving ones; he delivered them out of the hand of the wicked. Light is sown for the righteous, and joy for the upright in heart. Rejoice in the Lord, ye righteous; and give thanks to his holy name.

## Psalm xcviii. A Psalm.

O sing unto the Lord a new song; for he hath done marvellous things: his right hand, and his holy arm, hath wrought salvation for him. The Lord hath made known his salvation: his righteousness hath he revealed in the sight of the nations. He hath remembered his lovingkindness and his faithfulness toward the house of Israel: all the ends of the earth have seen the salvation of our God. Shout for joy unto the Lord, all the earth; break forth into exultation, and sing praises. Sing praises unto the Lord with the lyre; with the lyre and the sound of song. With trumpets and the sound of the horn shout for joy before the king, the Lord. Let the sea roar, and the fulness thereof, the world, and they that dwell therein. Let the streams clap their hands, let the mountains exult together before the Lord, for he cometh to judge the earth: he will judge the world with righteousness, and the peoples with equity.

## Psalm xcix.

The Lord reigneth; let the peoples tremble; he sitteth above the cherubim; let the earth be moved. The Lord is great in Zion; and he is high above all the peoples. Let them give thanks to thy great and dreaded name; holy is he. And the strength of a king that loveth justice thou didst establish in equity; thou hast wrought justice and righteousness in Jacob. Exalt ye the Lord our God, and worship at his footstool: holy is he. Moses and Aaron among his priests,

וְאַהֲרֹן בְּכֹהֲנָיו וּשְׁמוּאֵל בְּקֹרְאֵי שְׁמוֹ קֹרְאִים אֶל־יְיָ
וְהוּא יַעֲנֵם: בְּעַמּוּד עָנָן יְדַבֵּר אֲלֵיהֶם שָׁמְרוּ עֵדֹתָיו
וְחֹק נָתַן־לָמוֹ: יְיָ אֱלֹהֵינוּ אַתָּה עֲנִיתָם אֵל נֹשֵׂא הָיִיתָ
לָהֶם וְנֹקֵם עַל־עֲלִילוֹתָם: רוֹמְמוּ יְיָ אֱלֹהֵינוּ וְהִשְׁתַּחֲווּ
לְהַר קָדְשׁוֹ כִּי קָדוֹשׁ יְיָ אֱלֹהֵינוּ:

תהלים כט

מִזְמוֹר לְדָוִד הָבוּ לַייָ בְּנֵי אֵלִים הָבוּ לַייָ כָּבוֹד וָעֹז:
הָבוּ לַייָ כְּבוֹד שְׁמוֹ הִשְׁתַּחֲווּ לַייָ בְּהַדְרַת־קֹדֶשׁ: קוֹל
יְיָ עַל הַמָּיִם אֵל־הַכָּבוֹד הִרְעִים יְיָ עַל־מַיִם רַבִּים:
קוֹל־יְיָ בַּכֹּחַ קוֹל יְיָ בֶּהָדָר: קוֹל יְיָ שֹׁבֵר אֲרָזִים
וַיְשַׁבֵּר יְיָ אֶת־אַרְזֵי הַלְּבָנוֹן: וַיַּרְקִידֵם כְּמוֹ־עֵגֶל לְבָנוֹן
וְשִׂרְיוֹן כְּמוֹ בֶן־רְאֵמִים: קוֹל־יְיָ חֹצֵב לַהֲבוֹת אֵשׁ:
קוֹל יְיָ יָחִיל מִדְבָּר יָחִיל יְיָ מִדְבַּר קָדֵשׁ: קוֹל יְיָ
יְחוֹלֵל אַיָּלוֹת וַיֶּחֱשֹׂף יְעָרוֹת וּבְהֵיכָלוֹ כֻּלּוֹ אֹמֵר
כָּבוֹד: יְיָ לַמַּבּוּל יָשָׁב וַיֵּשֶׁב יְיָ מֶלֶךְ לְעוֹלָם: יְיָ עֹז
לְעַמּוֹ יִתֵּן יְיָ ׀ יְבָרֵךְ אֶת־עַמּוֹ בַשָּׁלוֹם:

לְכָה דוֹדִי לִקְרַאת כַּלָּה · פְּנֵי שַׁבָּת נְקַבְּלָה: לכה
שָׁמוֹר וְזָכוֹר בְּדִבּוּר אֶחָד · הִשְׁמִיעָנוּ אֵל הַמְיֻחָד · יְיָ
אֶחָד וּשְׁמוֹ אֶחָד · לְשֵׁם וּלְתִפְאֶרֶת וְלִתְהִלָּה: לכה
לִקְרַאת שַׁבָּת לְכוּ וְנֵלְכָה · כִּי הִיא מְקוֹר הַבְּרָכָה ·

and Samuel among them that call upon his name, called upon the Lord, and he answered them. He spake unto them in the pillar of cloud: they kept his testimonies, and the statute that he gave them. Thou didst answer them, O Lord our God: a forgiving God thou wast unto them, though thou tookest vengeance on their misdeeds. Exalt ye the Lord our God, and worship at his holy mount; for the Lord our God is holy.

Psalm xxix. A Psalm of David.

Give unto the Lord, O ye children of the mighty, give unto the Lord glory and strength. Give unto the Lord the glory due unto his name; worship the Lord in the beauty of holiness. The voice of the Lord is upon the waters: the God of glory thundereth, even the Lord upon the great waters. The voice of the Lord is powerful; the voice of the Lord is full of majesty. The voice of the Lord breaketh the cedars; yea, the Lord breaketh in pieces the cedars of Lebanon. He maketh them also to skip like a calf; Lebanon and Sirion like a young wild-ox. The voice of the Lord cleaveth flames of fire; the voice of the Lord maketh the wilderness to tremble; the Lord maketh tremble the wilderness of Kadesh. The voice of the Lord maketh the hinds to travail, and strippeth the forests bare: and in his temple everything saith, Glory. The Lord sat as king at the flood; yea, the Lord sitteth as king for ever. The Lord will give strength unto his people; the Lord will bless his people with peace.

*Come, my friend, to meet the bride; let us welcome the presence of the Sabbath.

"Observe" and "Remember the Sabbath day," the only God caused us to hear in a single utterance†: the Lord is One, and his name is One to his renown and his glory and his praise. Come, etc.

---

* In this poem, written in the form of an acrostic on the name of the author, R. Shelomo Halevi (Alkabets), the Sabbath is personified as a bride, whose visit to the faithful of Israel it is desired to honour and welcome.

† A reference to the Midrashic explanation (see "Talmud Shevuoth, 20 b) of the discrepancy between the two versions of the Fourth Commandments in Exodus xx. 8 and Deut. v. 12.

מֵרֹאשׁ מִקֶּדֶם נְסוּכָה · סוֹף מַעֲשֶׂה בְּמַחֲשָׁבָה
תְּחִלָּה: לכה

מִקְדַּשׁ מֶלֶךְ עִיר מְלוּכָה · קוּמִי צְאִי מִתּוֹךְ הַהֲפֵכָה · רַב
לָךְ שֶׁבֶת בְּעֵמֶק הַבָּכָא · וְהוּא יַחֲמוֹל עָלַיִךְ
חֶמְלָה: לכה

הִתְנַעֲרִי מֵעָפָר קוּמִי · לִבְשִׁי בִּגְדֵי תִפְאַרְתֵּךְ עַמִּי · עַל-
יַד בֶּן-יִשַׁי בֵּית הַלַּחְמִי · קָרְבָה אֶל-נַפְשִׁי גְאָלָהּ: לכה

הִתְעוֹרְרִי הִתְעוֹרְרִי · כִּי בָא אוֹרֵךְ קוּמִי אוֹרִי · עוּרִי
עוּרִי שִׁיר דַּבֵּרִי · כְּבוֹד יְיָ עָלַיִךְ נִגְלָה: לכה

לֹא תֵבֹשִׁי וְלֹא תִכָּלְמִי · מַה תִּשְׁתּוֹחֲחִי וּמַה תֶּהֱמִי · בָּךְ
יֶחֱסוּ עֲנִיֵּי עַמִּי · וְנִבְנְתָה עִיר עַל-תִּלָּהּ: לכה

וְהָיוּ לִמְשִׁסָּה שֹׁאסָיִךְ · וְרָחֲקוּ כָּל-מְבַלְּעָיִךְ · יָשִׂישׂ עָלַיִךְ
אֱלֹהָיִךְ · כִּמְשׂוֹשׂ חָתָן עַל-כַּלָּה: לכה

יָמִין וּשְׂמֹאל תִּפְרוֹצִי · וְאֶת-יְיָ תַּעֲרִיצִי · עַל יַד-אִישׁ בֶּן
פַּרְצִי · וְנִשְׂמְחָה וְנָגִילָה: לכה

בּוֹאִי בְשָׁלוֹם עֲטֶרֶת בַּעְלָהּ · גַּם בְּשִׂמְחָה וּבְצָהֳלָה · תּוֹךְ
אֱמוּנֵי עַם סְגֻלָּה · בּוֹאִי כַלָּה · בּוֹאִי כַלָּה: לכה

*On the entry of Mourners into the Synagogue they are greeted thus:*

הַמָּקוֹם יְנַחֵם אֶתְכֶם בְּתוֹךְ שְׁאָר אֲבֵלֵי צִיּוֹן וִירוּשָׁלָיִם:

תהלים צ״ב

מִזְמוֹר שִׁיר לְיוֹם הַשַּׁבָּת: טוֹב לְהֹדוֹת לַיהוָֹה וּלְזַמֵּר
לְשִׁמְךָ עֶלְיוֹן: לְהַגִּיד בַּבֹּקֶר חַסְדֶּךָ וֶאֱמוּנָתְךָ בַּלֵּילוֹת:

Come, let us go to meet the Sabbath, for it is a well-spring of blessing; from the beginning, from of old it was ordained,—last in production, first in thought. Come, etc.

O sanctuary of our King, O regal city, arise, go forth from thy overthrow; long enough hast thou dwelt in the valley of weeping; verily he will have compassion upon thee. Come, etc.

Shake thyself from the dust, arise, put on the garments of thy glory, O my people! Through the son of Jesse, the Bethlehemite, draw Thou nigh unto my soul, redeem it.

Come, etc.

Arouse thyself, arouse thyself, for thy light is come: arise, shine; awake, awake; give forth a song; the glory of the Lord is revealed upon thee. Come, etc.

Be not ashamed, neither be confounded. Why art thou cast down, and why art thou disquieted? The poor of my people trust in thee, and the city shall be builded on her own mound. Come, etc.

And they that spoil thee shall be a spoil, and all that would swallow thee shall be far away: thy God shall rejoice over thee, as a bridegroom rejoiceth over his bride. Come, etc.

Thou shalt spread abroad on the right hand and on the left, and thou shalt reverence the Lord. Through the off-spring of Perez we also shall rejoice and be glad. Come, etc.

Come in peace, thou crown of thy husband, with rejoicing and with cheerfulness, in the midst of the faithful of the chosen people: come, O bride; come, O bride. Come, etc.

*On the entry of Mourners into the Synagogue they are greeted thus*:

May the Almighty comfort you among the other mourners for Zion and Jerusalem.

Psalm xciii. A Psalm, A Song for the Sabbath Day.

It is a good thing to give thanks unto the Lord, and to sing praises unto thy name, O Most High: to declare thy lovingkindness in the morning, and thy faithfulness every

עֲלֵי־עָשׂוֹר וַעֲלֵי־נָבֶל עֲלֵי הִגָּיוֹן בְּכִנּוֹר: כִּי שִׂמַּחְתַּנִי
יְהוָֹה בְּפָעֳלֶךָ בְּמַעֲשֵׂי יָדֶיךָ אֲרַנֵּן: מַה־גָּדְלוּ מַעֲשֶׂיךָ
יְהוָֹה מְאֹד עָמְקוּ מַחְשְׁבֹתֶיךָ: אִישׁ בַּעַר לֹא יֵדָע וּכְסִיל
לֹא־יָבִין אֶת־זֹאת: בִּפְרֹחַ רְשָׁעִים כְּמוֹ־עֵשֶׂב וַיָּצִיצוּ
כָּל־פֹּעֲלֵי אָוֶן לְהִשָּׁמְדָם עֲדֵי־עַד: וְאַתָּה מָרוֹם לְעֹלָם
יְהוָֹה: כִּי הִנֵּה אֹיְבֶיךָ יְהוָֹה כִּי־הִנֵּה אֹיְבֶיךָ יֹאבֵדוּ
יִתְפָּרְדוּ כָּל־פֹּעֲלֵי אָוֶן: וַתָּרֶם כִּרְאֵים קַרְנִי בַּלֹּתִי
בְּשֶׁמֶן רַעֲנָן: וַתַּבֵּט עֵינִי בְּשׁוּרָי בַּקָּמִים עָלַי מְרֵעִים
תִּשְׁמַעְנָה אָזְנָי: צַדִּיק כַּתָּמָר יִפְרָח כְּאֶרֶז בַּלְּבָנוֹן יִשְׂגֶּה:
שְׁתוּלִים בְּבֵית יְהוָֹה בְּחַצְרוֹת אֱלֹהֵינוּ יַפְרִיחוּ: עוֹד
יְנוּבוּן בְּשֵׂיבָה דְּשֵׁנִים וְרַעֲנַנִּים יִהְיוּ: לְהַגִּיד כִּי־יָשָׁר
יְהוָֹה צוּרִי וְלֹא עַוְלָתָה בּוֹ:

תהלים צ״ג

יְהוָֹה מָלָךְ גֵּאוּת לָבֵשׁ לָבֵשׁ יְהוָֹה עֹז הִתְאַזָּר אַף־
תִּכּוֹן תֵּבֵל בַּל־תִּמּוֹט: נָכוֹן כִּסְאֲךָ מֵאָז מֵעוֹלָם אָתָּה:
נָשְׂאוּ נְהָרוֹת יְהוָֹה נָשְׂאוּ נְהָרוֹת קוֹלָם יִשְׂאוּ נְהָרוֹת
דָּכְיָם: מִקֹּלוֹת מַיִם רַבִּים אַדִּירִים מִשְׁבְּרֵי־יָם אַדִּיר
בַּמָּרוֹם יְהוָֹה: עֵדֹתֶיךָ נֶאֶמְנוּ מְאֹד לְבֵיתְךָ נַאֲוָה־קֹדֶשׁ
יְהוָֹה לְאֹרֶךְ יָמִים:

קדיש יתום, p. 94 o.

night, with an instrument of ten strings and with a harp, with thoughtful music upon the lyre. For thou, O Lord, hast made me rejoice through thy work: I will exult in the works of thy hands. How great are thy works, O Lord: thy thoughts are very deep. A brutish man knoweth it not, neither does a fool understand this: when the wicked sprang up as the grass, and all the workers of iniquity flourished, it was that they might be destroyed for ever. But thou, O Lord, art on high for evermore. For, lo, thine enemies, O Lord, for, lo, thine enemies shall perish; all the workers of iniquity shall be scattered. But my horn hast thou exalted, like that of the wild-ox: I am anointed with fresh oil. Mine eye also hath seen my desire on mine enemies; mine ears have heard my desire of them that rose up against me, doers of evil. The righteous shall spring up like a palm-tree; he shall grow tall like a cedar in Lebanon. Planted in the house of the Lord, they shall blossom in the courts of our God. They shall still shoot forth in old age; they shall be full of sap and green: to declare that the Lord is upright: he is my rock, and there is no unrighteousness in him.

## Psalm xciii.

The Lord reigneth; he hath robed him in majesty; the Lord hath robed him, yea, he hath girded himself with strength: the world also is set firm, that it cannot be moved. Thy throne is set firm from of old: thou art from everlasting. The streams have lifted up, O Lord, the streams have lifted up their voice; the streams lift up their roaring. Than the voices of many waters, mighty waters, breakers of the sea, more mighty is the Lord on high. Thy testimonies are very faithful: holiness becometh thine house, O Lord, for evermore.

*Mourner's Kaddish*, p. 122b.

*Reader.*

בָּרְכוּ אֶת־יְיָ הַמְבֹרָךְ׃

*Cong. and Reader.*

בָּרוּךְ יְיָ הַמְבֹרָךְ לְעוֹלָם וָעֶד׃

*Congregation in an undertone.*

יִתְבָּרַךְ וְיִשְׁתַּבַּח וְיִתְפָּאַר וְיִתְרוֹמַם וְיִתְנַשֵּׂא שְׁמוֹ שֶׁל־מֶלֶךְ מַלְכֵי הַמְּלָכִים הַקָּדוֹשׁ בָּרוּךְ הוּא׃ שֶׁהוּא רִאשׁוֹן וְהוּא אַחֲרוֹן וּמִבַּלְעָדָיו אֵין אֱלֹהִים׃ סֹלּוּ לָרֹכֵב בָּעֲרָבוֹת בְּיָהּ שְׁמוֹ וְעִלְזוּ לְפָנָיו׃ וּשְׁמוֹ מְרוֹמָם עַל־כָּל־בְּרָכָה וּתְהִלָּה׃

בָּרוּךְ שֵׁם כְּבוֹד מַלְכוּתוֹ לְעוֹלָם וָעֶד׃ יְהִי שֵׁם יְיָ מְבֹרָךְ מֵעַתָּה וְעַד עוֹלָם׃

בָּרוּךְ אַתָּה יְיָ אֱלֹהֵינוּ מֶלֶךְ הָעוֹלָם׃ אֲשֶׁר בִּדְבָרוֹ מַעֲרִיב עֲרָבִים בְּחָכְמָה פּוֹתֵחַ שְׁעָרִים וּבִתְבוּנָה מְשַׁנֶּה עִתִּים וּמַחֲלִיף אֶת־הַזְּמַנִּים וּמְסַדֵּר אֶת־הַכּוֹכָבִים בְּמִשְׁמְרוֹתֵיהֶם בָּרָקִיעַ כִּרְצוֹנוֹ׃ בּוֹרֵא יוֹם וָלָיְלָה גּוֹלֵל אוֹר מִפְּנֵי־חֹשֶׁךְ וְחֹשֶׁךְ מִפְּנֵי־אוֹר׃ וּמַעֲבִיר יוֹם וּמֵבִיא לָיְלָה וּמַבְדִּיל בֵּין יוֹם וּבֵין לָיְלָה יְיָ צְבָאוֹת שְׁמוֹ׃ אֵל חַי וְקַיָּם תָּמִיד יִמְלוֹךְ עָלֵינוּ לְעוֹלָם וָעֶד׃ בָּרוּךְ אַתָּה יְיָ׃ הַמַּעֲרִיב עֲרָבִים׃

אַהֲבַת עוֹלָם בֵּית יִשְׂרָאֵל עַמְּךָ אָהָבְתָּ׃ תּוֹרָה וּמִצְוֹת חֻקִּים וּמִשְׁפָּטִים אוֹתָנוּ לִמַּדְתָּ׃ עַל־כֵּן יְיָ אֱלֹהֵינוּ בְּשָׁכְבֵנוּ וּבְקוּמֵנוּ נָשִׂיחַ בְּחֻקֶּיךָ׃ וְנִשְׂמַח בְּדִבְרֵי תוֹרָתְךָ וּבְמִצְוֹתֶיךָ לְעוֹלָם וָעֶד׃ כִּי הֵם חַיֵּינוּ וְאֹרֶךְ יָמֵינוּ וּבָהֶם נֶהְגֶּה יוֹמָם וָלָיְלָה׃ וְאַהֲבָתְךָ אַל־תָּסִיר מִמֶּנּוּ לְעוֹלָמִים׃ בָּרוּךְ אַתָּה יְיָ׃ אוֹהֵב עַמּוֹ יִשְׂרָאֵל׃

*Reader.* — Bless ye the Lord who is to be blessed.

*Cong. and Reader.* —Blessed is the Lord who is to be blessed for ever and ever.

*Congregation, in an undertone.*

Blessed, praised, glorified, exalted and extolled be the name of the supreme King of kings, the Holy One, blessed be he, who is the first and the last, and beside him there is no God. Extol ye him that rideth upon the heavens by his name Jah, and rejoice before him. His name is exalted above all blessing and praise. Blessed be His name, whose glorious kingdom is for ever and ever. Let the name of the Lord be blessed from this time forth and for evermore.

Blessed art thou, O Lord our God, King of the universe, who at thy word bringest on the evening twilight, with wisdom openest the gates of the heavens, and with understanding changest times and variest the seasons, and arrangest the stars in their watches in the sky, according to thy will. Thou createst day and night; thou rollest away the light from before the darkness, and the darkness from before the light; thou makest the day to pass and the night to approach, and dividest the day from the night, the Lord of hosts is thy name; a God living and enduring continually, mayest thou reign over us for ever and ever. Blessed art thou, O Lord, who bringest on the evening twilight.

With everlasting love thou hast loved the house of Israel, thy people; a Law and commandments, statutes and judgments hast thou taught us. Therefore, O Lord our God, when we lie down and when we rise up we will meditate on thy statutes: yea, we will rejoice in the words of thy Law and in thy commandments for ever; for they are our life and the length of our days, and we will meditate on them day and night. And mayest thou never take away thy love from us. Blessed art thou, O Lord, who lovest thy people Israel.

(*When Prayers are not said with the Congregation, add:—*

אֵל מֶלֶךְ נֶאֱמָן:)

דברים ו׳ ד־ט׳

שְׁמַע יִשְׂרָאֵל יְהוָה אֱלֹהֵינוּ יְהוָה ׀ אֶחָד:

בָּרוּךְ שֵׁם כְּבוֹד מַלְכוּתוֹ לְעוֹלָם וָעֶד:

וְאָהַבְתָּ אֵת יְהוָה אֱלֹהֶיךָ בְּכָל־לְבָבְךָ וּבְכָל־נַפְשְׁךָ וּבְכָל־מְאֹדֶךָ: וְהָיוּ הַדְּבָרִים הָאֵלֶּה אֲשֶׁר אָנֹכִי מְצַוְּךָ הַיּוֹם עַל־לְבָבֶךָ: וְשִׁנַּנְתָּם לְבָנֶיךָ וְדִבַּרְתָּ בָּם בְּשִׁבְתְּךָ בְּבֵיתֶךָ וּבְלֶכְתְּךָ בַדֶּרֶךְ וּבְשָׁכְבְּךָ וּבְקוּמֶךָ: וּקְשַׁרְתָּם לְאוֹת עַל־יָדֶךָ וְהָיוּ לְטֹטָפֹת בֵּין עֵינֶיךָ: וּכְתַבְתָּם עַל־מְזֻזוֹת בֵּיתֶךָ וּבִשְׁעָרֶיךָ:

דברים י״א י״ג־כ״א

וְהָיָה אִם־שָׁמֹעַ תִּשְׁמְעוּ אֶל־מִצְוֹתַי אֲשֶׁר אָנֹכִי מְצַוֶּה אֶתְכֶם הַיּוֹם לְאַהֲבָה אֶת־יְהוָה אֱלֹהֵיכֶם וּלְעָבְדוֹ בְּכָל־לְבַבְכֶם וּבְכָל־נַפְשְׁכֶם: וְנָתַתִּי מְטַר־אַרְצְכֶם בְּעִתּוֹ יוֹרֶה וּמַלְקוֹשׁ וְאָסַפְתָּ דְגָנֶךָ וְתִירֹשְׁךָ וְיִצְהָרֶךָ: וְנָתַתִּי עֵשֶׂב בְּשָׂדְךָ לִבְהֶמְתֶּךָ וְאָכַלְתָּ וְשָׂבָעְתָּ: הִשָּׁמְרוּ לָכֶם פֶּן־יִפְתֶּה לְבַבְכֶם וְסַרְתֶּם וַעֲבַדְתֶּם אֱלֹהִים אֲחֵרִים וְהִשְׁתַּחֲוִיתֶם לָהֶם: וְחָרָה אַף־יְהוָה בָּכֶם וְעָצַר אֶת־הַשָּׁמַיִם וְלֹא־יִהְיֶה מָטָר וְהָאֲדָמָה לֹא תִתֵּן אֶת־יְבוּלָהּ

(*When Prayers are not said with the Congregation, add*: God, faithful King!)

Deut. vi. 4—9

Hear, O Israel: the Lord our God, the Lord is One.

Blessed be His name, whose glorious kingdom is for ever and ever.

And thou shalt love the Lord thy God with all thine heart, and with all thy soul, and with all thy might. And these words, which I command thee this day, shall be upon thine heart: and thou shalt teach them diligently unto thy children, and shalt talk of them when thou sittest in thine house, and when thou walkest by the way, and when thou liest down, and when thou risest up. And thou shalt bind them for a sign upon thine hand, and they shall be for frontlets between thine eyes. And thou shalt write them upon the doorposts of thy house, and upon thy gates.

Deut. xi. 13—21.

And it shall come to pass, if ye shall hearken diligently unto my commandments which I command you this day, to love the Lord your God, and to serve him with all your heart and with all your soul, that I will give the rain of your land in its season, the former rain and the latter rain, that thou mayest gather in thy corn, and thy wine, and thine oil. And I will give grass in thy field for thy cattle, and thou shalt eat and be satisfied. Take heed to yourselves, lest your heart be deceived, and ye turn aside, and serve other gods, and worship them; and the anger of the Lord be kindled against you, and he shut up the heaven, that there be no rain, and that the land yield not her fruit; and ye perish

וַאֲבַדְתֶּם מְהֵרָה מֵעַל הָאָרֶץ הַטֹּבָה אֲשֶׁר יְהוָה נֹתֵן
לָכֶם: וְשַׂמְתֶּם אֶת־דְּבָרַי אֵלֶּה עַל־לְבַבְכֶם וְעַל־נַפְשְׁכֶם
וּקְשַׁרְתֶּם אֹתָם לְאוֹת עַל־יֶדְכֶם וְהָיוּ לְטוֹטָפֹת בֵּין
עֵינֵיכֶם: וְלִמַּדְתֶּם אֹתָם אֶת־בְּנֵיכֶם לְדַבֵּר בָּם בְּשִׁבְתְּךָ
בְּבֵיתֶךָ וּבְלֶכְתְּךָ בַדֶּרֶךְ וּבְשָׁכְבְּךָ וּבְקוּמֶךָ: וּכְתַבְתָּם
עַל־מְזוּזוֹת בֵּיתֶךָ וּבִשְׁעָרֶיךָ: לְמַעַן יִרְבּוּ יְמֵיכֶם וִימֵי
בְנֵיכֶם עַל הָאֲדָמָה אֲשֶׁר נִשְׁבַּע יְהוָה לַאֲבֹתֵיכֶם
לָתֵת לָהֶם כִּימֵי הַשָּׁמַיִם עַל־הָאָרֶץ:

במדבר טו לז־מא

וַיֹּאמֶר יְהוָה אֶל־מֹשֶׁה לֵּאמֹר: דַּבֵּר אֶל־בְּנֵי יִשְׂרָאֵל
וְאָמַרְתָּ אֲלֵהֶם וְעָשׂוּ לָהֶם צִיצִת עַל־כַּנְפֵי בִגְדֵיהֶם
לְדֹרֹתָם וְנָתְנוּ עַל־צִיצִת הַכָּנָף פְּתִיל תְּכֵלֶת: וְהָיָה
לָכֶם לְצִיצִת וּרְאִיתֶם אֹתוֹ וּזְכַרְתֶּם אֶת־כָּל־מִצְוֹת יְהוָה
וַעֲשִׂיתֶם אֹתָם וְלֹא תָתוּרוּ אַחֲרֵי לְבַבְכֶם וְאַחֲרֵי עֵינֵיכֶם
אֲשֶׁר־אַתֶּם זֹנִים אַחֲרֵיהֶם: לְמַעַן תִּזְכְּרוּ וַעֲשִׂיתֶם
אֶת־כָּל־מִצְוֹתָי וִהְיִיתֶם קְדֹשִׁים לֵאלֹהֵיכֶם: אֲנִי יְהוָה
אֱלֹהֵיכֶם אֲשֶׁר הוֹצֵאתִי אֶתְכֶם מֵאֶרֶץ מִצְרַיִם לִהְיוֹת
לָכֶם לֵאלֹהִים אֲנִי יְהוָה אֱלֹהֵיכֶם:

אֱמֶת וֶאֱמוּנָה כָּל־זֹאת וְקַיָּם עָלֵינוּ כִּי הוּא יי אֱלֹהֵינוּ

quickly from off the good land which the Lord giveth you. Therefore shall ye lay up these my words in your heart and in your soul; and ye shall bind them for a sign upon your hand, and they shall be for frontlets between your eyes. And ye shall teach them your children, talking of them when thou sittest in thine house, and when thou walkest by the way, and when thou liest down, and when thou risest up. And thou shalt write them upon the door posts of thine house, and upon thy gates; that your days may be multiplied, and the days of your children, upon the land which the Lord sware unto your fathers to give them, as the days of the heavens above the earth.

Numbers xv. 37—41.

And the Lord spake unto Moses, saying, Speak unto the children of Israel, and bid them that they make them a fringe upon the corners of their garments throughout their generations, and that they put upon the fringe of each corner a cord of blue; and it shall be unto you for a fringe, that ye may look upon it, and remember all the commandments of the Lord, and do them; and that ye go not about after your own heart and your own eyes, after which ye use to go astray that ye may remember and do all my commandments, and be holy unto your God. I am the Lord your God, who brought you out of the land of Egypt, to be your God: I am the Lord your God.

True and trustworthy is all this, and it is established with us that he is the Lord our God, and there is none beside

וְאֵין זוּלָתוֹ וַאֲנַחְנוּ יִשְׂרָאֵל עַמּוֹ ׃ הַפּוֹדֵנוּ מִיַּד מְלָכִים מַלְכֵּנוּ הַגּוֹאֲלֵנוּ מִכַּף כָּל־הֶעָרִיצִים ׃ הָאֵל הַנִּפְרָע לָנוּ מִצָּרֵינוּ וְהַמְשַׁלֵּם גְּמוּל לְכָל־אוֹיְבֵי נַפְשֵׁנוּ ׃ הָעֹשֶׂה גְדוֹלוֹת עַד־אֵין חֵקֶר וְנִפְלָאוֹת עַד־אֵין מִסְפָּר ׃ הַשָּׂם נַפְשֵׁנוּ בַּחַיִּים וְלֹא־נָתַן לַמּוֹט רַגְלֵנוּ ׃ הַמַּדְרִיכֵנוּ עַל־בָּמוֹת אוֹיְבֵינוּ וַיָּרֶם קַרְנֵנוּ עַל־כָּל־שׂנְאֵינוּ ׃ הָעֹשֶׂה־לָּנוּ נִסִּים וּנְקָמָה בְּפַרְעֹה אוֹתֹת וּמוֹפְתִים בְּאַדְמַת בְּנֵי־חָם ׃ הַמַּכֶּה בְעֶבְרָתוֹ כָּל־בְּכוֹרֵי מִצְרָיִם וַיּוֹצֵא אֶת־עַמּוֹ יִשְׂרָאֵל מִתּוֹכָם לְחֵרוּת עוֹלָם ׃ הַמַּעֲבִיר בָּנָיו בֵּין גִּזְרֵי יַם־סוּף אֶת־רוֹדְפֵיהֶם וְאֶת־שׂוֹנְאֵיהֶם בִּתְהוֹמוֹת טִבַּע ׃ וְרָאוּ בָנָיו גְּבוּרָתוֹ שִׁבְּחוּ וְהוֹדוּ לִשְׁמוֹ וּמַלְכוּתוֹ בְּרָצוֹן קִבְּלוּ עֲלֵיהֶם ׃ מֹשֶׁה וּבְנֵי יִשְׂרָאֵל לְךָ עָנוּ שִׁירָה בְּשִׂמְחָה רַבָּה ׃ וְאָמְרוּ כֻלָּם ׃

מִי־כָמֹכָה בָּאֵלִם יְהוָה מִי כָּמֹכָה נֶאְדָּר בַּקֹּדֶשׁ נוֹרָא תְהִלֹּת עֹשֵׂה פֶלֶא ׃

מַלְכוּתְךָ רָאוּ בָנֶיךָ בּוֹקֵעַ יָם לִפְנֵי מֹשֶׁה ׃ זֶה אֵלִי עָנוּ ׃ וְאָמְרוּ ׃ יְהוָה יִמְלֹךְ לְעֹלָם וָעֶד ׃

וְנֶאֱמַר כִּי־פָדָה יְיָ אֶת־יַעֲקֹב וּגְאָלוֹ מִיַּד חָזָק מִמֶּנּוּ ׃ בָּרוּךְ אַתָּה יְיָ ׃ גָּאַל יִשְׂרָאֵל ׃

him, and that we, Israel, are his people. It is he who redeemed us from the hand of kings, even our King, who delivered us from the grasp of all the terrible ones; the God, who on our behalf dealt out punishment to our adversaries, and requited all the enemies of our soul; who doeth great things past finding out, yea, and wonders without number; who holdeth our soul in life, and hath not suffered our feet to be moved; who made us tread upon the high places of our enemies, and exalted our horn over all them that hated us; who wrought for us miracles and vengeance upon Pharaoh, signs and wonders in the land of the children of Ham; who in his wrath smote all the first-born of Egypt, and brought forth his people Israel from among them to everlasting freedom; who made his children pass between the divisions of the Red Sea, but sank their pursuers and their enemies in the depths. Then his children beheld his might; they praised and gave thanks unto his name, and willingly accepted his sovereignty. Moses and the children of Israel sang a song unto thee with great joy, saying, all of them,

Who is like unto thee, O Lord, among the mighty ones? Who is like unto thee, glorious in holiness, revered in praises, doing wonders?

Thy children beheld thy sovereign power, as thou didst cleave the sea before Moses: they exclaimed, This is my God! and said, The Lord shall reign for ever and ever.

And it is said, For the Lord hath delivered Jacob, and redeemed him from the hand of him that was stronger than he. Blessed art thou, O Lord, who hast redeemed Israel.

הַשְׁכִּיבֵנוּ יְיָ אֱלֹהֵינוּ לְשָׁלוֹם וְהַעֲמִידֵנוּ מַלְכֵּנוּ לְחַיִּים · וּפְרוֹשׂ עָלֵינוּ סֻכַּת שְׁלוֹמֶךָ וְתַקְּנֵנוּ בְּעֵצָה טוֹבָה מִלְּפָנֶיךָ וְהוֹשִׁיעֵנוּ לְמַעַן שְׁמֶךָ · וְהָגֵן בַּעֲדֵנוּ וְהָסֵר מֵעָלֵינוּ אוֹיֵב דֶּבֶר וְחֶרֶב וְרָעָב וְיָגוֹן · וְהָסֵר שָׂטָן מִלְּפָנֵינוּ וּמֵאַחֲרֵינוּ · וּבְצֵל כְּנָפֶיךָ תַּסְתִּירֵנוּ כִּי אֵל שׁוֹמְרֵנוּ וּמַצִּילֵנוּ אָתָּה כִּי אֵל מֶלֶךְ חַנּוּן וְרַחוּם אָתָּה · וּשְׁמוֹר צֵאתֵנוּ וּבוֹאֵנוּ לְחַיִּים וּלְשָׁלוֹם מֵעַתָּה וְעַד עוֹלָם · וּפְרוֹשׂ עָלֵינוּ סֻכַּת שְׁלוֹמֶךָ · בָּרוּךְ אַתָּה יְיָ · הַפּוֹרֵשׂ סֻכַּת שָׁלוֹם עָלֵינוּ וְעַל כָּל־עַמּוֹ יִשְׂרָאֵל וְעַל־יְרוּשָׁלָיִם :

*On* שַׁבָּת :—

שמות לא ט״ז־י״ז

וְשָׁמְרוּ בְנֵי־יִשְׂרָאֵל אֶת־הַשַּׁבָּת לַעֲשׂוֹת אֶת־הַשַּׁבָּת לְדֹרֹתָם בְּרִית עוֹלָם · בֵּינִי וּבֵין בְּנֵי יִשְׂרָאֵל אוֹת הִוא לְעֹלָם כִּי־שֵׁשֶׁת יָמִים עָשָׂה יְהוָֹה אֶת־הַשָּׁמַיִם וְאֶת־הָאָרֶץ וּבַיּוֹם הַשְּׁבִיעִי שָׁבַת וַיִּנָּפַשׁ :

Cause us, O Lord our God, to lie down in peace, and raise us up, O King, unto life. Spread over us the tabernacle of thy peace; direct us aright through thine own good counsel; save us for thy name's sake; be thou a shield about us; remove from us every enemy, pestilence, sword, famine and sorrow; remove also the adversary from before us and from behind us. O shelter us beneath the shadow of thy wings; for thou, O God, art our Guardian and our Deliverer; yea, thou, O Lord, art a gracious and merciful King; and guard our going out and our coming in unto life and unto peace from this time forth and for evermore; yea, spread over us the tabernacle of thy peace. Blessed art thou, O Lord, who spreadest the tabernacle of peace over us and over all thy people Israel, and over Jerusalem.

*On Sabbaths*:—

Exodus xxxi. 16, 17.

And the children of Israel shall keep the Sabbath, to observe the Sabbath throughout their generations, for an everlasting covenant. It is a sign between me and the children of Israel for ever, that in six days the Lord made the heavens and the earth, and on the seventh day he rested, and ceased from his work.

*On* פֶּסַח, שָׁבֻעוֹת *and* סֻכּוֹת:—

וַיְדַבֵּר מֹשֶׁה אֶת־מֹעֲדֵי יְהוָֹה אֶל־בְּנֵי יִשְׂרָאֵל׃

*On* רֹאשׁ הַשָּׁנָה:—

תִּקְעוּ בַחֹדֶשׁ שׁוֹפָר בַּכֶּסֶה לְיוֹם חַגֵּנוּ׃ כִּי חֹק לְיִשְׂרָאֵל הוּא מִשְׁפָּט לֵאלֹהֵי יַעֲקֹב׃

*On* יוֹם כִּפּוּר:—

כִּי בַיּוֹם הַזֶּה יְכַפֵּר עֲלֵיכֶם לְטַהֵר אֶתְכֶם מִכֹּל חַטֹּאתֵיכֶם לִפְנֵי יְהוָֹה תִּטְהָרוּ׃

חֲצִי קַדִּישׁ, *p.* 37.

*On Festivals say the appropriate* עֲמִידוֹת.

אֲדֹנָי שְׂפָתַי תִּפְתָּח וּפִי יַגִּיד תְּהִלָּתֶךָ׃

בָּרוּךְ אַתָּה יְיָ אֱלֹהֵינוּ וֵאלֹהֵי אֲבוֹתֵינוּ ׳ אֱלֹהֵי אַבְרָהָם אֱלֹהֵי יִצְחָק וֵאלֹהֵי יַעֲקֹב ׳ הָאֵל הַגָּדוֹל הַגִּבּוֹר וְהַנּוֹרָא אֵל עֶלְיוֹן ׳ גּוֹמֵל חֲסָדִים טוֹבִים וְקוֹנֵה הַכֹּל ׳ וְזוֹכֵר חַסְדֵי אָבוֹת וּמֵבִיא גוֹאֵל לִבְנֵי בְנֵיהֶם לְמַעַן שְׁמוֹ בְּאַהֲבָה ׳

*On* שַׁבַּת שׁוּבָה *say*:—

זָכְרֵנוּ לְחַיִּים מֶלֶךְ חָפֵץ בַּחַיִּים ׳ וְכָתְבֵנוּ בְּסֵפֶר הַחַיִּים לְמַעַנְךָ אֱלֹהִים חַיִּים׃

מֶלֶךְ עוֹזֵר וּמוֹשִׁיעַ וּמָגֵן ׳ בָּרוּךְ אַתָּה יְיָ ׳ מָגֵן אַבְרָהָם׃

*On Passover, Pentecost and Tabernacles, say:—*

And Moses declared the set feasts of the Lord unto the children of Israel.

*On New Year:—*

Blow the horn on the new moon, at the beginning of the month, for our day of festival: for it is a statute for Israel, a decree of the God of Jacob.

*On the Day of Atonement:—*

For on this day shall atonement be made for you to cleanse you; from all your sins shall ye be clean before the Lord.

*Kaddish, p.* 37.

*On Festivals say the appropriate Amidoth.*

O Lord, open thou my lips, and my mouth shall declare thy praise.

Blessed art thou, O Lord our God and God of our fathers, God of Abraham, God of Isaac, and God of Jacob, the great, mighty and revered God, the most high God, who bestowest lovingkindnesses, and possessest all things, who rememberest the pious deeds of the patriarchs, and in love wilt bring a redeemer to their children's children for thy name's sake.

*On the Sabbath of Penitence say:—*

Remember us unto life, O King, who delightest in life, and inscribe us in the book of life, for thine own sake, O living God.

O King, Helper, Saviour and Shield. Blessed art thou, O Lord, the Shield of Abraham.

אַתָּה גִּבּוֹר לְעוֹלָם אֲדֹנָי מְחַיֵּה מֵתִים אַתָּה רַב לְהוֹשִׁיעַ׃

*From* שַׁבַּת בְּרֵאשִׁית *until the First Day of* פֶּסַח *say:—*

מַשִּׁיב הָרוּחַ וּמוֹרִיד הַגֶּשֶׁם׃

מְכַלְכֵּל חַיִּים בְּחֶסֶד מְחַיֵּה מֵתִים בְּרַחֲמִים רַבִּים · סוֹמֵךְ נוֹפְלִים וְרוֹפֵא חוֹלִים וּמַתִּיר אֲסוּרִים וּמְקַיֵּם אֱמוּנָתוֹ לִישֵׁנֵי עָפָר · מִי כָמוֹךָ בַּעַל גְּבוּרוֹת וּמִי דּוֹמֶה לָּךְ · מֶלֶךְ מֵמִית וּמְחַיֶּה וּמַצְמִיחַ יְשׁוּעָה ·

*On* שַׁבַּת שׁוּבָה *say:—*

מִי כָמוֹךָ אַב הָרַחֲמִים זוֹכֵר יְצוּרָיו לַחַיִּים בְּרַחֲמִים ·

וְנֶאֱמָן אַתָּה לְהַחֲיוֹת מֵתִים · בָּרוּךְ אַתָּה יְיָ · מְחַיֵּה הַמֵּתִים׃

אַתָּה קָדוֹשׁ וְשִׁמְךָ קָדוֹשׁ וּקְדוֹשִׁים בְּכָל־יוֹם יְהַלְלוּךָ סֶּלָה · בָּרוּךְ אַתָּה יְיָ · הָאֵל הַקָּדוֹשׁ׃

*On* שַׁבַּת שׁוּבָה *conclude the Blessing thus:—*

הַמֶּלֶךְ הַקָּדוֹשׁ׃

אַתָּה קִדַּשְׁתָּ אֶת־יוֹם הַשְּׁבִיעִי לִשְׁמֶךָ · תַּכְלִית מַעֲשֵׂה שָׁמַיִם וָאָרֶץ · וּבֵרַכְתּוֹ מִכָּל־הַיָּמִים וְקִדַּשְׁתּוֹ מִכָּל־הַזְּמַנִּים · וְכֵן כָּתוּב בְּתוֹרָתֶךָ׃

Thou, O Lord, art mighty for ever, thou quickenest the dead, thou art mighty to save.

*From the Sabbath after the Eighth Day of Solemn Assembly until the First Day of Passover say:—*

Thou causest the wind to blow and the rain to fall.

Thou sustainest the living with lovingkindness, quickenest the dead with great mercy, supportest the falling, healest the sick, loosest the bound, and keepest thy faith to them that sleep in the dust. Who is like unto thee, Lord of mighty acts, and who resembleth thee, O King, who killest and quickenest, and causest salvation to spring forth?

*On the Sabbath of Penitence say:—*

Who is like unto thee, Father of mercy, who in mercy rememberest thy creatures unto life?

Yea, faithful art thou to quicken the dead. Blessed art thou, O Lord, who quickenest the dead.

Thou art holy, and thy name is holy, and holy beings praise thee daily. (Selah.) Blessed art thou, O Lord, the holy God.

*On the Sabbath of Penitence conclude the Blessing thus:*

the holy King.

Thou didst hallow the seventh day unto thy name, as the end of the creation of heaven and earth; thou didst bless it above all days, and didst hallow it above all seasons; and thus it is written in thy Law:

וַיְכֻלּוּ הַשָּׁמַיִם וְהָאָרֶץ וְכָל צְבָאָם: וַיְכַל אֱלֹהִים בַּיּוֹם הַשְּׁבִיעִי מְלַאכְתּוֹ אֲשֶׁר עָשָׂה וַיִּשְׁבֹּת בַּיּוֹם הַשְּׁבִיעִי מִכָּל־מְלַאכְתּוֹ אֲשֶׁר עָשָׂה: וַיְבָרֶךְ אֱלֹהִים אֶת־יוֹם הַשְּׁבִיעִי וַיְקַדֵּשׁ אֹתוֹ כִּי בוֹ שָׁבַת מִכָּל־מְלַאכְתּוֹ אֲשֶׁר־בָּרָא אֱלֹהִים לַעֲשׂוֹת:

אֱלֹהֵינוּ וֵאלֹהֵי אֲבוֹתֵינוּ · רְצֵה בִמְנוּחָתֵנוּ קַדְּשֵׁנוּ בְּמִצְוֹתֶיךָ וְתֵן חֶלְקֵנוּ בְּתוֹרָתֶךָ · שַׂבְּעֵנוּ מִטּוּבֶךָ וְשַׂמְּחֵנוּ בִּישׁוּעָתֶךָ וְטַהֵר לִבֵּנוּ לְעָבְדְּךָ בֶּאֱמֶת · וְהַנְחִילֵנוּ יְיָ אֱלֹהֵינוּ בְּאַהֲבָה וּבְרָצוֹן שַׁבַּת קָדְשֶׁךָ · וְיָנוּחוּ בָהּ יִשְׂרָאֵל מְקַדְּשֵׁי שְׁמֶךָ · בָּרוּךְ אַתָּה יְיָ · מְקַדֵּשׁ הַשַּׁבָּת:

רְצֵה יְיָ אֱלֹהֵינוּ בְּעַמְּךָ יִשְׂרָאֵל וּבִתְפִלָּתָם · וְהָשֵׁב אֶת־הָעֲבוֹדָה לִדְבִיר בֵּיתֶךָ · וְאִשֵּׁי יִשְׂרָאֵל וּתְפִלָּתָם בְּאַהֲבָה תְקַבֵּל בְּרָצוֹן · וּתְהִי לְרָצוֹן תָּמִיד עֲבוֹדַת יִשְׂרָאֵל עַמֶּךָ ·

*On* רֹאשׁ חֹדֶשׁ *and* חוֹל הַמּוֹעֵד *of* פֶּסַח *and of* סֻכּוֹת *say* אֱלֹהֵינוּ וכו׳,

וְתֶחֱזֶינָה עֵינֵינוּ בְּשׁוּבְךָ לְצִיּוֹן בְּרַחֲמִים · בָּרוּךְ אַתָּה יְיָ · הַמַּחֲזִיר שְׁכִינָתוֹ לְצִיּוֹן:

מוֹדִים אֲנַחְנוּ לָךְ שָׁאַתָּה הוּא יְיָ אֱלֹהֵינוּ וֵאלֹהֵי אֲבוֹתֵינוּ לְעוֹלָם וָעֶד · צוּר חַיֵּינוּ מָגֵן יִשְׁעֵנוּ אַתָּה הוּא

And the heaven and the earth were finished and all their host. And on the seventh day God had finished his work which he had made; and he rested on the seventh day from all his work which he had made. And God blessed the seventh day, and he hallowed it, because he rested thereon from all his work which God had created and made.

Our God and God of our fathers, accept our rest; sanctify us by thy commandments, and grant our portion in thy Law; satisfy us with thy goodness, and gladden us with thy salvation; purify our hearts to serve thee in truth; and in thy love and favour, O Lord our God, let us inherit thy holy Sabbath; and may Israel, who hallow thy name, rest thereon. Blessed art thou, O Lord, who halowest the Sabbath.

Accept, O Lord our God, thy people Israel and their prayer; restore the service to the oracle of thy house; receive in love and favour both the fire-offerings of Israel and their prayer; and may the service of thy people Israel be ever acceptable unto thee.

*On New Moon and the Intermediate Days of Passover and Tabernacles say, "Our God . . . May our remembrance," p. 50.*

And let our eyes behold thy return in mercy to Zion. Blessed art thou, O Lord, who restoreth thy divine presence unto Zion.

We give thanks unto thee, for thou art the Lord our God and the God of our fathers for ever and ever; thou art the Rock of our lives, the Shield of our salvation through

לְדוֹר וָדוֹר · נוֹדֶה לְּךָ וּנְסַפֵּר תְּהִלָּתֶךָ עַל־חַיֵּינוּ הַמְּסוּרִים בְּיָדֶךָ וְעַל נִשְׁמוֹתֵינוּ הַפְּקוּדוֹת לָךְ · וְעַל נִסֶּיךָ שֶׁבְּכָל־יוֹם עִמָּנוּ וְעַל נִפְלְאוֹתֶיךָ וְטוֹבוֹתֶיךָ שֶׁבְּכָל־עֵת עֶרֶב וָבֹקֶר וְצָהֳרָיִם · הַטּוֹב כִּי לֹא־כָלוּ רַחֲמֶיךָ · וְהַמְרַחֵם כִּי לֹא־תַמּוּ חֲסָדֶיךָ מֵעוֹלָם קִוִּינוּ לָךְ׃

*On* חֲנֻכָּה *say* עַל הַנִּסִּים,

וְעַל־כֻּלָּם יִתְבָּרַךְ וְיִתְרוֹמַם שִׁמְךָ מַלְכֵּנוּ תָּמִיד לְעוֹלָם וָעֶד׃

*On* שַׁבַּת שׁוּבָה *say:—*

וּכְתוֹב לְחַיִּים טוֹבִים כָּל־בְּנֵי בְרִיתֶךָ׃

וְכֹל הַחַיִּים יוֹדוּךָ סֶּלָה · וִיהַלְלוּ אֶת־שִׁמְךָ בֶּאֱמֶת · הָאֵל יְשׁוּעָתֵנוּ וְעֶזְרָתֵנוּ סֶלָה · בָּרוּךְ אַתָּה יְיָ · הַטּוֹב שִׁמְךָ וּלְךָ נָאֶה לְהוֹדוֹת׃

שָׁלוֹם רָב עַל יִשְׂרָאֵל עַמְּךָ תָּשִׂים לְעוֹלָם · כִּי אַתָּה הוּא מֶלֶךְ אָדוֹן לְכָל הַשָּׁלוֹם · וְטוֹב בְּעֵינֶיךָ לְבָרֵךְ אֶת־עַמְּךָ יִשְׂרָאֵל בְּכָל־עֵת וּבְכָל־שָׁעָה בִּשְׁלוֹמֶךָ׃

בָּרוּךְ אַתָּה יְיָ · הַמְבָרֵךְ אֶת־עַמּוֹ יִשְׂרָאֵל בַּשָּׁלוֹם׃

*On* שַׁבַּת שׁוּבָה *say:*

בְּסֵפֶר חַיִּים בְּרָכָה וְשָׁלוֹם וּפַרְנָסָה טוֹבָה נִזָּכֵר וְנִכָּתֵב לְפָנֶיךָ אֲנַחְנוּ וְכָל־עַמְּךָ בֵּית יִשְׂרָאֵל לְחַיִּים טוֹבִים וּלְשָׁלוֹם · בָּרוּךְ אַתָּה יְיָ · עוֹשֵׂה הַשָּׁלוֹם׃

every generation. We will give thanks unto thee and declare thy praise for our lives which are committed unto thy hand, and for our souls which are in thy charge, and for thy miracles, which are daily with us, and for thy wonders and thy benefits which are wrought at all times, evening, morn and noon. O thou who are all-good, whose mercies fail not; thou, merciful Being, whose lovingkindness never cease, we have ever hoped in thee.

*On Chanukah say, "We thank thee," etc., p. 51, to "thy great name," p. 52.*

For all these things thy name, O our King, shall be continually blessed and exalted for ever and ever.

*On the Sabbath of Penitence say:—*

O inscribe all the children of thy covenant for a happy life.

And everything that liveth shall give thanks unto thee for ever, and shall praise thy name in truth, O God, our salvation and our help. Blessed art thou, O Lord, whose name is All-good, and unto whom it is becoming to give thanks.

Grant abundant peace unto Israel thy people for ever; for thou art the sovereign Lord of all peace; and may it be good in thy sight to bless thy people Israel at all times and at every hour with thy peace.

*On the Sabbath of Penitence say:—*

In the book of life, blessing, peace and good sustenance may we be remembered and inscribed before thee, we and all thy people the house of Israel, for a happy life and for peace. Blessed art thou, O Lord, who makest peace.

Blessed art thou, O Lord, who blessest thy people Israel with peace.

אֱלֹהַי · נְצוֹר לְשׁוֹנִי מֵרָע וּשְׂפָתַי מִדַּבֵּר מִרְמָה · וְלִמְקַלְלַי נַפְשִׁי תִדּוֹם וְנַפְשִׁי כֶּעָפָר לַכֹּל תִּהְיֶה: פְּתַח לִבִּי בְּתוֹרָתֶךָ וּבְמִצְוֹתֶיךָ תִּרְדּוֹף נַפְשִׁי · וְכֹל הַחוֹשְׁבִים עָלַי רָעָה מְהֵרָה הָפֵר עֲצָתָם וְקַלְקֵל מַחְשְׁבוֹתָם · עֲשֵׂה לְמַעַן שְׁמֶךָ עֲשֵׂה לְמַעַן יְמִינֶךָ עֲשֵׂה לְמַעַן קְדֻשָּׁתֶךָ עֲשֵׂה לְמַעַן תּוֹרָתֶךָ · לְמַעַן יֵחָלְצוּן יְדִידֶיךָ הוֹשִׁיעָה יְמִינְךָ וַעֲנֵנִי: יִהְיוּ לְרָצוֹן אִמְרֵי־פִי וְהֶגְיוֹן לִבִּי לְפָנֶיךָ יְיָ צוּרִי וְגֹאֲלִי: עֹשֶׂה שָׁלוֹם בִּמְרוֹמָיו הוּא יַעֲשֶׂה שָׁלוֹם עָלֵינוּ וְעַל כָּל־יִשְׂרָאֵל · וְאִמְרוּ אָמֵן:

יְהִי רָצוֹן לְפָנֶיךָ יְיָ אֱלֹהֵינוּ וֵאלֹהֵי אֲבוֹתֵינוּ שֶׁיִּבָּנֶה בֵּית הַמִּקְדָּשׁ בִּמְהֵרָה בְיָמֵינוּ · וְתֵן חֶלְקֵנוּ בְּתוֹרָתֶךָ: וְשָׁם נַעֲבָדְךָ בְּיִרְאָה כִּימֵי עוֹלָם וּכְשָׁנִים קַדְמוֹנִיּוֹת: וְעָרְבָה לַייָ מִנְחַת יְהוּדָה וִירוּשָׁלָיִם כִּימֵי עוֹלָם וּכְשָׁנִים קַדְמוֹנִיּוֹת:

*The Reader and Congregation repeat from* וַיְכֻלּוּ *to* לַעֲשׂוֹת, *p.* 117.

*From* בָּרוּךְ *to* מְקַדֵּשׁ הַשַּׁבָּת, *p.* 120, *is omitted when Prayers are not said with the Congregation.*

*Reader.* בָּרוּךְ אַתָּה יְיָ אֱלֹהֵינוּ וֵאלֹהֵי אֲבוֹתֵינוּ · אֱלֹהֵי אַבְרָהָם אֱלֹהֵי יִצְחָק וֵאלֹהֵי יַעֲקֹב · הָאֵל הַגָּדוֹל הַגִּבּוֹר וְהַנּוֹרָא אֵל עֶלְיוֹן קֹנֵה שָׁמַיִם וָאָרֶץ:

O my God! guard my tongue from evil and my lips from speaking guile; and to such as curse me let my soul be dumb, yea, let my soul be unto all as the dust. Open my heart to thy Law, and let my soul pursue thy commandments. If any design evil against me, speedily make their counsel of none effect, and frustrate their designs. Do it for the sake of thy name, do it for the sake of thy right hand, do it for the sake of thy holiness, do it for the sake of thy Law. In order that thy beloved ones may be delivered, O save with thy right hand and answer me. Let the words of my mouth and the meditation of my heart be acceptable before thee, O Lord, my Rock and my Redeemer. He who maketh peace in his high places, may he make peace for us and for all Israel, and say ye, Amen.

May it be thy will, O Lord our God and God of our fathers, that the temple may be speedily rebuilt in our days, and grant our portion in thy Law. And there we will serve thee with awe, as in the days of old, and as in ancient years. Then shall the offering of Judah and Jerusalem be pleasant unto the Lord, as in the days of old, and as in ancient years.

*The Reader and Congregation repeat from "And the heaven," to "and made," p.* 117.

*The following to "the Sabbath," p.* 120, *is omitted when Prayers are not said with the Congregation:—*

*Reader.*—Blessed art thou, O Lord our God and God of our fathers, God of Abraham, God of Isaac and God of Jacob, the great, mighty and revered God, the most High God, Possessor of heaven and earth.

*Reader and Congregation.* מָגֵן אָבוֹת בִּדְבָרוֹ מְחַיֵּה מֵתִים בְּמַאֲמָרוֹ הָאֵל (*On* שַׁבַּת שׁוּבָה *read* הַמֶּלֶךְ *for* הָאֵל) הַקָּדוֹשׁ שֶׁאֵין כָּמֽוֹהוּ הַמֵּנִיחַ לְעַמּוֹ בְּיוֹם שַׁבַּת קָדְשׁוֹ ׃ כִּי בָם רָצָה לְהָנִיחַ לָהֶם ׃ לְפָנָיו נַעֲבוֹד בְּיִרְאָה וָפַחַד וְנוֹדֶה לִשְׁמוֹ בְּכָל־יוֹם תָּמִיד מֵעֵין הַבְּרָכוֹת ׃ אֵל הַהוֹדָאוֹת אֲדוֹן הַשָּׁלוֹם מְקַדֵּשׁ הַשַּׁבָּת וּמְבָרֵךְ שְׁבִיעִי ׃ וּמֵנִיחַ בִּקְדֻשָּׁה לְעַם מְדֻשְּׁנֵי עֹֽנֶג ׃ זֵֽכֶר לְמַעֲשֵׂה בְרֵאשִׁית ׃

*Reader.* אֱלֹהֵֽינוּ וֵאלֹהֵי אֲבוֹתֵֽינוּ ׃ רְצֵה בִמְנוּחָתֵֽנוּ ׃ קַדְּשֵֽׁנוּ בְּמִצְוֹתֶֽיךָ וְתֵן חֶלְקֵֽנוּ בְּתוֹרָתֶֽךָ ׃ שַׂבְּעֵֽנוּ מִטּוּבֶֽךָ וְשַׂמְּחֵֽנוּ בִּישׁוּעָתֶֽךָ וְטַהֵר לִבֵּֽנוּ לְעָבְדְּךָ בֶּאֱמֶת ׃ וְהַנְחִילֵֽנוּ יְיָ אֱלֹהֵֽינוּ בְּאַהֲבָה וּבְרָצוֹן שַׁבַּת קָדְשֶֽׁךָ וְיָנֽוּחוּ בָהּ יִשְׂרָאֵל מְקַדְּשֵׁי שְׁמֶֽךָ ׃ בָּרוּךְ אַתָּה יְיָ ׃ מְקַדֵּשׁ הַשַּׁבָּת ׃

קַדִּישׁ תִּתְקַבַּל, *p.* 75.

*The following is not said on Festivals, on* שַׁבַּת חוֹל הַמּוֹעֵד *or on the evening after a Festival:—*

משנה שבת פ״ב

(א) בַּמֶּה מַדְלִיקִין וּבַמָּה אֵין מַדְלִיקִין ׃ אֵין מַדְלִיקִין לֹא בְלֶֽכֶשׁ וְלֹא בְחֹֽסֶן וְלֹא בְכַלָּךְ ׃ וְלֹא בִפְתִילַת הָאִידָן וְלֹא בִפְתִילַת הַמִּדְבָּר ׃ וְלֹא בִירוֹקָה שֶׁעַל פְּנֵי הַמָּֽיִם ׃ וְלֹא בְזֶֽפֶת וְלֹא בְשַׁעֲוָה ׃ וְלֹא בְשֶֽׁמֶן קִיק וְלֹא בְשֶֽׁמֶן שְׂרֵפָה ׃ וְלֹא בְאַלְיָה וְלֹא בְחֵֽלֶב ׃ נַחוּם הַמָּדִי אוֹמֵר מַדְלִיקִין בְּחֵֽלֶב

*Reader and Cong.*—He with his word was a shield to our forefathers, and by his bidding will quicken the dead; the holy God (*on the Sabbath of Penitence* say, "holy King"), like unto whom there is none; who giveth rest to his people on his holy Sabbath day, because he took pleasure in them to grant them rest. Him we will serve with fear and awe, and daily and constantly we will give thanks unto his name in the fitting forms of Blessings. He is the God to whom thanksgivings are due, the Lord of peace, who halloweth the Sabbath and blesseth the seventh day, and in holiness giveth rest unto a people sated with delights, in remembrance of the creation.

*Reader*s Our God and God of our fathers, accept our rest; sanctify us by thy commandments, and grant our portion in thy Law; satisfy us with thy goodness, gladden us with thy salvation; purify our hearts to serve thee in truth; and in thy love and favour, O Lord our God, let us inherit thy holy Sabbath; and may Israel, who hallow thy name, rest thereon. Blessed art Thou, O Lord, who hallowest the Sabbath.

*Kaddish, p.* 75.

*The following is not said on Festivals, on the Intermediate Sabbath of a Festival, or on the evening after a Festival.*

Mishnah, Treatise Sabbath, ch. ii.

1. With what materials may the Sabbath lamp be lighted, and with what may it not be lighted? It may not be lighted with cedar-bast, nor with uncombed flax, nor with floss silk, nor with willow fibre, nor with nettle fibre, nor with water-weeds (all these forming imperfect wicks). It may also not be lighted with pitch, nor with liquid wax, nor with oil made from the seeds of the cotton plant, nor with oil which, having been set apart as a heave-offering and having become defiled, is condemned to be destroyed by burning, nor with the fat from the tails of sheep, nor with tallow. Nahum the Mede says one

מְבֻשָּׁל׳ וַחֲכָמִים אוֹמְרִים אֶחָד מְבֻשָּׁל וְאֶחָד שֶׁאֵינוֹ מְבֻשָּׁל אֵין מַדְלִיקִין בּוֹ: (ב) אֵין מַדְלִיקִין בְּשֶׁמֶן שְׂרֵפָה בְּיוֹם טוֹב׳ רַבִּי יִשְׁמָעֵאל אוֹמֵר אֵין מַדְלִיקִין בְּעִטְרָן מִפְּנֵי כְבוֹד הַשַּׁבָּת׳ וַחֲכָמִים מַתִּירִין בְּכָל הַשְּׁמָנִים בְּשֶׁמֶן שֻׁמְשְׁמִין בְּשֶׁמֶן אֱגוֹזִים בְּשֶׁמֶן צְנוֹנוֹת בְּשֶׁמֶן דָּגִים בְּשֶׁמֶן פַּקֻּעוֹת בְּעִטְרָן וּבְנֵפְט׳ רַבִּי טַרְפוֹן אוֹמֵר אֵין מַדְלִיקִין אֶלָּא בְּשֶׁמֶן זַיִת בִּלְבָד: (ג) כָּל הַיּוֹצֵא מִן הָעֵץ אֵין מַדְלִיקִין בּוֹ אֶלָּא פִשְׁתָּן׳ וְכָל הַיּוֹצֵא מִן הָעֵץ אֵינוֹ מִטַּמֵּא טֻמְאַת אֹהָלִים אֶלָּא פִשְׁתָּן׳ פְּתִילַת הַבֶּגֶד שֶׁקִּפְּלָהּ וְלֹא הִבְהֲבָהּ׳ רַבִּי אֱלִיעֶזֶר אוֹמֵר טְמֵאָה הִיא וְאֵין מַדְלִיקִין בָּהּ׳ רַבִּי עֲקִיבָא אוֹמֵר טְהוֹרָה הִיא וּמַדְלִיקִין בָּהּ: (ד) לֹא יִקּוֹב אָדָם שְׁפוֹפֶרֶת שֶׁל בֵּיצָה וִימַלְּאֶנָּה שֶׁמֶן וְיִתְּנֶנָּה עַל פִּי הַנֵּר בִּשְׁבִיל שֶׁתְּהֵא מְנַטֶּפֶת וַאֲפִילוּ הִיא שֶׁל חֶרֶס׳ וְרַבִּי יְהוּדָה מַתִּיר׳ אֲבָל אִם חִבְּרָהּ הַיּוֹצֵר מִתְּחִלָּה מֻתָּר מִפְּנֵי שֶׁהוּא כְּלִי אֶחָד׳ לֹא יְמַלֵּא אָדָם קְעָרָה שֶׁמֶן וְיִתְּנֶנָּה בְּצַד הַנֵּר וְיִתֵּן רֹאשׁ הַפְּתִילָה בְּתוֹכָהּ בִּשְׁבִיל שֶׁתְּהֵא שׁוֹאֶבֶת׳ וְרַבִּי יְהוּדָה מַתִּיר: (ה) הַמְכַבֶּה אֶת הַנֵּר מִפְּנֵי שֶׁהוּא מִתְיָרֵא מִפְּנֵי גוֹיִם מִפְּנֵי לִסְטִים מִפְּנֵי רוּחַ רָעָה אוֹ בִּשְׁבִיל הַחוֹלֶה שֶׁיִּישַׁן פָּטוּר׳ כְּחָס עַל הַנֵּר כְּחָס עַל הַשֶּׁמֶן כְּחָס עַל הַפְּתִילָה חַיָּב׳ רַבִּי יוֹסֵי פּוֹטֵר בְּכֻלָּן חוּץ מִן הַפְּתִילָה מִפְּנֵי שֶׁהוּא עוֹשָׂהּ פֶּחָם: (ו) עַל שָׁלשׁ עֲבֵרוֹת נָשִׁים מֵתוֹת בִּשְׁעַת לֵדָתָן׳ עַל שֶׁאֵינָן זְהִירוֹת בְּנִדָּה בְּחַלָּה וּבְהַדְלָקַת הַנֵּר: (ז) שְׁלשָׁה דְבָרִים צָרִיךְ אָדָם לוֹמַר בְּתוֹךְ בֵּיתוֹ עֶרֶב שַׁבָּת עִם חֲשֵׁכָה׳ עִשַּׂרְתֶּם עֵרַבְתֶּם הַדְלִיקוּ אֶת הַנֵּר׳ סָפֵק חֲשֵׁכָה סָפֵק אֵינָהּ חֲשֵׁכָה אֵין מְעַשְּׂרִין

may use tallow when it has been boiled, but the other sages say, that whether so prepared or not, it may not be used.

2. On a festival one may not use such consecrated oil as has been condemned, after defilement, to be burnt. R. Ishmael says, one may not, from respect to the Sabbath, use tar. The sages permit the use of all kinds of oil; the oil of sesamum, of nuts, of radish seeds, of fish, of colocynth seeds, as well as tar and naphtha. R. Tarphon says, one may use no other than olive oil for lighting the Sabbath lamp.

3. No part of a tree may be used as a wick for lighting, with the exception of flax (spoken of in Joshua ii: 6 as "the flax of a tree"); nor is any part of a tree, if used in the construction of a tent, capable of acquiring pollution according to the law concerning the pollution of tents, except flax. If a slip of cloth has been folded but not singed, R. Eliezer says it may become unclean, and may not be used as a wick for lighting; R. Akiba says it remains clean, and may be used.

4. One may not perforate an egg-shell, fill it with oil, and place it above the opening of the lamp, so that drops of oil may fall therein; he may not even employ an earthenware vessel in this manner; but R. Jehudah permits it. If, however, the potter had originally joined the two parts, then it is allowed, because it is actually only one vessel. A person may not fill a bowl with oil, place it by the side of the lamp, and put the end of the wick into it, so that it may draw the oil to the flame; but R. Jehudah permits it.

5. He who extinguishes the light, because he is in fear of heathens, of robbers, or of an evil spirit, or to enable a sick person to sleep, is absolved; if his object is to save the lamp, the oil, or the wick, he is guilty of a breach of the Sabbath law. R. José absolves from such guilt in every case except in that of the one whose object is to save the wick, because by thus extinguishing it, he converts it into a coal.

6. For three transgressions women die in childbirth: because they have been negligent in regard to their periods of separation, in respect to the consecration of the first cake of dough, and in the lighting of the Sabbath lamp.

7. Three things a man must say to his household on Sabbath eve towards dusk: Have ye separated the tithe? Have ye made the Erub? Kindle the Sabbath lamp. If it be doubtful whether it is dark, that which is certainly untithed must not then

אֶת הַהֹדִי וְאֵין מַטְבִּילִין אֶת הַכֵּלִים וְאֵין מַדְלִיקִין אֶת הַנֵּרוֹת · אֲבָל מְעַשְּׂרִין אֶת הַדְּמַאי וּמְעָרְבִין וְטוֹמְנִין אֶת הַחַמִּין׃

הלמוד מסכת ברכות

אָמַר רַבִּי אֶלְעָזָר אָמַר רַבִּי חֲנִינָא · תַּלְמִידֵי חֲכָמִים מַרְבִּים שָׁלוֹם בָּעוֹלָם · שֶׁנֶּאֱמַר וְכָל בָּנַיִךְ לִמּוּדֵי יְיָ וְרַב שְׁלוֹם בָּנָיִךְ · אַל תִּקְרָא בָּנָיִךְ אֶלָּא בּוֹנָיִךְ׃ שָׁלוֹם רָב לְאֹהֲבֵי תוֹרָתֶךָ וְאֵין לָמוֹ מִכְשׁוֹל׃ יְהִי־שָׁלוֹם בְּחֵילֵךְ שַׁלְוָה בְּאַרְמְנוֹתָיִךְ׃ לְמַעַן אַחַי וְרֵעָי אֲדַבְּרָה־נָּא שָׁלוֹם בָּךְ׃ לְמַעַן בֵּית־יְיָ אֱלֹהֵינוּ אֲבַקְשָׁה טוֹב לָךְ׃ יְיָ עֹז לְעַמּוֹ יִתֵּן יְיָ יְבָרֵךְ אֶת־עַמּוֹ בַשָּׁלוֹם׃

*The Reader, taking a cup of wine in his hand, says;—*

בָּרוּךְ אַתָּה יְיָ אֱלֹהֵינוּ מֶלֶךְ הָעוֹלָם · בּוֹרֵא פְּרִי הַגָּפֶן׃

בָּרוּךְ אַתָּה יְיָ אֱלֹהֵינוּ מֶלֶךְ הָעוֹלָם · אֲשֶׁר קִדְּשָׁנוּ בְּמִצְוֹתָיו וְרָצָה בָנוּ · וְשַׁבַּת קָדְשׁוֹ בְּאַהֲבָה וּבְרָצוֹן הִנְחִילָנוּ זִכָּרוֹן לְמַעֲשֵׂה בְרֵאשִׁית · כִּי הוּא יוֹם תְּחִלָּה לְמִקְרָאֵי קֹדֶשׁ זֵכֶר לִיצִיאַת מִצְרָיִם · כִּי־בָנוּ בָחַרְתָּ וְאוֹתָנוּ קִדַּשְׁתָּ מִכָּל־הָעַמִּים וְשַׁבַּת קָדְשְׁךָ בְּאַהֲבָה וּבְרָצוֹן הִנְחַלְתָּנוּ · בָּרוּךְ אַתָּה יְיָ · מְקַדֵּשׁ הַשַּׁבָּת׃

---

עָלֵינוּ לְשַׁבֵּחַ לַאֲדוֹן הַכֹּל לָתֵת גְּדֻלָּה לְיוֹצֵר בְּרֵאשִׁית · שֶׁלֹּא עָשָׂנוּ כְּגוֹיֵי הָאֲרָצוֹת וְלֹא שָׂמָנוּ

be tithed, vessels must not be immersed to purify them from their defilement, nor must the Sabbath lamps be lighted: but that which is doubtfully untithed may be tithed, the Erub may be made, and hot victuals may be covered to retain their heat.

## Talmud Babli. End of Treatise Berachoth.

R. Eleazar said in the name of R. Chanina, The disciples of the sages increase peace throughout the world, as it is said, and all thy children shall be taught of the Lord; and great shall be the peace of thy children. (Read not here *banayich,* thy children, but *bonayich,* thy builders).—Great peace have they who love thy Law; and there is no stumbling for them. Peace be within thy rampart, prosperity within thy palaces. For my brethren and companions' sakes I would fain speak peace concerning thee. For the sake of the house of the Lord our God I would seek thy good. The Lord will give strength unto his people; the Lord will bless his people with peace.

*The Reader, taking a cup of wine in his hand, says:—*

Blessed art thou, O Lord our God, King of the universe, who createst the fruit of the vine.

Blessed art thou, O Lord our God, King of the Universe, who hast sanctified us by thy commandments and hast taken pleasure in us, and in love and favour hast given us thy holy Sabbath as an inheritance, a memorial of the creation—that day being also the first of the holy convocations, in remembrance of the departure from Egypt. For thou hast chosen us and sanctified us above all nations, and in love and favour hast given us thy holy Sabbath as an inheritance. Blessed art thou, O Lord, who hallowest the Sabbath.

---

It is our duty to praise the Lord of all things, to ascribe greatness to him who formed the world in the beginning, since he hath not made us like the nations of other lands,

כְּמִשְׁפְּחוֹת הָאֲדָמָה · שֶׁלֹּא שָׂם חֶלְקֵנוּ כָּהֶם וְגוֹרָלֵנוּ כְּכָל הֲמוֹנָם · וַאֲנַחְנוּ כּוֹרְעִים וּמִשְׁתַּחֲוִים וּמוֹדִים לִפְנֵי מֶלֶךְ מַלְכֵי הַמְּלָכִים הַקָּדוֹשׁ בָּרוּךְ הוּא · שֶׁהוּא נוֹטֶה שָׁמַיִם וְיוֹסֵד אָרֶץ · וּמוֹשַׁב יְקָרוֹ בַּשָּׁמַיִם מִמַּעַל · וּשְׁכִינַת עֻזּוֹ בְּגָבְהֵי מְרוֹמִים : הוּא אֱלֹהֵינוּ · אֵין עוֹד · אֱמֶת מַלְכֵּנוּ · אֶפֶס זוּלָתוֹ · כַּכָּתוּב בְּתוֹרָתוֹ · וְיָדַעְתָּ הַיּוֹם וַהֲשֵׁבֹתָ אֶל־לְבָבֶךָ כִּי יְיָ הוּא הָאֱלֹהִים בַּשָּׁמַיִם מִמַּעַל וְעַל־הָאָרֶץ מִתָּחַת. אֵין עוֹד:

עַל־כֵּן נְקַוֶּה לְךָ יְיָ אֱלֹהֵינוּ לִרְאוֹת מְהֵרָה בְּתִפְאֶרֶת עֻזֶּךָ · לְהַעֲבִיר גִּלּוּלִים מִן הָאָרֶץ וְהָאֱלִילִים כָּרוֹת יִכָּרֵתוּן · לְתַקֵּן עוֹלָם בְּמַלְכוּת שַׁדַּי וְכָל־בְּנֵי בָשָׂר יִקְרְאוּ בִשְׁמֶךָ · לְהַפְנוֹת אֵלֶיךָ כָּל־רִשְׁעֵי אָרֶץ : יַכִּירוּ וְיֵדְעוּ כָּל־יוֹשְׁבֵי תֵבֵל כִּי לְךָ תִּכְרַע כָּל־בֶּרֶךְ תִּשָּׁבַע כָּל־לָשׁוֹן : לְפָנֶיךָ יְיָ אֱלֹהֵינוּ יִכְרְעוּ וְיִפֹּלוּ · וְלִכְבוֹד שִׁמְךָ יְקָר יִתֵּנוּ · וִיקַבְּלוּ כֻלָּם אֶת־עֹל מַלְכוּתֶךָ · וְתִמְלוֹךְ עֲלֵיהֶם מְהֵרָה לְעוֹלָם וָעֶד · כִּי הַמַּלְכוּת שֶׁלְּךָ הִיא וּלְעוֹלְמֵי עַד תִּמְלוֹךְ בְּכָבוֹד : כַּכָּתוּב בְּתוֹרָתֶךָ · יְיָ יִמְלֹךְ לְעוֹלָם וָעֶד : וְנֶאֱמַר · וְהָיָה יְיָ לְמֶלֶךְ עַל־כָּל־הָאָרֶץ בַּיּוֹם הַהוּא יִהְיֶה יְיָ אֶחָד וּשְׁמוֹ אֶחָד :

and hath not placed us like other families of the earth, since he hath not assigned unto us a portion as unto them, nor a lot as unto all their multitude. For we bend the knee and offer worship and thanks before the supreme King of kings, the Holy One, blessed be he, who stretched forth the heavens and laid the foundations of the earth, the seat of whose glory is in the heavens above, and the abode of whose might is in the loftiest heights. He is our God; there is none else: in truth he is our King: there is none besides him; as it is written in his Law, And thou shalt know this day, and lay it to thine heart, that the Lord he is God in heaven above and upon the earth beneath: there is none else.

We therefore hope in thee, O Lord our God, that we may speedily behold the glory of thy might, when thou wilt remove the abominations from the earth, and the idols will be utterly cut off, when the world will be perfected under the kingdom of the Almighty, and all the children of flesh will call upon thy name, when thou wilt turn unto thyself all the wicked of the earth. Let all the inhabitants of the world perceive and know that unto thee every knee must bow, every tongue must swear. Before thee, O Lord our God, let them bow and fall; and unto thy glorious name let them give honour; let them all accept the yoke of thy kingdom, and do thou reign over them speedily, and for ever and ever. For the kingdom is thine, and to all eternity thou wilt reign in glory; as it is written in thy Law, The Lord shall reign for ever and ever. And it is said, and the Lord shall be king over all the earth: in that day shall the Lord be One, and his name One.

## קַדִּישׁ יָתוֹם

*Mourner.* יִתְגַּדַּל וְיִתְקַדַּשׁ שְׁמֵהּ רַבָּא בְּעָלְמָא דִּי־בְרָא כִרְעוּתֵהּ · וְיַמְלִיךְ מַלְכוּתֵהּ בְּחַיֵּיכוֹן וּבְיוֹמֵיכוֹן וּבְחַיֵּי דְּכָל־בֵּית יִשְׂרָאֵל בַּעֲגָלָא וּבִזְמַן קָרִיב · וְאִמְרוּ אָמֵן:

*Cong. and Mourner.* יְהֵא שְׁמֵהּ רַבָּא מְבָרַךְ לְעָלַם וּלְעָלְמֵי עָלְמַיָּא ·

*Mourner.* יִתְבָּרַךְ וְיִשְׁתַּבַּח וְיִתְפָּאַר וְיִתְרוֹמַם וְיִתְנַשֵּׂא וְיִתְהַדַּר וְיִתְעַלֶּה וְיִתְהַלַּל שְׁמֵהּ דְּקֻדְשָׁא · בְּרִיךְ הוּא · לְעֵלָּא מִן־כָּל־בִּרְכָתָא וְשִׁירָתָא תֻּשְׁבְּחָתָא וְנֶחֱמָתָא דִּי־ אֲמִירָן בְּעָלְמָא · וְאִמְרוּ אָמֵן:

*Cong.* יְהִי שֵׁם יְיָ מְבֹרָךְ מֵעַתָּה וְעַד עוֹלָם:

*Mourner.* יְהֵא שְׁלָמָא רַבָּא מִן־שְׁמַיָּא וְחַיִּים עָלֵינוּ וְעַל־ כָּל־יִשְׂרָאֵל · וְאִמְרוּ אָמֵן:

*Cong.* עֶזְרִי מֵעִם יְיָ עֹשֵׂה שָׁמַיִם וָאָרֶץ:

*Mourner.* עֹשֶׂה שָׁלוֹם בִּמְרוֹמָיו הוּא יַעֲשֶׂה שָׁלוֹם עָלֵינוּ וְעַל כָּל־יִשְׂרָאֵל · וְאִמְרוּ אָמֵן:

---

יִגְדַּל אֱלֹהִים חַי וְיִשְׁתַּבַּח · נִמְצָא וְאֵין עֵת אֶל־מְצִיאוּתוֹ:
אֶחָד וְאֵין יָחִיד כְּיִחוּדוֹ · נֶעְלָם וְגַם אֵין סוֹף לְאַחְדּוּתוֹ:
אֵין לוֹ דְּמוּת הַגּוּף וְאֵינוֹ גוּף · לֹא נַעֲרוֹךְ אֵלָיו קְדֻשָּׁתוֹ:

*The following Kaddish is said by a Mourner:—*

*Mourner.*—Magnified and sanctified be his great name in the world which he hath created according to his will. May he establish his kingdom during your life and during your days, and during the life of all the house of Israel, even speedily and at a near time, and say ye, Amen.

*Cong. and Mourner.*—Let his great name be blessed for ever and to all eternity.

*Mourner.*—Blessed, praised and glorified, exalted, extolled and honoured, magnified and lauded be the name of the Holy One, blessed be he; though he be high above all the blessings and hymns, praises and consolations, which are uttered in the world; and say ye, Amen.

*Cong.*—Let the name of the Lord be blessed from this time forth and for evermore.

*Mourner.*—May there be abundant peace from heaven and life for us and for all Israel; and say ye, Amen.

*Cong.*—My help is from the Lord, who made heaven and earth.

*Mourner.*—He who maketh peace in his high places, may he make peace for us and for all Israel; and say ye, Amen.

---

1. Magnified and praised be the living God: he is, and there is no limit in time unto his being.

2. He is One, and there is no unity like unto his unity; inconceivable is he, and unending is his unity.

3. He hath neither bodily form nor substance: we can compare nought unto him in his holiness.